THE RATTLING CHAINS

Also by NICHOLAS HALASZ

Roosevelt Through Foreign Eyes

Nobel

In the Shadow of Russia

Dreyfus

The Rattling Chains

*Slave Unrest and Revolt
in the Antebellum South*

by NICHOLAS HALASZ

DAVID McKAY COMPANY, INC.　　New York

THE RATTLING CHAINS

COPYRIGHT © 1966 BY NICHOLAS HALASZ

Library of Congress Catalog Card Number, 66-21760

MANUFACTURED IN THE UNITED STATES OF AMERICA

VAN REES PRESS • NEW YORK

To Eva Zeisel

Puzzled, she induced me
to explore the subject
of this book.

ACKNOWLEDGMENTS

I FEEL deeply indebted to Edward J. Foote who, with his literary sensitivity and sympathetic understanding put the manuscript of this book in its final shape.

Robert Halasz advised me in researching the broader historical background of the subject. He read the manuscript, chapter by chapter, and checked for accuracy. His comments greatly helped me in organizing the material.

I welcome the opportunity to thank the librarians in charge of the American History Room of the New York Public Library. For two years, while I did a large part of the research for this book, they helped me with expert guidance, friendliness, and prompt service.

CONTENTS

THE RATTLING CHAINS

I

THE SLAVE:
A NEW AMERICAN COMMODITY

"In no instance can it be said to be a more plain and lamentable truth, that the love of money is the root of all evil, than when it urges men to trade in the bodies and souls of their fellow creatures."

Alexander Hewitt, *An Historical Account of the Rise and Fall of the Colonies of South Carolina and Georgia.*

I N the spring of 1526, a small vessel brought about five hundred Spanish colonists from Hispaniola in the West Indies to the coast of what is now South Carolina with the intention of establishing sugarcane plantations there. With them they brought some one hundred Negroes, the first black slaves to reach continental North America. The Indians of South Carolina must have been surprised to see black men and women chained together, their moans mingling with the cracking whips over their heads.

Before long a disease to which Indians and Negroes were immune began to thin the group of Spaniards. Many of the white men remained in their huts, and grave markers began to dot the settlement. The slaves discovered that once out of the tiny colony they could easily find a friendly Indian and be guided to freedom. Those slaves caught in an attempt to flee were tortured horribly by the white men, but the threat of torture did not deter the South Carolina slaves from taking the risk and running away.

By the end of the first summer, the white leaders of the pioneer slave colony had decided against spending a damp autumn there with such reduced numbers. The Indians witnessed the colonists' reembarkation and the failure of the first plantation in what is now the United States. The wilderness reclaimed its realm. The Negro slaves who escaped were Americans, seventy-five years before the first settlements in Virginia.

It was not until 1619 that Negro slaves were introduced to a permanent American colony, twelve years after the settlement of Jamestown by the English. In that year, John Smith, founder of the colony, mentions a report by one John Rolfe that "about the last August came in a Dutch man of warre that sold us twenty negars." Others describe the ship as a Dutch trading vessel hailing from the West Indies. There was little demand for black slaves in Virginia at the time, and four years elapsed before the next slave trader brought his human cargo into Jamestown. He sold few Negroes.

After 1635, slave ships were arriving every year, but in spite of this, interest in maintaining slaves for labor on the plantations and as personal body servants remained small, and few slaves changed hands. By 1649, when the white population of the colony had grown to 15,000, the census still included only 100 Negroes.

In the early days the settlers in Virginia did not need abundant unskilled labor. They needed young men with a variety of skills who could live in or about the house as mem-

2

bers of the household and help with every duty around the farm. This need was met by indentured servants who had contracted for service, customarily with the captains of ships sailing for Virginia. The captain would credit the passage and sell the contract to the highest bidder when he reached Virginia. The contract bound the man to servitude for two to seven years, or sometimes longer, after which he was to be furnished by his master with a piece of land, the tools of his trade, and a certain amount of money, food, and clothes.

In 1619, the same year that the first group of Negroes were disembarking at Jamestown, more than 1,200 permanent settlers arrived from England with 100 of these "disorderly persons" to be employed as servants by order of the King. Among these "disorderly persons" were a good many convicts, but then and later about half of the English immigrants could not pay their passage over the Atlantic and sailed on credit. Upon arrival some paid the debt against the obligation of servitude for a definite time, regulated by the statutes. This system of indentured servitude continued into the nineteenth century. A report of Governor William Berkeley in 1671 stated that the total population of 40,000 Virginians included 6,000 indentured servants and 2,000 Negro slaves. A white servant could be used for many tasks, if only because he understood what the master wanted. On the other hand, if he chose to run away, he easily disappeared from sight.

Another reason why Virginians at first preferred indentured servants to slaves was the uncertain legal status of the Negro. Not even the official records called them slaves; they were always known as "Negro servants." In fact, it was not until 1661—more than forty years after the first slave had entered Jamestown—that the Virginia General

3

Assembly recognized the existence of slavery by ruling on the legal rights of children born as a result of miscegenation. It was decided that the status of the mother determined whether the child would be slave or free.

Another problem concerning the status of the Negro disquieted the Virginians. What if a black slave became Christian, married a black girl, also Christian, and had a child baptized? Puzzled Virginians wanted to know if a child born in Virginia from Christian parents could be a slave. The decision came from London, stating that if not a Christian when first purchased, the Negro and all his descendants could be hereditary slaves.

In Virginia, where slavery had been recognized on economic grounds, the Negro slave was a lifetime servant who was absolutely incapable of supporting his offspring, or so the accepted argument went. The master, therefore, did it for him and was compensated by the servitude of the children. On this basis, Virginia recognized the heredity of slavery in 1662, Maryland in 1664, and South Carolina in 1712.

Shortly after the official recognition of slavery in the Virginia colony, Gloucester County recorded, in 1663, the first known conspiracy of slaves to rebel.

Revealed by a white servant known only as Berkenhead, it was apparently a naïve plot of servants and Negro slaves to overthrow their masters and set themselves free. The revolt was set for the 13th of September, 1663, but it was crushed while still only in the planning stages. The General Assembly ordered the date of its occurrence to be annually "kept holy ... it being the day those villains intended to put the plot into execution," to commemorate "so transcendent a favour as the preserving of all we have from utter ruin."

4

The gratefulness of the Assembly to Berkenhead for delivering the colony from what it regarded as the ultimate abhorrence was such that it granted the informer 5,000 pounds of tobacco and his freedom.

After this initial conspiracy, twenty-five years passed before there was another slave disturbance serious enough to be recorded. Again, the conspiracy was effectively cut off before it could be well organized. In April of 1688 at James City, Virginia, the County of Westmoreland convicted a Negro for inciting his fellow slaves. The vicious cruelty of the punishment is recorded matter-of-factly in the court documents:

> It appeared that Sam Negro to Richard Metcalfe hath several times endeavoured to promote a Negro Insurrection in this colony. It is therefore ordered to deter him and others from the like evil practice for time to come that he be by the sheriff of James City County, or his Deputy severally whipt at a cart tayle from the prison round about the town, and then to the Gallows, and from thence to the prison againe and that hee be conveyed by the sheriff of Westmoreland County to that county and he is ordered to whip him severely at the next Court to be held for that County, and that hee have a halter about his necke during that time, and afterwards that hee have a strong Iron collar affixed about his necke with four spriggs which collar hee is never to take or gett off nor to goe off his master or masters plantacon during all the time hee shall live, and if hee shall goe off his said master or masters plantacon or get off his collar then to be hanged.

It is easy to understand why the Virginia settlers did not voluntarily start replacing indentured farm and domestic servants with black slaves. Agriculture in Virginia was no more suited for slave labor than it was in Maryland or North

Carolina at the middle of the seventeenth century; intensive cultivation of tobacco on the small farms that were then the rule was best done by contracted servants and hired hands. The slave master might live in luxury and enjoy to some extent his power and wealth, but he would never know life without the fear that led him to carry his firearms with him wherever he went, even to social functions in neighboring plantations and to church on Sunday.

It was the royal authority in London that created a situation which at last left the American farmer no other choice but to buy Negro slaves. In 1672, the Africa Company was registered in London as the agency for transporting Negroes from Guinea to the overseas colonies. King Charles II was the principal shareholder in the company; by 1702, under Queen Anne, the largest share of the royal revenues would be obtained from this source. Upon the chartering of the Company, the King sent instructions to the governor of the colony of Virginia to promote the importation of slaves for the profit of the Company. The Board of Trade assisted in the venture, as its largest profits, too, were realized from the sale of slaves. It put another form of pressure on the settlers; by design, it reduced the emigration of indentured servants to a trickle to force the reluctant colonists to rely on slave labor.

Even with these sanctions taken against them, the colonists did not cease protesting against a mass influx of slaves. Their Assembly in Virginia tried for a hundred years to find ways to control this plague after the Africa Company began its operations. That their efforts were finally frustrated, can be seen from a letter written by a cleric of Westover, Virginia, the Rev. Peter Fontaine, on March 30, 1757, complaining to his brother of the impossibility of resisting:

6

THE SLAVE: A NEW AMERICAN COMMODITY

... our Assembly, foreseeing the ill consequences of importing such members amongst us, hath often attempted to lay a duty upon them which would amount to a prohibition, such as ten or twenty pounds a head, but no governor dare pass such a law, having instructions to the contrary from the Board of Trade at home. By this means they are forced upon us, whether we will or not ... this of course draws us all into the original sin and curse of the country of purchasing slaves.

The large number of black slaves imported in the interest of the mother country made the expansion of tobacco farms possible; thus a vicious circle was begun. Slavery also made possible the growing of rice on extensive landholdings in South Carolina. And subsequently the plantation economy which required large working forces with great endurance and physical strength became prevalent throughout the South.

Simple uprisings on board American slavers were abundant toward the middle of the eighteenth century, and accounts disclose that they often succeeded. If American commanders and crew were less vigilant than those of other nationalities, it was not from the lack of having been properly warned. Shipowners were well aware of the dangers to their precious property and underlined admonishments of caution to the captains with great earnestness. The warning of Samuel Waldo, a prosperous shipowner of Boston, on March 12, 1734, was typical of the kind of precaution that had to be taken throughout the century to assure a safe passage for slavers:

For your own Safety as well as mine You'll have the needful Guard over your Slaves, and put not too much confidence in the Women nor Children lest they happen to be Instrumental to your being surprised which may be fatall.

7

Waldo probably knew of cases in which female slaves and children, having been left unchained, had heeded the suggestions of a slave leader in preparing a revolt, though no such case has been found on the records.

Uprisings were certainly regular hazards of slavers navigating close to the African shores, as has been pointed out. But the number of these that succeeded in getting the better of American vessels is, curiously enough, far above normal for ships of the period.

Captain Murrel of the *Clare* lost his ship in this way off the coast of Guinea in 1729, after setting sail for home. The *Clare,* the record reports,

> was not got 10 Leagues in her Way before the Negroes rose, and making themselves Masters of the Gunpowder and Fire arms, the Captain and Ships Crew took to their Long Boat, and got ashore near Cape Coast Castle. The Negroes ran the Ship on shore within a few Leagues of the said Castle, and made their Escape.

A variation on the pattern of uprising aboard the slavers is provided by the record of the misfortune of Captain William Atkinson of the *Katherine,* sailing from Boston in 1729. In this case the slaves took advantage of a mutiny on ship that was not of their own making to escape:

> Captain Atkinson had earlier been reported to have stolen many Negroes on the Guinea coast. On his last voyage there, the crew probably thought they should be given a share of the illicit profit of the undertaking, for they mutinied and threw the captain into the sea. Some of the slaves on board the *Katherine* were able to escape in the disorder, and these fugitives informed on the crew. The mutineers had been seized in Antigua and jailed by the time the report was recorded in July 1726.

The report of the Newport Customs House in 1730 is the source of the following dramatic story, in which the ingenuity of a Yankee captain and his mates prevailed over the attempts of their cargo of slaves to take command of the ship *Little George* after a mutiny:

> The *Little George* had sailed from the Guinea coast for Rhode Island in June of 1730, with 96 slaves aboard, of whom 35 were men. The latter somehow "got off their iron" on June 6 at dawn. Captain George Scott, the mates, and a cabin boy barricaded themselves in the cabin, while the slaves tried to turn the ship towards shore. After four days the whites noticed that the ship had returned to the same point where it had lain when the slaves had taken over. While they navigated, the slaves "were continually heaving down Billets of Wood, and Water into the cabin, with the intention to Disable us and spoil our small arms," Captain Scott reported.
>
> However, the captain and crew came up with a plan of their own. They bored holes through the bottom of the vessel and let in about three feet of water. Then the captain called to the slaves and stated that he would sink the ship with all of them. The frightened slaves were cajoled into promising to land the ship and leave it intact. The captain shouted navigating directions through the closed cabin door and when the ship was beached the slaves hastened onto shore and disappeared.
>
> Natives drawn by the spectacle of the beached ship then thronged the shore, excited by the prospect of seizing the ship and its treasures. They fired on the vessel and were preparing to climb aboard when an English ship approached and saved the embattled crew members, who had survived their nine-day imprisonment in the cabin by eating stored rice and water.

The *Newport Mercury* of 1765 printed an extraordinary account of one of the numerous shipside revolts that was subdued during the eighteenth century:

Captain Esek Hopkins, on commission from a trader in Providence, R.I., had lost most of the crew and officers of his brig *Sally* through illness. When his ship had loaded its cargo on the African coast and set sail for the American continent, the Captain selected a few slaves who looked more alert than the rest and allowed them to move about the ship at will, in return for their acting as crew members. The slaves freed their fellows in irons and rose up against the captain and the white crew; the latter however, were armed to the teeth, conscious of the danger that free slaves on board represented; they were especially careful because of their reduced number and the advantage that the more than 100 slaves on the ship held over them. Hopkins and his men met the attack with murderous fire, killing or forcing overboard eighty.

Captain Hopkins may have gambled on the likelihood that the benefits of a privileged position on the ship would have broken the solidarity of the slave ranks and also dispelled the fears and suspicions of those still in chains. The severity of punishment meted out to the surviving slaves was mitigated by the desire of the captain to deliver as much of his saleable "merchandise" as possible to his masters in Rhode Island.

The pages of *The News Letter* of Boston swarm with names of captains of the century: Captain Bear of a Rhode Island Vessel, slave revolt off Cape Coast Castle in 1747, captain and crew slaughtered; Captain Nicoll of a New York ship, slave revolt in 1761, crew and vessel saved, forty slaves killed, the rest surrendered; Captain Harris of a Boston ship, slave revolt in 1766 on the Gambia River, captain and crew murdered, thirty slaves escaped, the rest recaptured by several vessels lying nearby.

Despite the great losses risked and suffered through such incidents, the trade continued unrelentingly, buoyed by the enormous profits and expanding markets. It is hard to realize that such losses were calculated almost entirely in human lives, but they were. The normal cost can be roughly calculated by a letter dated Barbados, February 28, 1758, from Captain Joseph Harrison of the *Rainbow* to a business partner, describing a typical profit venture in the trade from Angola:

> I purchased eight slaves on the windward coast, and 261 at Benin, besides 5400 weight of ivory. Leaving the river November 9th, we arrived at St. Thomas Dec. 17th, from whence our three vessels saild, Jan. 4th. I have buried all my officers, except my first and third mate and gunner. Having lost since left Liverpool 25 white people and 44 Negroes. The Negroes rose on us after we left St. Thomas'; they killed my linguister whom I got at Benin, and we then secured them without farther loss.

The loss of life among slavers and their crews was nothing in comparison to the terrible massacres of black people caused in the vise of trade. It is apt to recall the figures used by Sir Fowell Buxton before the House of Commons in the early nineteenth century to visualize the carnage:

> The whole wastage of the traffic is seven tenths, that is to say, for every ten Negroes whom Africa parts with, America receives only three; the other seven die....

Slaves were customarily given a few days to recover after their long voyages. They ate good food, put colorful cloth around their loins, and washed themselves. A mixture of lemon juice and gunpowder was used to make their muscles swell; pimento rubbed on their gums masked the ravages of scurvy. Niceties of this sort may have been physically comforting, but they were also disquieting. Even those who did not believe they were being prepared to be eaten, suspected sinister intentions behind the traders' kindness.

Auctions of slaves and colonial products were advertised in local papers. West Indian Negroes and those being resold knew the procedure and followed the course of such auctions with interest, though many of the bewildered, homesick African Negroes were terrified into insensibility. More experienced slaves listened carefully to the proceedings of the auctions and exhibited pride when high bids proved their worth, not so much from vanity as from the certainty that, as valuable property, they could expect special consideration from their new masters.

Professional buyers probably calculated the value of slaves on the basis of life expectancy. According to Ulrich Bonnell Phillips, "probably not half of those who had been seized in Africa were alive in America at the end of three or four years." Children under fourteen, men over thirty, and women over twenty-two had very little value. Yet some bargain hunters knew that inferior slaves, bought for almost nothing, could be restored to health and eventually sold at an enormous profit. Unforeseen disappointments often awaited the buyers at auctions, however, if the slaves they bought did not live long enough to justify the considerable financial outlay necessary for their purchase.

Planters usually put new slaves and experienced ones together in their settlements to ease the shock of adjustment to a new environment. Experienced planters encouraged their slaves to interrupt work to sing and dance in order to combat the disease of melancholy which often impaired the newcomers' strength and sapped their will to live. Poor masters could not afford such leniency. Dependent upon a considerable investment, they exacted as much work as possible from the slaves.

Planters ran a special risk when they bought slaves from the West Indies; the natives there had received a taste of what was to be their lot in life and had come to know the domineering influence of the white man. The atmosphere of the West Indian islands was always charged with the incitements of slave revolts, mass escapes, and slave hunts; Negroes there were forced to witness horrible executions of alleged rebels, though such punishments proved that well-acclimated slaves who had seen the punishments were even more prone to insurrection than the newcomers from Africa. Nevertheless, they were better workers than the newcomers, and planters preferred them. Greed for profit was stronger than the fear of revolt.

The revolts on the islands affected the slaveholding colonies of America directly. Frightened West Indian planters from time to time pulled up their roots and took their implements and slaves to less turbulent areas on the mainland. These new residents, with their stories of slave treachery, served as a living warning to the colonial planters not to become complacent. And conversely, notwithstanding the immense danger of talking about such matters, slaves of the newcomers also found ways to spread the news of the uprisings that had forced their masters to flee.

In the 1730s, drought, hurricane, and locusts plagued the Danish West Indies. The slaves' staple food, corn, was destroyed. On the island of St. John, the 1,000 slaves working on over 100 sugar plantations faced starvation. The planters knew enough to expect trouble when the food supply was low; only the slim luxury of being fed and cared for made slavery bearable. Hoping to forestall unrest among the

13

slaves, the Danish governor prescribed severe punishment for slaves caught attempting to flee: they were to be seared three times with a red-hot iron and then hanged; Negroes who knew of a conspiracy but failed to report it were to be branded on the forehead in addition to receiving a hundred lashes.

Installation of this reign of terror as a preventive "remedy" precipitated a slave rebellion which, because of its closeness to the North American continent, its long duration, and the great difficulties of the whites in overcoming it, had a particular impact on the southern English colonies.

On November 23, 1733, about a dozen Negroes carrying wood stormed Governor Gardelin's office in St. John. Once inside the building, they removed sugarcane knives from under the wood they were carrying and murdered the guards, subsequently rushing to the guardroom where off-duty guards were sleeping and killing them all. Meanwhile, a group of slaves who knew how to handle guns fired three salvos as a signal for all the slaves of the island to rise. The plantation Negroes killed every white man they could find, and survivors were forced to row in hasty retreat to the neighboring island of St. Thomas for help. The commander there dispatched eighteen soldiers whose number was supplemented by friendly blacks. They opened a counterattack in the dense jungle bush of the island, but found that they were too few in number to penetrate it effectively.

Sixteen marines taken from an English ship in the harbor at St. Thomas were recruited by the Danish commander. They landed on St. John, and formed a patrol to reconnoiter. The patrol was immediately ambushed; four were killed and the rest withdrew. The captain of the English ship had evidently taken part in this action on his own responsibility, for he then lifted anchor and sailed away. The slaves remained safely hidden in their stronghold.

Throughout the next winter the slaves remained in the bush, venturing out to plunder food and warm clothing. No help was forthcoming from distant Denmark, which was short of ships and soldiers. Realizing this, the Danish commander turned to the French in Martinique for help, promising them as bounty four-fifths of all slaves captured. In April of 1734, two French boats landed at St. John carrying 220 Creoles and some officers who were veterans of other campaigns against fugitive slaves. The Danes themselves added seventy-four West Indian Negroes to the expeditionary force. Led by the French commander himself, the armed men climbed steep mountains and combed the forests and valleys of the island in search of the slaves. They killed and captured a great many of them and ultimately broke the backbone of the insurrection. Yet in August of the same year, nine months after the beginning of the revolt, fourteen slaves were still known to be at large, and one-fourth of the Danish population of the island had already perished in the unrest of the rebellion.

Despite the widespread spirit of rebellion in the West Indies, planters of South Carolina and the French colony of Louisiana had for many years bought slaves at Barbados. There were certain signal advantages in making transactions there which were established by successful petition to Louis XIV by Governor Bienville of Louisiana in 1712. Under the terms of the agreement, Indian slaves from the mainland could be traded for Negro slaves from the islands at the ratio of three Indians for one Negro. In the petition to the King this scheme was justified by Bienville with an ingenious argument:

The Indian when in the West Indies will not be able to run away, the country being unknown to them, and the Negroes will not dare become fugitives in Louisiana, because the Indians would kill them.

In South Carolina, however, colonists did not have the security for their slaves that they found in Louisiana. Their deadly enemies, the Yamassee Indians, encouraged Negro slaves to flee, promising to guide them to freedom in the Spanish colony of Florida. Sometimes the Indians kept these Negroes and assimilated them into their tribe; at other times they used them as their own slaves, treating them with exemplary fairness. But often, pressure from the Spanish planter was too strong to resist, and the Indians sold the runaways to them. These Spanish planters were accustomed to buying fugitives from Indians without asking them where they came from even if, from time to time, they ran into trouble with their own governors, when the English colonists sought to reclaim their property.

English planters deeply resented this lax policy on the part of the Spanish colonists, who were members of a nation that allowed slaveholding and slave trading itself, but would not return fugitive slaves. They considered it an execrable crime against the rights of property, one that in the long run would endanger slaveholders everywhere. If slaves were allowed and encouraged to flee their plantations, the momentary advantages of buying cheap slaves from the Indians in the Spanish fashion were not worth the danger that such an act created to the institution of slaveholding.

Such counsel on the part of the English colonists might have prevailed over Spanish governors of Florida if Spanish policy had been decided by the propertied classes. But the Spanish King still ruled his kingdom virtually as a family estate. This had been made clear in 1688 when King Philip V had issued an order automatically setting runaway slaves free and barring their sale, purchase, or return. Spanish planters in Florida, who were willing to admit fugitives but were used to reenslaving them, were disturbed by the order and often evaded it. Spanish governors pursued a vacillating policy. The King was far away, the powerful planters, nearby.

Thus the Yamassee Indians were a particular point of conflict between the English and Spanish colonists, providing a catalytic agent for bad feeling between the two pioneer communities. This tribe was hostile to the South Carolinians anyway, since the colonists were expanding their plantations into Indian territory at the beginning of the eighteenth century. Furthermore, the Yamassees brought hundreds of thousands of valuable skins to the trading post at Charleston, but were being offered increasingly less useful items in exchange, such as trinkets, mirrors, and ribbons. By intoxicating the Indians at the post before they dealt with them, white traders persuaded them to accept unfair barter rates for their pelts, thus forcing the Indians to buy what they actually needed on credit and making them deeply indebted to the white colony.

Mounting bitterness over their mistreatment had culminated in a mass attack on the South Carolina colony at the turn of the century. After a long military campaign Governor Craven defeated the Yamassee and forced them over the Savannah River, which constituted the limit of the English colony at that time, and into Spanish territory.

The Spanish, on their side of the Savannah, received the Yamassee triumphantly, ringing bells and firing guns in celebration. The Indians were allowed to settle there and, in a move designed to produce more harassment for the English, were kept well armed by the Spanish so that they could periodically issue forth from their sanctuary to invade English settlements on the other side of the river.

The South Carolina settlers, knowing the rebellious temper of their West Indian slaves, were fearful that they might conspire with the Yamassee, who had been thus installed as a guerrilla force, or, even worse, might rise up during an Indian raid to massacre the whites and run away. To prevent this, the colonists turned South Carolina into an armed camp. Every white man was a member of the militia, carrying arms by day and patrolling the settlement by night.

In 1733, the King of Spain reissued his order concerning the freeing of runaway slaves, and the governor of Florida no longer dared evade it. The province of South Carolina and the Savannah region had always been considered by the Spanish to be theirs, so that there always had been latent hostility towards the English. With the added bad feeling on the part of the South Carolinians prompted by the newly enforced Spanish edict luring their slaves away, war appeared imminent.

The Florida garrison of the Spanish was weak, their armed forces being sparsely distributed among their many possessions in the Western Hemisphere. The governor of the colony accordingly decided that, with the alternatives of freedom and newly acquired property under the Spanish or torture and death under the South Carolinians, no one would fight the English with more determination than the Negroes.

With this thought in mind, Governor Montiano in 1726 established a military colony of the fugitive slaves to the north of St. Augustine, and named it Fort Mosa.

This fort, founded as an ill-judged gambit in the colonial

strategies of two great European powers, inspired a great slave revolt which, later inflated by rumor and exaggeration, lingered for many years in the memories of the southern states.

Thirty-eight Negro families who had been converted to Catholicism were moved to Fort Mosa, or Negro Fort, as it was generally called. The settlers were allotted food, tools, furniture, and some land, which they cultivated with great industry and spectacular results. A battery of four cannon was mounted about the fortified town they inhabited. Other Negroes were settled in villages and organized into a military company, trained by the Spanish army, but led by Negro officers.

This Negro garrison, made up of fugitive slaves from Spanish colonies, was considered a provocation and a mortal danger by the English colonists in South Carolina. Fort Mosa stood as a beacon, guiding all slaves to freedom.

These fears turned out to be well justified. On September 9, 1737, eleven years after the setting up of the garrison at Fort Mosa, a group of Negroes in Stono, South Carolina, attacked the town warehouse, taking guns and ammunition and setting fire to the building. Having heard of the free Negro settlement in Florida from the Indians, they had determined to join it, elected a leader and set out on the road, with colors flying and drums beating. On the way, they attacked farms and killed all white men on them. Their plan was to seize all supplies they could lay their hands on, order all slaves they fell in with to join them, and burn down houses and barns within their reach.

The long column of Negroes attracted the attention of two distinguished travelers, Governor Bull and a Mr. Golightly, who were riding to Charleston that Sunday morning. Golightly immediately galloped eight miles to Wilton, the nearest white settlement, where he found the settlers in church. A militia was hastily formed, and rode out to encounter the Negroes. They reached them sooner than expected, for the Negroes had taken a rest, and were indulging in wildly intoxicated dancing and singing, having come upon several barrels of rum in a farmhouse. The fugitives were secretly encircled, and several rapid volleys fired into their midst, killing and wounding many of them. The rest of the mob fled into the woods, but were later captured and stood trial for rebellion. In all, forty-four Negroes and twenty-one whites lost their lives in the revolt.

The whites hoped that the slaves would be discouraged from further uprising by the news of the Stono massacre, but apparently they were not, for the Georgia records note a new uprising in South Carolina less than a year later. In the beginning of June, 1738, more than 150 runaway slaves were reported to have met near Charleston and turned south to march towards Florida and Fort Mosa. However, these were quickly detected and pursued by bands of white men. The slaves could not live off the land because the corn was not yet ripe. They also lacked weapons to defend themselves or procure food by force. By June 9, fifty of them had been taken prisoner, "whom they were daily hanging, ten a day."

Florida and the bordering English colonies were made a zone of combat by the war of Jenkins' Ear, in 1739. Though the conflict had been kindled by the allegation of an English captain that his ear had been cut off by the Spanish, the real issue at stake was the British monopoly of the Asiento—granted at the Treaty of Utrecht in 1713. Parliament, under relentless pressure of British merchants, had deprived the Africa Company of the monopoly and made the slave trade free to all British merchants. Spain used this action as a pretext to declare the British slave monopoly in Spanish territory void altogether.

One consequence of the war was an offensive launched in 1740 by General James Oglethorpe, governor of the newly founded English colony of Georgia, to capture St. Augustine. Oglethorpe, it will be seen, was also a great visionary, but in this military venture he hoped to end the threat of the Spanish and Yamassee Indians once and for all. He commanded a British regiment, some South Carolina militia, a company of immigrant Scottish Highlanders, and a group of Creek Indians. In their march to St. Augustine, the detachment stormed Fort Mosa, but found it deserted. The Spanish had evacuated both the troops and the townspeople.

Oglethorpe's campaign in Florida failed, however, because the navy was unable to cooperate as planned. The general was forced to withdraw his troops from Florida, and the Spanish resettled Fort Mosa. The fort held out as a Negro settlement until 1763, when Spain finally ceded Florida to the British, resettling the free Negroes of Fort Mosa in Cuba.

Upon his return to England, Oglethorpe organized a group of influential philanthropists, bound together by their disgust with the revival of slave trade which the colonization of America had brought about. The general's experience in the South had refuted the widely held argument that only black slaves had the physical endurance to turn the wilderness into fertile farms. Even if this argument had in fact been true, these philanthropists wondered at the morality of showering untold misery on the natives of Africa merely for the improved prosperity of white colonists in America. And had not General Oglethorpe's own experience confirmed that a reliance on slave labor, in addition to being wrong in itself, exposed the colonists to danger to life and property, and to their own moral corruption?

An opportunity arose for the Oglethorpe group to attempt to prove that the tide of slave trade was not irresistible; it might be even reversed if it could be proved that the colonies could thrive without importing black slaves.

At that time, the English public was aroused by a new current of religious persecution on the Continent. Oglethorpe joined such religious groups as the Society for the Propagation of the Gospel in Foreign Parts in collecting funds and petitioning King George II for a colonial charter to settle the Protestant refugees in America.

A subtle interpretative shading in the purpose of the charter made the idea of banning the importation and trading of slaves to the colony palatable to the English government:

> Experience has shewn that the manner of settling Colonys and Plantation with Black Slaves and Negroes hath obstructed the increase of English and Christian inhabitants the rein who alone can in case of War be relyed on for Defence and Security of the same.

In their efforts to secure support of the colony by the King and Parliament, the philanthropists resorted to diplomacy, but their resolve not to admit Negro slaves into the colony rested actually on their desire to protect it from the same dread of slave rebellions as afflicted the settlers in South Carolina. The Scots in Georgia truly expressed this intention when they protested the softening of the prohibition, stating: the Negroes "are thrown amongst us to be our Scourge one Day or other for our sins; and as Freedom to them must be as dear as to us, what a Scene of Horror must it bring about."

Although the settlers were to serve imperial and financial interests, "working peacefully on their piece of land they will defend in war," Oglethorpe and the Trustees firmly resolved that the settlement "was not to be rich but a Godly Colony." Named for George II and chartered in 1732, the Colony of Georgia posed a challenge to the spirit of the age by denying the validity of the assumption that happiness is best pursued through acquisition and unrestrained economic ambition.

The charter of this utopia attracted a strange assortment of people. The largest group of refugees were Salzburg Lutherans, who had chosen exile in preference to conversion to Catholicism. They harkened to the words of the charter that "forever thereafter there shall be liberty of conscience allowed in the worship of God."

Moravian Brethren from Germany also decided to go. They were governed solely by divine inspiration, determined by drawing lots among the faithful.

The Waldenses, descendants of an old group of religious heretics of Europe, persecuted since the Crusades, contributed their interests in raising silkworms and making wine. The population of the original colony also included some survivors of the Jacobite rising of 1715 in Scotland, and a group of Portuguese Jews fleeing the Inquisition. In addition to these, regular English immigrants who paid their own way followed later.

Oglethorpe must have realized the perplexity of the situation as he led the first group of colonists in 1733. Spain, the fountainhead of modern slavery, had established a sanctuary for fugitive slaves in Fort Mosa. England, the largest slave-trading nation in the world, had set up a colony in which slavery was illegal. Yet, this colony of Georgia was to be a buffer between the settlement of slaveholders in South Carolina and the free Negroes in Fort Mosa!

The many inherent contradictions of the colony revealed

themselves when the hostility of Jenkins' Ear broke out between England and Spain in 1739. The Moravian Brethren refused to take up arms. When this act of conscientious objection was pronounced unfair to the other settlers, they left the colony entirely and went to Pennsylvania. The labor shortage created by the war was used as a pretext by some of the remaining colonists to borrow slaves from Carolina traders, in an indirect violation of the charter of Georgia. The importation and trade in slaves was prohibited but, as these men discovered, "borrowing" slaves was not. Boot-legging made its appearance. Evergrowing numbers of colonists petitioned the Trustees to lift all limitation on property ownership. Well-to-do immigrants coveted Indian lands which Oglethorpe had solemnly sworn in the charter to protect.

The Rev. George Whitefield, deacon of the Anglican Church, on a visit to Oglethorpe's colony in 1740 expressed the hope that the young people of the colony would eventually realize its moral principles:

> The colony could never prosper till this generation was all worn out, like the Israelites in the wilderness.

But he was mistaken. The failure of the first generation saved the next one from being tested.

* * *

When he returned to the Georgian town of Frederica, after the disastrous Florida campaign of 1740, General Oglethorpe was informed that a strange man had been captured by English orders on the charge of being a French agent. The man had cut his hair in the Indian manner, painted his face and body as the Indians did, and wore only a shirt and flap.

"He is an ugly little man," Oglethorpe was told, "but his politeness which dress or imprisonment could not disguise, attracted the notice of every gentleman in Frederica and gained him the favor of many visits and conversations."

The man's name was William Gottlieb Priber, a German from Saxony, alleged, but never proved, to be a Jesuit. He had won the friendship of the Cherokees among whom he had lived since 1737 and was accepted as one of them. He was held in great respect as an advisor to the Cherokee king. Priber spoke English, Dutch, French, and Latin fluently and had finished a Cherokee-French dictionary that he planned to publish in Europe.

On Priber's person had been found a manuscript, ready for the press, entitled "Paradise." According to those who had either read his manuscript or heard him explain his ideas, Priber's "Paradise" was to be a communistic society in which all things, including women, would be held in common; children would be reared by the community.

Oglethorpe had an interview with the prisoner. It is not known whether or not he had an opportunity to glance at Priber's manuscript, but if he had, the strange man would have appeared to him as a kind of caricature of himself, embodying the reverse side of all the ideas and concepts that he was trying to realize in Georgia.

Both men believed in establishing a new civilization on virgin soil, free from the corruption of the old world. Oglethorpe's society was to be peopled by religious idealists, whereas Priber's was to be based on the men of Nature, soon to be called "noble savages" by the philosophes of Europe.

Significantly, there was to be no place for slavery in either community. Georgia was planned by Oglethorpe as a white society, but Priber wanted it to be part of a great Indian empire fashioned of a confederation of southern Indians.

It was Priber's conviction that "before this century is passed, the Europeans (meaning white men) will have a very small footing on this continent." On about the same territory, between the Savannah and Altamaha rivers, both men intended to reserve a refuge for debtors and the persecuted, but Priber would also include criminals and *wished to also invite the slaves "who would fly thither from justice or their Masters."*

Both men strove to protect the Indians from the fraud and greed of the white man. Oglethorpe set an official price for their furs, and prohibited the sale of alcoholic beverages to them; Priber taught them to use weights and measures and constructed steelyards (balances) for their use.

However, Oglethorpe wanted to preserve the Indian friendship with the British, while Priber advised them to trade with both the English and the French on the same footing "so as to be caressed, courted, and receive presents from both," and insisted that they should give away no more land and divest themselves of alliances with Europeans. English traders thus had good reason to imprison Priber.

"A very extraordinary man," Oglethorpe said after the interview. He himself was a general and governor of the new colony (though about to return to England to defend the failure of his military campaign); Priber, in spite of his erudition and fine manners, was only an adventurer. Yet the general must have felt that they both had failed at the same undertaking.

Oglethorpe departed in 1743 from the colony he had founded. Soon after, greedy settlers began to appropriate Indian lands, endangering the peace with the Indians; seven years later, the Trustees of the Georgia Colony returned their charter to the Government.

Georgia, obviously, survived Oglethorpe. But his "Godly Colony" became a land of plantations and Negro slavery.

William Gottlieb Priber, it is reported, died in prison. His dream of the Indian empire free from black slaves died with him.

Of his manuscript "Paradise," nothing is known; it disappeared without a trace after his death.

II

EARLY LAWS AND UPRISINGS

"A conspiracy of ambition and avarice of kings and maitresses; venal corruption of public men, the open profligacy of the courts, the greedy cupidity of trade, conspired in exercizing dominion over the civilized community."

Frederick Bancroft, *Slave Trading in the Old South.*

L AW, public opinion, and the solidarity of his fellow slave owners supported the master in wielding practically limitless power and authority over his slaves.

But an irrepressible doubt sapped his exterior power and often made him insecure. Was there, perhaps, an element in slavery that ran counter to the laws of humanity?

This feeling, though at most times subconscious, caused a master to *expect* rebellion, and, expecting it, to apply preventive remedies. The slightest signs of dissatisfaction or ˈessness: innocent gestures, facial expressions, fragments ˈersations overheard in slave quarters, were inter- ˈnously by the sensitive and suspicious occu- ˈntation house. Often under scrutiny the slave ˈpicions unintentionally through a variety ˈsion, unconscious spite, a perverse

28

desire to provoke just what his master feared, or, on the contrary, a self-conscious will to act as his master would want him to act.

In contemporary records we read over and over of "conspiracies nipped in the bud," or "revolts prevented at the last minute," and of the resulting reprisals that took the lives of many slaves. It should be borne in mind that the ultimate reality of these abortive conspiracies originated more often than not in the master's mind. The severe measures applied as punishment served as a cathartic release of the master's own fantasies, tensions, and terrors.

In the eighteenth century, Britain was almost continuously at war with one or the other European powers in the Western Hemisphere. In the resulting confusion, the periodic threat of invasion was added to the many terrors that plagued the colonists' minds. It was easy to imagine the opportunities that such troubles would present to the slaves for mass escape or rebellion; easier still, the dreadful possibility of collusion between invader and slave—and, indeed, some foreign armies did appeal to the slaves to rise. Such pressures produced startling reprisals for slave conspiracies which probably never existed in fact.

Documented cases of insurrection in the early days of the colonies are few and far between; in almost every case, there is doubt as to the veracity of the incidents—though their occurrence generally resulted in strengthened repressive measures against slaves.

Virginia showed a typical trend in this respect. There, the law had imposed few restrictions on the movements of slaves until about 1680, when the increasing influx of Negroes had begun to disquiet the whites. At that time dreadful rumors of conspiracies began to spread, and appropriate measures were taken to prevent revolts. The settlements were regularly patrolled, Negro quarters being searched for unlawful assemblies, and constables were empowered to arrest "all such persons or strolling slaves and servants without passes, and to take them to justice to be whipped not exceeding twenty lashes." But, according to James Curtis Ballagh in an evaluation from which the preceding is taken, the times remained remarkably calm:

> Though a number of attempted or supposed conspiracies were discovered during the 17th and 18th centuries, no actual insurrection worthy of the name occurred. Between 1680 and 1726 were a number of scares from Negro assemblies and plots ... but insurrection was more of an anticipated danger than an actual one.

Nevertheless, in 1723 a law was passed by the Virginia Assembly declaring that a conspiracy to rebel by five or more Negroes or slaves was punishable by death. How little "conspiracy" there had to be in order to warrant the death penalty may be gathered from a letter written by Lieutenant Governor Robert Dinwiddie many years later, during the French and Indian War, when he was stirred up by the impact of a British setback on the Ohio River. Dinwiddie was addressing the letter to a colonel of the Virginia troops, whose son had been ambushed at his home by Negroes "in a body." The Negroes had been arrested, a measure approved by the Lieutenant Governor. He added that:

> If found guilty of the Expressions mentioned I expect you will send for a Com'o to try them, and an Example of one or two at first may prevent those creatures enter'g into Combinat's and wicked Designs ... These poor creatures imagine the French will give them their freedom.

Here, the classical pattern of Negro revolt is illustrated at its simplest: political unrest and the hope of emancipation to be granted by foreign forces caused a slight disturbance among the Negroes; doubtless this "conspiracy" of Negroes —little more than a haphazard gathering of slaves—was punished with all the ruthlessness sanctioned by the law, and the "example of one or two at first" efficiently made.

A senseless incident of suppression occurred in Maryland, as a consequence of what is described as a "great consternation" that seems to have taken hold of the people of the colony. To quote from the records of the 1739 Maryland Council:

> Slaves and convicts were watched, the militia was ready to quell any insurrections. Soon rumors began to spread of Negroes holding tumultous meetings in several parts.

From all available accounts, it is apparent that these rumors had no foundation in fact. However, in 1739 loyal slaves in Prince George's County told of a "most wicked and dangerous conspiracy" they knew of on the part of the county's Negroes, whose purpose was to usurp the power of the whites and possess themselves of the country. The governor issued a proclamation urging the county officials to "aid in averting such great dangers."

The Council later stated that the cause of the fevered rumors was some trivial local excitement among a few Negroes, certainly no massive planned conspiracy. However, the same record relates that at least one of the slaves, the "leader," was tried and executed; he could not be resurrected when an inquiry into the same insurrection by the Maryland House of Delegates the next year found that it "failed to find anything which could be in any way presumed to have endangered the welfare of the province."

Another "conspiracy," this one in New Orleans, illustrates the tendency of ill-informed colonists to grasp at the slightest whisper of dissent in times of trouble and turn it into palpable evidence of revolt.

The population of the French colony of Louisiana had long lived in terror of the fierce Natchez Indians, who had massacred the French at Fort Rosalie, in 1729. While the colonists were awaiting reinforcements from France and the West Indies to help subdue the Indians, a slave rebellion was reported in 1730, called Zamba's Plot. This is what happened, to quote from the *Magazine of American History*, vol. XII.

> Soldiers in New Orleans had stopped a Negro woman on the street and had ordered her to bring them firewood. When she refused to do as she was told, one of the soldiers slapped her face; after this the woman was reported to have screamed in colloquial New Orleans French that though the soldiers might beat her then and there, Frenchmen would not beat Negroes long. She was arrested and questioned as to the meaning of the remarks, but denied knowing anything. She excused her words as being uttered in anger, meaning nothing. A French planter, Le Page, insisted to the Governor that a conspiracy might be afoot. He asked power to investigate and was granted it. The same night, with his servant, he went to the Negro quarter of New Orleans searching for any cabin with a sign of light, which would betray the presence of several Negroes assembled. He found a light burning in the Cabin of Zamba, a powerful Negro overseer who, it was rumored had been deported to America from West Africa after driving the French out of his country. On the ship *Annibal* he was discovered plotting a revolt and had been put in chains. Zamba, after his arrival in New Orleans, had gained the leadership of the most alert slaves through his strength and intelligence. The Frenchman Le Page overheard Zamba talking over a "plan" with

two other Negroes—for a revolt led by eight reliable men, six of whom were known to Le Page.

The following night Le Page returned to find all eight of the ringleaders assembled in Zamba's cabin where he overheard a decision to delay the rising until after the harvest.

The next day, the Governor and Le Page agreed to arrest the conspirators singly so that it would not be noticed that they had disappeared. After their arrest, none of the eight would acknowledge any part in a conspiracy, though finally on being told that Le Page had spied on his cabin, Zamba reportedly exclaimed "Le Page? He knows everything!" This was interpreted as admission of guilt; the rest of the "conspirators" broke down under torture. Three were convicted and broken on the wheel. A woman was also hanged.

There were no institutional regulations in English law in regard to the status of the slave. When modern slavery made its first powerful inroads into the conduct of business and public life, a basic concept was applied to the slave from which were to be derived the complexities of his relationship to the institutions of the people into whose world he came.

A legal fiction was accepted—that the Negro slave was not a person, but chattel. English law did not interfere with a property owner's handling of his goods and chattels.

The American colonists inherited this concept, though it flagrantly contradicted their senses. This contradiction infected their legal, social, religious, intellectual, and psychological achievements. Gustave de Beaumont saw this dilemma on his travels in America, and reported to the French Academy of Moral and Political Sciences that it was "easy for American legislators to declare that the slaves had no 'patrie,' nor society or family. But how to allow him to multiply without being a father, mother, children, brothers,

sisters, and, consequently, having family affections and interests? They made the slaves things; but by that they did
not deprive them of intelligence and sentiments inherent in
human nature."

Colonial legislatures passed a number of acts pertaining
to slaves, mostly for the purpose of public safety. These
acts also provided for a certain uniformity of treatment of
slaves outside their master's jurisdiction and set some limit
to the power of a master over his slave. These acts were
based very much on the assumption that the slave was
human, in one way, since fear of slave conspiracies was their
main concern, and only humans are able to conspire.

Yet, by recognizing that slaves could be clearly distinguished by the color of their skin from the free population,
these local regulations excluded Negroes from the rest of
the community. The earliest slave code, enacted in Virginia
in 1667, clearly stated this principle by discriminating against
colored peoples, even when freed: it banished white men or
women who married Negroes, Indians, or mulattoes. Both
slaves and free Negroes were dealt the death penalty for the
following offenses: murder, rape of a white woman, burning
wheat worth $50 or more, beating a white person, or inciting
to rebellion. On the other hand, the code declared that "killing a slave by extremity of correction was not a felony."

South Carolina codified its regulations in 1712. A runaway
slave was to be whipped in public for twenty days; on repeti-
tion, the letter "R" was to be branded on his right cheek.
On a third offense, if absent over thirty days, he was to lose
one ear. For the fourth offense he was to be castrated. A
woman's punishment on first and subsequent attempts of
escape was: the whip, "R" branded on left cheek, left ear
cut off. The owner who refused to inflict these measures was

to be fined; he also lost ownership of the slave. Anyone enticing slaves to run away was to receive the death penalty.

All Negro houses were to be searched for weapons and stolen goods. Punishments for theft were: whipping for the first offense; loss of one ear for the second, nose slit for the third offense, death penalty for the fourth. No slave was allowed to operate a boat, buy, sell, or wear fine cloth.

The master, if he killed his slave intentionally, had to pay a fine of 50 pounds sterling.

The code was revised in 1739: it forbade, under penalty of $100 and six months in prison, teaching a slave to read and write, as well as to give him alcoholic beverages. On the other hand it increased the fine of the master who had intentionally killed his slave to 700 pounds (he received no punishment if the slave died as a consequence of punishment). It forbade work on Sunday, and more than fifteen hours work a day in summer, fourteen hours in winter. The court having jurisdiction in cases involving the slave codes consisted of the justice of the peace, two justices, and two freeholders. The court was open to the slave only in one instance: if he sued for his freedom.

The slave code in other colonies was in essence the same as in South Carolina. It was usually amended after a case of alleged or actual conspiracy or revolt. In the years of relative calm, masters and authorities would relax their application of the harsh measures of the code. It would be almost forgotten, until a new scare resulted in a new wave of restrictions and punishments.

Pennsylvania abolished the death penalty for crimes committed by slaves in 1705, under Quaker influence.

The New England states, which had very few Negro slaves, assigned the trial of slaves charged with crimes punishable with death to regular courts (except for Rhode Island). All enacted laws that he who wilfully killed a slave received the same punishment as if he had killed a white man. In New England a black slave could testify even against a white person.

The colonies dealt differently with the slaves because local conditions varied, but surges of fear dictated cruel treatment in all, even where the laws had generally been lenient.

In the years when large or frequent fires visited a region, rumor usually had it that arsonists had been at work and the blame fell on the slaves, whom people suspected with good reason of harboring evil intentions against the white people. Periodically, the slaves were accused of poisoning or attempting to poison their masters or the whole white community. How much truth was in such accusations and whether slaves became arsonists or poisoners from personal grudges or as rebels one cannot state, however, with any assurance.

An added source of fear towards the middle of the eighteenth century for the white people of the colonies was the fact that the Negro population was growing faster than that of the whites. Several states made efforts to limit the importation of slaves; in South Carolina, fear of revolts prompted such measures. In Maryland and North Carolina, restrictions were urged by the farmers for other reasons, economic ones —they had run into debt to the traders by buying slaves entirely or partly on credit. In New England states, slavery had never been popular, the climate and soil not being favorable for its establishment, but the states had prospered on the slave trade; even little Rhode Island had 150 slave ships. Though a source of wealth in Massachusetts also, slavery was restricted within that state by a clever manipulation of the customs tariff—the fee paid upon the entry of a slaver into harbor was refunded if the ship later proceeded to another destination.

The Virginia law, passed in 1723, which set a death penalty for "conspiracy" also limited the number of slaves in the colony, though this of course was bound to meet with resistance from the London Board of Trade and the Africa Company, both anxious to sustain profits from slaving. The courts ordered the slaves suspected of involvement in conspiracies to be *sold and transported out of the colony*, thereby reducing the number of slaves in direct proportion to the number of "conspiracies" uncovered.

The increasingly strict regulations on the movements of slaves and the severity of punishment for any slave meeting did not prevent the continuation of one form of protest—flight. Bands of fugitives collected in the hills and forests, where they became bandits, since they could sustain themselves only by looting the settlements. In one such case, about 1729, Negro and Indian fugitives in the Virginia Blue Ridge Mountains apparently tried to create a self-sufficient community. Besides guns and ammunition, they had collected agricultural tools when discovered in 1729 by a group of armed white men who had surprised and overcome them after a long search.

The presence of free Negroes in their colony was a particular irritation to the Virginia colonists. When news of revolts or rumors of conspiracies were heard, the first reaction was to suspect free Negroes as the instigators. The Virginia House of Burgesses resolved to fix a perpetual brand on free Negroes and mulattoes, to distinguish them from other free men, since they "always did, and ever will adhere to and favor the slaves." Thus, in its secondary aspect, the slave problem was also a problem of coexistence between the races. Freedom for a Negro slave was never to make him equal to a white man.

To state that slavery is inhuman is to forget that this institution appeared at certain stages of social development almost everywhere. Slavery is human—all too human.

Basically, its origins can be traced to wars in which, for economic reasons, the victor took prisoners instead of killing them. This he did not only because he could use hands to work in a developing agricultural economy (whereas slaves had been a burden to tribes living off hunting and fishing), but also because the possession of slaves signaled a certain status.

To be a slave meant to enter a miserable existence at the bottom of any society. In Africa, however, a slave was a member of the household; he might own property and could marry and become integrated in the society. In Ashanti, he inherited property from his master.

When the slave trade tore the Negro from a world alive with the spirit of his ancestors, a world where he knew traditions, customs, and language to give his life purpose, he was thrust into a void. His lot was made worst if he had been selected for transport to North American colonies, for in these shipments there was often an intentional scrambling, and groups of Negroes speaking different dialects often commanded a higher price than those who came from the same tribe; for the traders and masters knew that difficulty in communication with others of his kind made Negro slaves less able to conspire. The Negro sold into slavery in the former British colonies of North America lost everything that had made him a social being: his family and kinship ties, his tribal religion, the means to communicate his fears or hopes, his name, and all that could give his life meaning or guidance.

A Negro sold in Spanish America or Brazil fared far better, though not because the master there was less cruel or greedy than the slaveholder in the Anglo-Saxon colonies. Indeed, a slave in North America was, in general, better fed than one in the Spanish-Portuguese colonies, and, though his living conditions might be miserable enough, they compared favorably with those of industrial workers in western Europe at the beginning of the nineteenth century.

But in Spanish-Portuguese America, two powerful institutions, both jealously clinging to their power, interfered with master-slave relations: the government and the church. In those countries, medieval slavery was still lingering on when its modern variation began to offer a huge income to the trade and the state. Therefore, strict regulations of the status of slaves existed and could be applied to the new influx. A slave was baptized before being shipped to a Spanish colony, and thus could not be considered a chattel. He was a being, not a commodity. He had rights, though they were clearly limited, and he was legally enabled to exercise them.

A Negro in Latin America was deemed free until he could be proven to have been a slave. A Negro who could not prove that he had been freed was deemed a slave in North America.

The Spanish code of 1789 prescribed that the child of a slave was to be baptized. Slaves were married in church. The church held concubinage to be a sin, and the code admonished masters not to tolerate it.

One of the gravest consequences of the Anglo-Saxon concept that Negroes were not legal persons was that the children of a slave could be sold from their mother, and wives (married only by the master and under his consent) could be sold from their husbands. Families thus lost track of each other, often forever. This was not the case in Latin America. After marriage, man and wife could be sold only together. If they had served different masters, the master of the woman slave had to allow her to join her husband, whose master had to reimburse the former owner for his loss. Manumission was encouraged by church and lay authorities and was socially approved. It behooved a good citizen to free his slaves at family events. A child's freedom could also be bought at his baptism for a nominal sum. Once freed, a Negro became equal with other free citizens, in contrast to the practice in the United States where, especially in the South, intolerance to free Negroes never ceased and they in no case attained the status of a white man.

The Spanish code also gave the slave the right to own property and to work extra hours to buy his freedom. Under the Anglo-Saxon definition, of course, a chattel could not have these or other rights.

In the American South, special courts sat in judgment over crimes removed from the jurisdiction of the master. In cases of wanton murder of a slave, the master had to stand trial. But a slave or a Negro could not testify against a white man, and a white would never, in actual practice, bear witness against his fellow, so the procedure was a mere form. The Spanish code left regular courts to judge these cases, and the black slave could bear witness against the master. Moreover, the code created the position of "Protector" for the slaves, whose duty was to watch over their treatment and represent them in case of abuse.

In Brazil, African slaves of the same dialect and tribe were left together as a rule, so that they could identify with their own group, and salvage its folklore, habits, and practices, even though they became mingled with Christian traditions.

The Spanish code and the Catholic church further alleviated the welfare of the slave by forbidding work not only on Sundays, but on the thirty rubricked days in the church calendar. Altogether, the slave had 134 days at his disposal to cultivate his own plot of land and to pursue his chosen recreation.

III

CONTROVERSY BEGINS

"Who are you, who pretend to judge another man's happiness; that state, which each man under the guidance of his Maker forms for himself, and not one man for another? ... To know what constitutes mine or your happiness is the sole perogative of Him who created us, and cast us in so various and different molds. Did your slaves ever complain to you of their unhappiness amidst their native woods and deserts?"

B ISHOP William Warburton's voice in 1766 was only one reed among a growing chorus; as the eighteenth century moved into its second half, the moral opposition to this barbarous institution at last began to consolidate. First the Quakers warned members of their community against taking part in the trade and subsequently against having slaves at all; other Christian leaders in England, like Warburton, tried to rouse public indignation.

Public controversy in England over slavery and the slave trade had been provoked for the first time, as a result of the introduction of certain general ideas about humanity that determined the rights of every man by the mere fact that he was, indeed born a man. In France enlightened circles also reacted with sympathy to the outrage and made valuable efforts to spread their views on the right of Negro slaves to their freedom. But it was in America that the rights of man first became the basis for a political movement that was to give history a new turn. The American colonists insisted on these rights and eventually resolved to use force to establish them.

The rebellious colonists were ready by the time of the Revolution to include slavery as an institution imposed upon the reluctant colonies largely by outside interests, in opposition to the principles which gave their grievances their broad moral basis. The real reason was that the colonies had become saturated with slaves, and several of them had already petitioned for a restriction on slave imports to their harbors. Even in South Carolina, traders and planters found that they had overinvested in the commodity, and that further imports would lower the prices of slaves and inflate their investment; in Virginia, which had been reluctant to accept the "original sin and curse" in the first place, the natural increase of the slave population was now considered sufficient to assure an adequate slave force.

Many slaveholders in Virginia and in Maryland felt that the material benefits of slavery were being overshadowed by the adverse moral effects of the institution. Colonel William Byrd expressed this sentiment in 1736 justly:

> They blow up the pride, and ruin the Industry of our White people, who seeing a Rank of poor Creatures below them, detest work for fear it should make them look like slaves.

Byrd, and many others like him, approved the earlier attempt of Georgia to prohibit slavery in her charter and repeated the common lament—also used to account for the indolence of New York youth—that slavery had a corrupting influence on the young. Byrd included another argument against slavery:

> in case there should arise a Man of desperate fortune, such a man might be dreadfully mischievous before any opposition could be found against him, and tinge our Rivers, as wide as they are, with blood. We have mountains in Virginia to which they might retire as safely and do as much mischief as they do in Jamaica.

Byrd's "wide rivers" were planters' rivers, and the slave was considered as a dangerous and explosive outside element. Clearly, he did not belong in Virginia.

Nevertheless, while the Virginia House of Burgesses in 1772 went so far as to label the slave trade "that inhuman and impolite commerce," it would not condemn slavery itself as inhuman. Those leaders of the colonies who signed and helped draft the Declaration of Independence were determined to do so in a form that would give a moral justification to the effort of the colonies to free themselves from the mother country. This they did by declaring all men to be created equal and free to revolt against oppression. But in framing the words of the document, the founders had to grapple with a great problem: how to remain consistent with the principles of the Declaration while at the same time assuring its acceptance by all parties to it.

Such revolutionary statesmen as James Otis, leader of the radicals of New England, recognized that the Negro had, after all, an inalienable right to freedom, but all the founding fathers knew that the consent of all thirteen colonies was inevitably needed to make independence a reality. Thomas Jefferson himself recognized the real dilemma: it lay in the almost insurmountable difficulty of persuading southern colonies to accept the abolition of slavery, balanced by the absolute necessity of being consistent with the basic principles of the Declaration of Independence. In a preliminary draft of the Declaration, an attempt was made to give satisfaction to both sides of the question by attributing the slave trade entirely to the King and Parliament and overlooking the fact that American traders had participated vigorously in it:

> He [the King] has waged civil war against human nature itself, violating its most sacred rights of life and liberty, in the persons of a distant people, who never offended him; captivating and carrying them into slavery in another hemisphere, or to incur miserable death in their transportation thither. This piratical warfare, the opprobrium of infidel powers, is the warfare of the Christian King of Great Britain; determined to keep open a market where MEN should be bought and sold, he prostituted his negative for suppressing every legislative attempt to prohibit or to restrain this execrable commerce.

In the closing sentences of this trial paragraph of the Declaration, Jefferson spelled out the great fear of the American colonists that the royal authority might enroll and arm the slaves against them. At the beginning of the Revolution, there were persistent rumors that one or another of the governors had already called upon the slaves working on the plantations of rebels to come over to the King's standards and join the loyalists and that some Tory commanders had begun to train fugitive slaves as British volunteers:

> and, that this assemblage of horrors might want no fact of distinguished dye, he is now exciting those very people to rise in arm among us, and to purchase that liberty of which he has deprived them, thus paying off former crimes, committed against the liberties of one people, with crimes which he urges them to commit against the lives of another.

However, the representatives of South Carolina and Georgia would not sign their names to the Declaration with the condemnation of slavery included in it; Jefferson knew this, and knew that there were also sensitive northern interests involved. "Our Northern brethren," he wrote, "also, I believe felt a little tender under those censures; for though their people had very few slaves themselves, yet they had been pretty considerable careers of them to others."

So that all the colonies might join the sovereign nations of the world as the United States, the paragraph was simply dropped, and the Declaration of Independence left the entire issue of slavery unbroached in any detail. However, it was manifestly true to any onlooker that even without direct references to slavery, the Declaration had explicitly justified revolt against any of the oppressors of men's inalienable rights; it would have been surprising if the slaves did not heed it as an eloquent invitation to insurrection.

Indeed, slaves in Massachusetts considered the Declaration an important enough assurance of their equal rights to freedom with the American colonists, that in 1777 they submitted a petition to the Council of the Massachusetts House of Representatives, remonstrating that:

> They cannot but express their Astonishment that It has Never bin Considered that Every Principle from which America has Acted in the Course of their unhappy Difficulties with Great Britain Pleads Stronger than a thousand arguments in favor of our petitions.

The petition from the slaves demonstrated that their rights to freedom needed to be stated and satisfied with far more cogency than that of the colonists. It appears that this petition may have formed the basis for Jefferson's statement on the subject years later.

What an incomprehensible machine is man who can endure toil, famine, stripes, imprisonment, and death itself, in vindication of his liberty; and the next moment be deaf to all those motives whose power supported him through his trials, and inflict on his fellow man a bondage, one hour of which is fraught with more misery than ages of that which he rose in rebellion to oppose.

In 1775, the Revolutionary War appeared about to secure for the slave his inalienable rights—but the Declaration left them undeclared.

In that year, the Continental Congress' Committee of Safety resolved to admit free Negroes into the army and navy of the insurgent colonies.

At first, Washington refused to allow the enlistment of Negroes, free or slave; he changed his mind, however, when Lord Dunmore, the Governor of Virginia, and Sir Henry Clinton of New York, both loyalists fighting for the King of England, issued proclamations offering freedom to slaves who enlisted in the Royal Army. Washington then resolved that freed Negroes could be accepted into the Continental Armies.

Prior to this decision, Connecticut and Rhode Island had already promised freedom to all slaves who joined the revolutionary forces.

The promise of freedom was thus offered to Negroes in four states by either British and colonial factions, and it inspired a mass movement that seemed shortly about to eradicate the institution of slavery even before it could be legally abolished: about 5,000 Negroes heeded Lord Dunmore's call at Norfolk; hundreds joined the British in every northern state. In South Carolina 25,000 were reported to have gone over. Many more slaves would have responded to the call for recruits during the early part of the Revolution if it had been issued as a part of a general policy everywhere, especially after the initial victories of British troops over American, and if the British had been able to organize and care properly for the masses of slaves that flocked to the royal standard. However, British appeals to the slaves remained confined to the states mentioned, and were made only sporadically; a large number of Negroes were taken to Canada and the West Indies for military service, and eventually settled in Sierra Leone, but due to lack of care and inefficiency, infectious diseases ravaged the masses of the Negro volunteers with frightful loss of lives.

Alexander Hamilton petitioned in 1779 to admit unfreed slaves into the armies in addition to the freed Negroes already assisting in the American cause, urging Congress to "give them their freedom with their swords." Hamilton's plan was actually to admit slaves into the armies, with the understanding that freedom would be granted them upon their discharge. He warned Congress to disregard "the thousand arguments (of southern slaveholders) that an unwillingness to part with property of so valuable a kind will furnish." "If we do not take them," he added, "the enemy probably will." But South Carolina was adamant in her refusal to allow Negroes into the armies, as one of her spokesmen, Charles Lee, insisted:

> So much depends on opinion, and the opinion which the slaves will entertain of our superiority or inferiority, will naturally keep pace, with our maintaining or giving ground.

Another gentleman from South Carolina, Colonel John Laurens, one of General Washington's aides-de-camp made energetic attempts to convince his home state to relent. British forces in South Carolina were enlisting slaves who ran away from their masters. There were so few white men in proportion to black slaves that most of them had to stay on the plantations to guard their property. Laurens proposed to Congress to advise South Carolina and Georgia to supplement their manpower with Negroes. Congress in 1779 approved the colonel's proposition, whereupon he tried personally to soften the resistance of the Deep South to release slaves for service in the army.

When his efforts proved fruitless and the South Carolinian and Georgian planters remained obdurate on the issue of releasing what they considered their personal and valuable property, he was bound to report his failure to Washington. In July, 1782, Washington replied sagely:

> I must confess that I am not at all astonished at the failure of your plan. That spirit of freedom which at the commencement of this contest would have gladly sacrificed everything to the attainment of its object, has long since subsided. It is not the public, but the private interest, which influences the generality of mankind, nor can the Americans boast of exception.

Nevertheless, Negroes were accepted not only into regiments of northern states, but even those of Virginia as the war dragged on. The New England states organized Negroes into separate regiments. Elsewhere, they were placed among the whites, mostly in labor units and the navy.

In 1778, Jefferson estimated that in Virginia alone, 30,000 slaves had left their masters—and the number of deserters in all the colonies was about 100,000 or close to 20 percent of the total number of Negroes in America. Of these, from 8,000 to 10,000 were Negroes who served in the Revolutionary armies. At the end of the war, Negroes who had taken part in the struggle on the side of the patriots were regarded with much good will by the American government and population. These Negroes received many of the privileges given to white veterans: they were granted the same warrant to land and certificate for severance pay, and also went through the same tribulations when the government was unable to honor these certificates. In the disorganized period which followed the war, they had the same difficulties in eking out a livelihood; many of them may have returned to their former masters, but much more often the reverse was true—masters simply reenslaved the discharged former slaves. After many complaints of such abuses, Virginia eventually empowered the Attorney General to prosecute masters who deprived Negro veterans of their freedom in this fashion.

Of slaves who decided to remain loyal and had chosen to enlist in British forces rather than the American, and who were, for one reason or another left in America after the war was ended, most were usually returned to slavery; the remainder became maroons, or wanderers, members of a kind of guerrilla pack roaming the countryside and foraging for its living. Such was the case of a group of Negroes in Georgia, where a band turned up shortly after the war. In 1786, the governor was called upon by many localities to suppress what was described by W. B. Stevens, as:

> corps of runaway negroes, the leaders of which, having been trained to arms by the British during the siege of Savannah, still called themselves the King of England's soldiers and ravaged both sides of the Savannah River, plundering and murdering to the great alarm of the people.

The presence of these maroons, who had chosen vagabondage as the one recourse to save themselves from reenslavement, prompted a large-scale search; in May of the same year, Lieutenant Colonel Howell leading an armed force discovered the maroon encampment on Bear Creek. The

Negroes fled as soon as they caught sight of the troops, scattered into the bush, and were pursued for about two miles. Many of them were killed and wounded; their encampment (which must have been a semi-permanent one as it was reported to have twenty-one houses) was burned; their provisions were taken, and their crops destroyed.

While the Revolution was in progress, few slave revolts were reported anywhere in the colonies. The opportunity presented for escape (and, possibly for freedom) by the enlistment policy of some of the states was too attractive. The hope of emancipation charged the air and frustrated the few who might have attempted rebellion. Added to this, the momentous nature of national events would have overshadowed the importance of local slave troubles, and it is altogether natural to assume that, when such troubles occurred, they were not usually printed in newspapers or otherwise recorded because of the lack of attention they received.

In the years leading up to the Revolutionary War, what widely scattered "troubles" involving slaves there were, must have sounded like a small-arms fire to the thundering cannon roar of political opinion which left the problem of the Negro entirely and now had different objectives in mind:

> 1767—In Virginia, near Alexandria; several overseers died, four Negroes executed, their heads cut off and fixed to the chimney of the courthouse; a northern newspaper, commenting on the incident, apprized that "it was expected that four more would soon meet the same fate."
>
> 1771—Georgia was experiencing troubles with fugitive slaves; the Council reported that it was engaging Indians to go out hunting "in order to discover the Camp of the Negroes," who were wandering in patrols along the Savannah River during the Christmas holidays that year.

1772—A Georgia Grand Jury was convened to consider the matter of fires set by fugitive slaves in a "Dwelling House near Black Creek."

1774—Negro slaves in St. Andrew's Parish, Georgia, rose and killed four whites, wounding three others. Two of the slaves were burnt alive.

In the long list of minor incidents, showing little inclination of the Negroes in this period to advance their claims, there was one exception: a revolt of some size was recorded in North Carolina in 1775. But even this disorder was believed by some to have been stirred up by a white leader in a responsible position.

According to one account, the Governor himself, Alexander Martin, incited the slaves to rise. Other sources accused a Connecticut commander of having had a hand in its organizing; in the investigation of rumors, it was discovered that the Negroes themselves in the region of the Tar River had plotted for an incident.

The details of the plot were simple: on a prearranged sign, Negroes were to murder the whites, running from plantation to plantation; then they were to march west, where they expected to be received and protected by inhabitants loyal to the British.

Whether it was the Governor or commander, Captain Johnson of White Haven, Conn., who was stirring up the blacks, was of no importance because on the evening before the projected insurrection, July 7, a slave disclosed the plot. Thereupon forty Negroes were rounded up, all of whom gave the same account of their organization:

They had been directed to fall ... on the white family, in which they resided, and, after destroying them, to set fire to the buildings, and proceed thus, from plantation to plantation, till they reached the back countries where they were promised to be received by persons, sent thither, and armed by government for their protection, and, as a reward for their exertion in the King's cause, they were to be enfranchised and settled beyond the mountains, in a free government of their own. In disarming them, a considerable quantity of arms and ammunition was secured.

It is well worth noting that the plan of the slaves in this instance, as in nearly all of those of the next half century, was directed towards settling a community of their own. Though individually freed slaves and Negro veterans of the Revolutionary War might look forward to a life in some way integrated with the whites, other slaves who planned to make themselves free by force had no such desire. This seems natural; if they had had any hope that the white man's law would bestow freedom on them, they would not have taken the heavy risk of revolting. Integrated life was never the object of the slave insurrections. This rudimentary instinct of the black community was echoed in more sophisticated terms by the white idealists who founded the country. Even Jefferson, almost half a century after the Declaration of Independence had been adopted (without his crucial clause concerning emancipation) could not imagine former masters and slaves living in the same community. In 1821, we find him writing:

> Nothing is more certainly written in the book of fate that these people are to be free. Nor is it less certain that the two races, equally free, cannot live in the same government. Nature, habit, opinion, has drawn indelible lines of distinction between them.

Half of Jefferson's prophecy has been proven just; the United States is still in the middle of a crucial national effort determined that the second half of the prophecy be proven unjust.

The convention convoked to write the Constitution of the United States in 1787 offered, from one point of view, the last opportunity for the peaceful abolition of slavery. The number of Negroes in the country was still not too high—there were 670,000 in 1790—to make the financial burden involved in such an act unbearable. As we have seen, most of the states and public opinion itself in many places, were losing interest in the institution. In theory, slavery could have been liquidated by the government itself, if it were to reimburse the masters for the financial loss. As other debts were to be, this also might have been assumed by the federal government. Added to these considerations was the powerful fact that the leaders of the most important southern state at the Convention, Virginia, spoke forcefully against slavery in the debates.

For the Convention, the question of slavery concerned first of all the balance of relative power between the states of the North and South, as expressed in the number of representatives each state was to send to the future House of Representatives, as well as in apportioning direct taxes.

The problem was a delicate one for the South. In their efforts to maintain themselves on a par with the North, southern leaders wanted slaves counted as *population* but were averse to recognizing them as *citizens* endowed with the right to vote.

The Pennsylvania delegate to the Convention, Gouverneur Morris, could not withhold his sarcasm at the spectacle of his countrymen trying to skirt the issue of their slaves' ambiguous status in the Constitution:

54

Upon what principle is it that the slaves shall be computed in the representation? Are they men? Then make them citizens and let them vote. Are they property? Why then is no other property included? ... The admission of slaves into the Representation when fairly explained comes to this: that the inhabitant of Georgia and S.C. who goes to the Coast of Africa, and in defiance of the most sacred laws of humanity tears away his fellow creatures from their dearest connections and damns them to the most cruel bondage, shall have more votes in a Gvt. instituted for protection of the rights of mankind, than the Citizen of Pa. or N. Jersey who views with a laudable horror so nefarious a practice ... He never would concur in upholding domestic slavery ... It was the curse of heaven on the States where it prevailed.

However, even Morris, who as envoy to France would cool much of President Washington's initial warmth towards the French Revolution, finally did "concur"; he was compelled as he said, "to declare himself reduced to the dilemma of doing injustice to the Southern States or to human nature, and he must therefore do it to the former." The "injustice" to the southern states, surely, was to allow them to perpetuate the "curse of heaven," the institution that would bring them so much sadness and shame in the years to come.

A compromise was accepted by the Convention. According to its terms, three-fifths of the number of slaves in a state were to be added to the number of free people and indentured servants to arrive at the basic figure for calculating the number of representatives a state should send to the House.

The controversy exploded again at the proposed prohibition of further import of slaves. Oliver Ellsworth of Connecticut protested the inconsistency of the proposition: "If [slavery] was to be considered in a moral light," he said, "we ought to go farther and free those already in the Country."

It was finally agreed to prohibit the import of slaves from abroad after twenty years had elapsed (that is, beginning on January 1, 1808), when most delegates believed slavery would have vanished from all the United States anyway.

Luther Martin of Maryland objected to injecting the problem of slavery in the Constitution in any form, since "it was inconsistent with the principles of the revolution and dishonorable to the American character to have such a feature in the Constitution." The feature Martin specifically alluded to was that "five slaves are to be counted as three free men in the apportionment of Representatives. It encourages slave trade, slaves enhancing the power of some states."

The North found itself objecting to one point towards the end of the Convention: the champions of state sovereignty in the South unexpectedly smuggled into the Constitution the power of the federal government to assist the states in the policing of their territory. Southerners surmised that this power might be useful in the future, when it was conceivable that state power might not be sufficient to subdue slave revolts.

"Shall one part of the U.S. be bound to defend another part, and that other part be at liberty not only to increase its own danger, but to withhold the compensation for the burden?" asked the Massachusetts delegate Rufus King ironically.

Nevertheless, the North gave in to southern demands, and the Constitution was drawn up to include the stipulation that the federal government should protect every state from domestic violence.

Thus, the document recognized that slavery was to be a continuing institution in the United States. General Washington had years before resignedly admitted that the spirit of freedom was subsiding; now his silence was incisive at the Convention, over which he himself was presiding.

Still, though its effects were postponed, the American Constitution was the first document of law to prohibit slave trading.

The existence of slavery itself was not seriously contested at the Constitutional Convention. Another opportunity had slipped by. But grave words of warning over the slave question were voiced by the Virginian delegate George Mason:

> As nations cannot be rewarded or punished in the next world, they must be in this. By an inevitable chain of causes and effects Providence punishes national sins by national calamities.

Mason's words were prophetic; he was a slaveholder himself, but Virginia at the time of the Convention had little interest in upholding the institution of slavery. No one could foresee that the Convention would provide the last chance for legal emancipation; no one could see that a few years later the cotton gin was to revolutionize the economy of the country, and, specifically, the agriculture of the South. Even in its primitive state, Eli Whitney's invention of 1793 made it possible for a single slave to clean fifty pounds of raw cotton in a day, while without it he could extract the seeds from only about one pound. When the invention was improved and harnessed to steam, it would clean a thousand pounds of cotton a day. The machine would make possible the growth of cotton on huge southern plantations. In cooperation with the thriving textile industry in England and mills in New England, it would give rise to a powerful national development of agriculture, industry, and overseas commerce. Through its efficacy, cotton was to become "king" all over the South. But it would require cheap and plentiful labor to meet the incredible magnitude of demand. The change in economy would radically alter Virginia's—and the South's—attitude towards slavery. So the cotton gin became the *deus ex machina* to rescue the institution from disrepair, and the Constitution had done nothing to prevent it. And, as a corollary, the Constitution indirectly caused a second blooming of slavery: since it prohibited the import of slaves from 1808 onward, the states of the upper South would become a virtual breeding paddock for slaves, and thrive on a huge interstate commerce in Negroes.

In their defense of slavery at the Convention, southern spokesmen were unimpressed by moral arguments against slavery. John Rutledge stood pat on the matter of economic interest:

> Religion and humanity had nothing to do with this question. Interest alone is the governing principle with nations. The true question at present is whether Southern States shall or shall not be parties to the Union.

A southern congressman insisted that, in fact, slavery was so well planted in the American states that it could not be eradicated:

> without tearing up by the roots their happiness, prosperity and tranquility; if it were an evil, it was one for which there was no remedy, and therefore, like wise men, they acquiesce in it.

Charles Pinckney came out flatly with brutal logic in his defiant justification of the system:

> If slavery were wrong, it was justified by the example of all the world: In all ages one-half of mankind have been slaves.

In the disillusioning atmosphere caused by these sentiments it would have been, perhaps, entirely out of place to remind these spokesmen of the southern viewpoint of their own earlier ideals when they had been fired by their awareness of serving as a model to the world in the framing of the rights of man. It would have been well to have recalled the feeling once put into words by Robert Livingston, one of the drafters of the Declaration of Independence:

> We must consider that we shall be as a city upon a hill. The eyes of all peoples are upon us, so that if we shall deal falsely with our God in this work we have undertaken, we shall be made a story and a byword throughout the world.

The enlightened men of Europe, and particularly of France, where the country was entering a revolutionary ferment of its own, received the American Constitution with mingled disappointment and incomprehension: they observed that it not only recognized the institution of slavery, but, by implication, promised federal help to states against risings for freedom.

The Abbé Grègoire, deputy from Lorraine, articulated Europe's sorrow and bitterness—"Blush, ye revolted colonists," wrote the great light of French spirit in 1788, "for having apostasized from your own principles."

IV

SAN DOMINGO:
SEEDS OF AMERICAN REVOLT

IN 1779, American forces under the command of Colonel Lincoln had combined with French troops under D'Estaing in mounting an attack on the besieged British stronghold of Savannah, a city of first importance in the southeast.

Count Pulaski had opened the assault with a furious charge at the head of about 200 horsemen. They had been annihilated by the well-intrenched forces of the British; Pulaski himself had lost his life. Seeing the nature of the disaster, D'Estaing and Lincoln resolved to lift the siege and withdraw, but their retreating troops were pursued and dangerously harassed by British grenadiers under Lieutenant Colonel Maitland. Only a resolute holding action on the part of rearguard Revolutionary forces saved the entire army from a full-scale rout.

The "Black Legion" of Viscount de Fontage, composed of about 800 free Negroes and mulattoes enlisted in San Domingo, covered the retreat with great bravery and success. A host of the petty officers of the Legion received citations for bravery from the command for their signal services.

These officers, trained in the hard-fighting discipline of the Revolution, were later to use their military skills to seize power in San Domingo for the blacks and assure the position of the extraordinary revolutionary figure, Dominique Toussaint L'Ouverture.

Though the presence and valor of this Negro regiment at the siege of Savannah may not have assumed any great significance to the slaves on the American continent—Negroes, after all, had served on both sides in the other battles of the Revolution, hoping to be rewarded with freedom—the tumultuous events in San Domingo were soon to inspire large-scale insurrections of slaves in the United States.

The background to the San Domingo uprisings, which dragged on for several years into the nineteenth century, was a complex mixture of political and historical tensions.

San Domingo had been the treasure island of Columbus which he had named Hispaniola. Buccaneers subsequently conquered the western half of the island, the fertile part of it, for France. The Spaniards squandered the entire native population of their half of the island and discovered the golden splendor of native civilization in Central and South America to replace it. The French did not dig for gold, but they transplanted sugarcane from Brazil and cultivated it in San Domingo with such success that sugar replaced almost entirely any other tropical plant. The French half of the island produced enough sugar to supply the needs of half of the world, while the Spanish part decayed.

In the eighteenth century young French aristocrats emigrated to the island in search of adventure, power, and wealth far away from the debauchery and boredom of army life in their own country. France seemed to be losing power and ambition and gave no opportunity to assert one's merit on the strength of vigor and character. By the end of the eighteenth century about 30,000 white men lived on the island—rich planters, former farmers swept off the land by sugar who now had become supervisors of the plantations, citizens engaged in commerce in the cities and harbors, craftsmen, and workers. Besides these, the officers and soldiers of the army and the employees of the civilian administration lived in the colony.

The French had several colonies in the West Indies like Guadeloupe and Martinique, but San Domingo's social stratification differed from all of them in one respect: it numbered among its citizens 25,000 mulattoes, almost equal to the size of the white population. The high percentage of mulattoes was the consequence of concubinage on the island, inevitable in a country where white men numbered twice as many as white women. Concubinage had become accepted there to the extent that special protection had been extended to mulattoes by French kings. Negro women eagerly sought the status of concubine, because by giving birth to the child of a white man, both mother and child were made free. Mulatto children could inherit land and slaves, which they proved they could manage efficiently and, it was said, more ruthlessly than white men. However, such mulattoes, though free, did not have the legal status of white men, being ineligible for appointment to public office.

In 1789, with the French Revolution's message of liberty, equality, and fraternity, a new era seemed to be dawning for all peoples and races whose rights and freedoms had been abrogated by the laws of the privileged. In Paris, the Society of Friends of the Blacks (Société des Amis des Noirs) was one of several societies that had discussed and prepared sweeping schemes for reform before the Revolution. It now was ready to implement its schemes with action. Its founders were the greatest figures of the opening phases of the Revolution: Lafayette, Condorcet, Necker, Sièyes, and Brissot. They had created the Society with the aim of propagating the abolition of slave trade, and Louis XVI had assured them of his good will in implementing its designs.

When the Constituent Assembly of the Revolution took up the proposition to issue a Declaration of the Rights of Man and of the Citizen, the powerful tribune, Mirabeau, interpreted it as meaning that "Every man, regardless of color, shall have equal rights to liberty." This alerted the planters from San Domingo and their representatives in Paris. They brought pressure to bear on the Assembly that the colonies be exempted from legislation derived from the principles of equality before the law, as they were laid down in the Declaration. They used weighty arguments: freedom for the slaves would bring chaos to the island, since they were not prepared to make orderly use of it, would ruin the economy and production of San Domingo, and deal a grave financial blow to France and her commerce.

But sons of rich mulattoes, who were studying in Paris, and mulattoes engaged in commerce there also hastened to avail themselves of the great opportunity to have their full citizenship recognized by law.

While these deliberations were going on in 1790, a young mulatto agitator and enthusiast made his way from Paris back to San Domingo to organize the petition for civil rights among his peers.

The mulatto, Vincent Ogé, did not wait until the Assembly had decided whether or not the principle of equality before the law would be extended to the colonies, but rushed home to San Domingo to herald and celebrate the news of freedom emanating from the Declaration itself. The civilian and military officials of the island reacted unfavorably to his elation, however. They had received no royal decree of reforms with respect to the status of the colonial population. They would not tolerate disturbance of the peace by Ogé. He was threatened with jail should he continue agitating. Ogé considered this an affront to the principles that inspirited France and resolved to organize the mulattoes to compel the local authorities to submit to the principles for which the French King and nation stood. Ogé set sail for the United States, bought arms for rum, smuggled them onto the island and began to organize a mulatto force in the mountains.

Meanwhile, the Revolution began to make inroads into the established ways of life of the whites in San Domingo. The poor whites felt much sympathy with the reforms expected from the new regime in France, but the planters wanted nothing of the sort in the colony. The colonial officers were dumbfounded, but as long as the King sanctioned the new institutions, they avoided airing their displeasure in public. In one thing all white men—rich and poor, civilian and military—were in agreement: to deny civil rights to the mulattoes; and, of course, to repress forever the idea of abolition of slavery.

The governor learned of the activities of Ogé and his mulatto confederates and sent out the militia to arrest them. The agitators fled into the Spanish part of the island. The governor demanded extradition and the Spanish high official promptly complied. Ogé was broken on the wheel; twenty of his fellow conspirators were hanged.

The news of these executions was received in Paris with a storm of protest. They were deemed an outrage to the spirit of the Revolution. The mulattoes were mourned as martyrs; popular dramas made Ogé a hero of freedom and attracted passionate audiences.

During this time, conservative influence was gaining in

the Assembly. The middle class began to be concerned with the violence and pressure of the populace; it strove to consolidate its acquisitions, and its representatives became extremely susceptible to such arguments as the planters' lobby reiterated: that the extensions of the Rights of Man to the colony would lead to bloody upheavals, and disaster to state finances. The sugar plantations, the planters' lobby argued, could not be run without slave labor. The immense source of income for the state and the possessions of persons who had invested capital and the life work of generations into them would be wiped out by emancipation or by revolt incited by ill-considered legislation of the Assembly in Paris. What these lobbyists wanted was autonomy for the colonies to legislate matters that concerned themselves and the status of their inhabitants. The planters received powerful support from commercial and shipping interests in their petitions. San Domingo required a slave importation of 30,000 yearly, because of the outrageous rate of mortality among the half million Negro slaves. The island thus represented a gigantic business in both ways, importing and transporting sugar from San Domingo and selling and shipping Negro slaves to the island.

The "Friends of the Blacks" became disheartened by the controversy, but not because of the strong opposition to their principles by colonial interests. The mulatto lobby deeply disturbed and disappointed the idealistic spirit of the great initiators of the Revolution, for the mulattoes opposed no less vehemently the emancipation of black slaves than the white planters, and protested the extension of full civil rights to the few free Negroes in San Domingo. These revolutionaries ran into irrational obstacles for the first time among the very group they most wanted to help.

"The colonies or the principles," the planters insisted: these were the only alternatives. Very few applauded the little known lawyer, Robespierre, when he took the defiant stand: "Let the colonies perish if they cost us our glory and our liberty!"

It came as no surprise that, in 1791, the National Assembly forged a compromise out of the opposing issues with which it was faced: a franchise was to be granted to mulattoes in the colonies, but only to such as were descended from free parents on both sides. This move elevated no more than a total of 400 mulattoes to the rights of full citizenship, but it broke through the barrier of color and in doing so infuriated the white planters since it infringed on their privileged colonial status. On the other hand, it quite naturally thrilled the mulattoes, even those who were not immediate beneficiaries of the law, because it established at last the principle that the color of skin was no bar to citizenship.

When this decree of May 15, 1791 arrived in San Domingo, white planters and poor whites began to antagonize and harass the mulattoes of the island, who then took up arms in the defense of their rights and demanded that the governor implement the law.

A very complicated situation thus arose, since planters and military chiefs of the island distrusted the poor whites, who claimed what the Revolution in France promised to confer, as much as they detested the claims of the mulattoes. To the former, they might grant the share in rights and power to which they were entitled; they would, however, deny such a share to men whose color was different from theirs:

> Believe not that the white creole will ever unite in the common cause with the man of color, although they are both proprietors, and have both the same interests to defend...

66

> Nothing can efface the unjust distinctions which keep him at
> so infinite a distance that the white would with less horror
> bear his enemies accuse him of a crime, than assert that a drop
> of African blood circulate in his veines.

So the Colonial Committee firmly reported in 1791. This
report gave an accurate picture of the feelings of the white
people of the island: their convictions were unchanged from
the day that the first news of the Revolution was brought to
San Domingo. The mulatto was not to be appeased in any
way. So believing, a royal officer had eloquently stated this
conviction to his superiors in France as the Revolution
began:

> The word "liberty" . . . is sowing a fatal seed, whose sprout-
> ing will be terrible. In France, where its application endangers
> despotism alone, we may hope for the best results. But here,
> where everything opposes the entire liberty of all classes, we
> should see only blood, carnage, and the certain destruction of
> one or other of those incompatible races of men which inhabit
> this colony. So long as there exists the opposition of white and
> black, so long it will be impossible to establish, upon a basis
> of liberty, any mutual support of existing society.

These forebodings appeared to be solidly rooted in prejudice—a prejudice which persevered even though it injured
economic interests. But a sudden danger to life and property,
to white and mulatto planters alike, made this same prejudice yield to common interest in defending them.

A Negro revolt flared up in the north of the island immediately after Vincent Ogé and his mulatto leaders had been
executed. It was a terrible outburst of blind fury, of vengeance, and destruction. It raged in the summer of 1791 and
more than two thousand white men, women, and children
were massacred. Within two months, 180 sugar plantations

and about 900 coffee, cotton, and indigo plantations were completely destroyed.

Why did this revolt occur?

Was it because sailors on ships arriving in San Domingo from France, startled at finding the Negroes in a bondage as if the Revolution had never occurred, had told the Negroes: "You are free before God and King"? Was it because these Negroes sensed the unrest among the white populace on the island, knew of the mulattoes' attempt to claim equality with the whites, but feared that they themselves would be tricked by these same mulattoes out of their own share in the freedoms coming from overseas?

The white planters, whatever the reason, were terrified by the revolt and turned to the mulattoes to combine against the common danger. These planters now readily recognized the rights France had accorded to the 400 mulattoes on the island whose parents had both been free.

The news of the revolt reached Paris just as the National Assembly was ready to close its sessions. The reports of the excesses roused such indignation in that body that even those members who had favored full freedom for the colonies began to see the situation in San Domingo in the light of the planter lobbyists. They had been cautioned against the emancipation of slaves—slaves, the planters insisted, who in their ignorance and savage instincts, would use their freedom for destructive ends. Now they were ready to believe the warnings. Under the impact of this bloody revolt, the Assembly decreed on September 24, 1791, that the right to decide on the status of inhabitants was reserved for the colonial assemblies; in addition, the execution of laws passed by the legislative body of France concerning political rights was to be delegated to these assemblies. The decree exempted decisions taken by colonial assemblies from the approval of the National Assembly and subjected them directly to the sanction of the King. This new order of authority had the effect of giving local planters free hand over slaves and mulattoes, since planters dominated the local assembly through a census on property. The planters were eager to read into the law an authorization for the local assembly to hold supreme power over the armed forces garrisoned on the island as well, but the military commander refused to accept this interpretation. So another tension was created between the planters on the one hand and the army command, supported by the poor whites, on the other.

The very complicated developments on San Domingo have direct relevance to slave revolts in the United States, and they cast a sharp focus on the hardships of self-liberation when attempted by a subject people and frustrated by a restricting emotional and intellectual heritage. These developments continued like shock waves received from the great upheaval in France, each shock having further repercussions on the social and political turmoil of the island.

The situation on the island had come to the point where there was slim hope left for peace and order. Seen through the eyes of contemporaries, the troubles could be resolved only through some form of repressive or revolutionary violence. A French colonial officer gave one analysis:

> You have three classes of brigands to fight. Firstly the white brigands, who are most to be feared (hostile to both white and mulatto planters). Leave them to be destroyed by the mulattoes, if you do not care to destroy them yourself. Next, with the aid of the mulattoes, you will reduce the rebel Negroes. After that you will gradually restore the old laws, and by that time you will be able to suppress the refractory element among the mulattoes themselves.

Another, and even more pessimistic, prophecy of what was to result from the San Domingan impasse was given by a colonist on his return to the island from Paris:

> One of the three things will follow: the whites will exterminate the whole mulatto caste; the mulattoes will destroy the whites; or the negroes will profit by these dissensions to annihilate both the whites and the mulattoes. But in any case, San Domingo should be erased from the maps of Europe.

Dissensions were again sharpened after King Louis XVI and his family attempted to flee France and, having been captured, were returned to Paris to be executed. The Jacobins ruling the France of the Republic had taken it for granted that the planters would side with the aristocrats in hostility to the revolutionary government, but it was inconceivable for the revolutionary leaders to find, as they now did, that the mulattoes of San Domingo were hoisting the Bourbon flag after the abolition of royalty, in recognition of the fact that they had received their (incomplete) freedom from the kings of France. Even more painful for the Jacobins was to read reports that Negro slaves who had participated in the bloody insurrection were fleeing in front of the army that pursued them to the Spanish sector of the island. There they were beginning to organize into a military force against the French sector. The Spanish supported this new body of Negro troops. The war of the European coalition against revolutionary France had begun, and invasion of French San Domingo would soon be in order when, it was foreseen, the war on the sea would be extended to colonial possessions in the Caribbean. "Our ancestors in Africa and here always lived under a king," the rebels argued. "If the French people killed theirs, we want to serve at least a Spanish king." So these Negro slaves justified their readiness to fight the revolution in the service of kings.

The Jacobins in Paris were aware that they could not defend their colonies overseas against the British, except for San Domingo. This island had a large free population to support the military and was rich enough to provide for its inhabitants through commerce. But its inhabitants had to be brought first into conformity with the regime in France so that the bulk of the people should feel that by defending the French rule they defended a better and more human life for themselves. The Convention duly sent 6,000 soldiers and a Commission to the island, the latter empowered to take the dispositions necessary to the effective defense of the island and to reorganize its administration and production.

The survey by the Commission brought to light a chaotic situation on San Domingo. French rule hardly reached further inland than the city regions along the coast. Whites and rich mulattoes crowded the harbor towns, most of them waiting for the British to protect them from slaves and revolution. In the mountains, slaves roamed over devastated plantations. Beyond the border, the Spanish were preparing invasion from the land, the British from the sea. The island had ceased to be a political unit even within the French sector. Steep mountain chains, and a rugged coast line divided it into isolated regions, each with different soil, climate, vegetation. Each section stood now under a different rule of suddenly emerged leaders, mulatto or Negro, most of whom had served in the French army on the Continent. What little contact they had with one another was hostile, more often than not. Each leader aspired to command the whole.

In the light of these facts, the Commission saw no other way to keep the colony for the Republic than to announce that all Negroes who would join the French to protect the island were to be freed. This the Commission carried out without waiting for the approval of the Convention in Paris, though the latter in 1794 issued a sweeping Proclamation; henceforth, "faithful to the Declaration of the Rights of Man slavery was abolished throughout the territory of the Republic." All inhabitants, without regard to color, were at last to be French citizens.

Into the chaotic vacuum created by the lack of firm authority and augmented by the confused state of civil affairs, now stepped a figure who was to dominate an unprecedented series of events in the history of rebellion in the Western Hemisphere: the great military commander, astute politician, and diplomat François Dominique Toussaint L'Ouverture.

Toussaint had risen from the low state of a slave coachman in San Domingo to a position of authority as a Negro leader in the Spanish sector of the island. He had fled there after the slave revolt of 1791 and was training Negro troops to fight the French. Upon the announcement that the Convention had declared equal rights for all, Toussaint again changed allegiance and led his troops over to French San Domingo under the flag of the Republic.

The Negro commander took his own initiative and either offered alliance to armed groups on the island or forced them to recognize his personal command and thus extended his rule over the northern sector. The south was at this time under the command of André Rigaud, a mulatto and a veteran of the Savannah campaign during the American Revolution. Rigaud, as a mulatto, considered it beneath his dignity to submit to Toussaint, an illiterate Negro. An internecine struggle between the two was to be injected into subsequent campaigns on the island, in which the great sea powers played favorites at the same time that they were threatening the autonomy of the entire island, north and south. However, the two leaders at first managed to cooperate to frustrate the long-awaited British advance on the colony in 1795. In this initial victory they were lent the substantial help of yellow fever. It devastated the invaders but the natives were immune.

Toussaint was well aware that, if he wished to extend and strengthen his rule, he ought to provide for the San Domingan population that had ceased to work during the Negro revolt. This population was now threatened by starvation. The island had never produced the food its inhabitants consumed; now, with the plantations destroyed, the situation was desperate. Toussaint hit upon a statesmanlike plan to convince the slaves to return to the fields and work again. The scheme was a compulsory share-cropping venture, and it worked well: the produce of the slaves was to serve to buy food, an exchange of goods which in peacetime had been transacted within the mercantile system of France. Now, however, in wartime conditions, French ships had not ventured across the ocean in large enough numbers to assure a two-way flow of goods. Toussaint solved the problem by extending commercial bonds with America, practically substituting her for France as a trading partner. Sugar had been shipped in large quantities to France before the war, but molasses, its by-product, France would not import in order to protect her own domestic cognac manufacturers; New England merchants had eagerly bought up the surplus molasses, distilled it into rum, carried the rum to Africa or Jamaica to buy slaves with it, shipped the slaves to the American slave markets and sold them. Such industries as distilleries quickly sprang up in New England. Mills, pouring out increased quantities of flour to be shipped on return voyages to San Domingo, also prospered. Officially, the huge business in rum was smuggling, but the prosperity of the two terminals rested upon its abundant and smooth flow. San Domingo was second only to England in the foreign commerce of America toward the end of the eighteenth century. It was this commerce which would, if reestablished, save the population of the island from starvation.

Toussaint managed a brilliant balance of his rule based on ambiguities of politics: Spain ceded the eastern half of the island to France in 1795; France and England were engaged in a gigantic duel close to the shores of America and in the Caribbean; America professed neutrality in the conflict, though most precariously in the case of San Domingo, whose trade the English badly wanted. Only America, however, could supply the food the island required while the war raged. Toussaint managed to convince France that he was exercising his power on her behalf, but at the same time let it be known to the English and Americans that his real intention was to make the island independent. This maneuver allowed America to continue feeding the island and importing its produce without being accused by the British of favoring the French.

The French government, accepting Toussaint's loyalty vows at face value, raised him to the rank of brigadier general in 1796. But in 1798 the Negro statesman concluded a secret agreement with the British whereby he granted an exclusive franchise for her foreign trade on the condition that all her forces be withdrawn from the island. Toussaint undertook the obligation, however, to allow the white and mulatto planters to return to cultivate their fields. When the secret of the monopoly leaked out to the Americans, they were invited to enter into the agreement and share the privileges with the British; Toussaint also promised to prevent all persons from leaving San Domingo whose presence might be dangerous in the slave regions of the United States and the British West Indies.

When the French suggested that Toussaint attack Jamaica or incite the slaves on that turbulent island to revolt, he could only refuse: he was bound to keep the secret agreement, of which the French were unaware. In this way, he was successful in balancing the claims of the various foreign powers in an arrangement suitable to him: his main consideration was to be trusted by any and all powers who might overthrow his rule. This aim he achieved for a long time, although it was always done by betraying whichever of the powers constituted the least danger to him at the particular moment. If Negro slaves hoped for assistance from Toussaint in their conspiracies, or the offer of refuge on his island if their revolts failed—as they often did—they had misplaced their hopes.

After consolidating his own position, in 1800 Toussaint prepared to launch an attack on André Rigaud, the mulatto leader, who still controlled the southern portion of the island and had been made a general by the French. He was certain that the British and Americans would now support him in his effort to dominate the whole island. He, therefore, organized an army of 15,000 for the attack on his archenemy.

Rigaud somehow managed to get possession of a copy of the secret agreement drawn up between Toussaint and the British and American governments. He exposed the Negro leader to both the French and the Negro slaves as a double traitor, who sold both the Negro state and the motherland, France, down the river to the British and Americans. With his methods uncovered, Toussaint could no longer afford to delay his attack on Rigaud. Aided by the U.S. Consul at Cape Francais, Edward Stevens, and American arms, ammunition, and food, Toussaint blockaded Rigaud's port at Les

Cayes. The American fleet sent gunboats to bombard the mulatto leader's stronghold at Jacmel (on the southern tip of the island). In August of 1800, Toussaint captured Les Cayes. Rigaud sought refuge in France, resolving to return to destroy the Negro leader.

In the same year—1800—Thomas Jefferson, the great friend of France and her Revolution, was elected to the American presidency. In 1793, Jefferson had written to Monroe:

> I became daily more and more convinced that all the West Indian Islands will remain in the hands of the people of colour, and a total expulsion of the whites sooner or later will take place.

The French commissioners were skeptical of Toussaint, who had pledged loyalty to France with one hand and signed secret agreements with other countries with the other. "I swear you that I will die before I will see snatched from my hands the sword, those arms, which France has confided to me for the triumph of liberty and equality," Toussaint had avowed in his 1796 message to the Directory; but the French commander on the island had reported that "San Domingo can be saved only by Republican bayonets," meaning bayonets wielded by French republicans, not island rebels. Yet those bayonets continued to be needed in Europe.

There was also a different sort of concern that began to exercise growing influence on American foreign policy vis-à-vis San Domingo at the beginning of Jefferson's first Administration. Dread was growing in the American South that risings of Negroes and mulattoes in the island might spark similar slave revolts in the United States. Jamaica had erupted periodically in slave revolts; bloody insurrections flared up on other islands of the West Indies, with refugees landing in America bringing tales with them of hideous cruelties and massacre. But in San Domingo, the colored masses had seized power and had kept it in their hands. Colored generals ran the country. Apparently they were there to stay. Refugees from this latest terror flocked to the United States by the thousands. In 1793 alone, 10,000 refugees had landed to seek exile in this country, usually in the southern cities, where they preferred the atmosphere and society as being more like their own. The early refugees who had not waited until the immediacy of the danger forced them to leave everything but their bare lives, brought along movable property, money, jewels, and slaves. The presence of these refugees, and conversations overheard among all white men, passed on to American slaves an idea of the kind of danger that was lurking for the whites in San Domingo.

"Negroes have wonderful art of communicating intelligence," a contemporary noted; "it will run several hundred miles in a week or fortnight." In this case, black maids and valets arriving in flight with their masters from San Domingo found means to break news to the slaves.

All of this must have served to give the American Negroes a very good idea of what had come to pass in the Caribbean.

The news of Toussaint's extraordinary feats put steel into the resolve of some alert Negroes, both free and slave, and eventually inspired their leaders to organized revolts. It also was received with legitimate terror by the white people of the South.

All slaves were now regarded with intense suspicion of ill intent; the faltering confidence of the whites distressed faithful slaves and disturbed all others. No one knew what could be done to dispel the suspicions; they lingered and the tensions generated between whites and Negroes in the South built up pressure because of them. A result of these pressures was irrational action: either masters acted rashly and imposed punishment for fictional rebellions, or slaves, acting contrarily, sought to justify the originally groundless suspicions of their masters by conspiring to run away, or rebel. Panic was again compounding the dangers of the slave state.

Fearing that the spirit of revolt would spread over the entire South as it had spread on the island of San Domingo, the whites reinforced the limitations of movements of slaves and mounted patrols to make an end to "relaxed observance" of the rules. These measures annoyed the southern Negroes intensely, and their increased bitterness was misinterpreted as an inclination to revolt.

The changed attitudes of both whites and Negroes at this time is evident from reports of antagonism which cropped up all over the eastern seaboard.

In May, 1792, sixteen Negroes in Hampton, Virginia, were arrested for plotting, though the court there found insufficient proof of guilt and merely advised selling the Negroes out of state. In the same county, a brawl was reported between a militiaman and a group of six Negroes who "struck him with their Clubs, but fortunately only knocked his hat ... the next day a party went in pursuit of them and apprehended five; they have undergone trial for their lives and three of them have been executed;" the sentence seems severe for the slight gesture of contempt it served. No merit was seen in recording the motive of the incident, for none was reported.

According to the report of a New York newspaper, the citizens of Charleston in 1793 had become "alarmed and the militia kept constant guard" because "the Negroes have become very insolent. It is said that the San Domingo Negroes have sown those seeds of revolt, and that a magazine has been attempted to be broken open."

On September 17 of the same year Negroes of Powhatan County, Virginia, met in an old schoolhouse, defying the prohibition of assembly without approval of their masters expressed in writing. According to the report made of the incident to the governor, these slaves "had confessed that three hundred was to meet there, while also several Negro foremen disappeared from the plantations." No reason for the meeting was given, but the fact that it occurred at all showed that Negroes were taking an unusual initiative.

The accomplished fact of the Negro establishment in San Domingo doubtless had its influence on such bold acts of slaves; they were at last being made to feel conscious that they were human beings, like the whites endowed with certain rights.

Through the summer of 1793, Virginia was seized by the jitters over impending slave insurrections. Militia commanders in her counties urged the governor to send them arms. The town of Petersburg petitioned the governor in strong terms, reminding him that "Our present unguarded and defenseless situation is almost a temptation, and tho' we believe it improbable that the negroes could ever make a stand, yet much mischief might be done by them, should they ever attempt an insurrection."

In Warwick County, the commander reported of actual attempts at disorders on the parts of slaves, but the insurrection was "timely suppressed in this county by executing one of the principal advisors." The commander was outspoken in attributing the unrest among the slaves to the "melancholy affair at Hispaniola."

Norfolk County also asked for arms "as we think the negroes have some thoughts of insurrection." Portsmouth asked for an entire "small battery and a company of men for constant duty," seeing significant and direct danger from Negroes brought over from San Domingo:

> Our town swarms with strange negroes, foreign and domestic, who have already begun hostilities upon themselves. Last night at half past eleven, 4 were found hanging twenty steps from my door, upon a cedar tree. What this may be a prelude to I am at a loss to conjecture ... We have many hundreds French negroes landed in this Town. It were 4 of them that was hung as above. They are divided. The Household family negroes are trusty and well disposed, but many others did belong to the insurrection in Hispaniola.

New Orleans had had lively communications with San Domingo, and enough refugee planters settled in Louisiana to implant fear in the citizens as well as in the Spanish authorities that the 25,000 Negro slaves living there might become susceptible to the ideas that had raised their fellow slaves on the island to the ruling caste. In 1795, there was a revolt on the plantation of Julian Poydras, "merchant, planter, poet, philanthropist and patriot" at Pointe Coupee. In one of his frequent absences from the estate, the slaves held a secret meeting at which they resolved to kill the whites. However, before they struck, one of their leaders turned informer. The ringleaders, three white men among them, were arrested, though this was not the end of the rebellion. A mob gathered to storm the jail and free the prisoners. A real battle unfolded in which twenty-five Negroes were slain and many wounded. The court found twenty-three Negroes guilty and condemned them to be hanged.

Under the impact of this revolt, Louisiana suspended the importation of slaves.

After conquering the Spanish half of San Domingo in 1801, Toussaint held the entire island through his policy of tolerating the advances of all powers involved in the fate of the island as insurance against conquest. In France, after the turn of the century, the declining revolution produced a new vigor in its new First Consul, the young general with a personal record of incredible victories—Napoleon. With the restoration of the French colonies in mind, Napoleon hastily issued a new proclamation: "Whatever may be your origin and your color, you are all Frenchmen; you are all free and equal." But he had to wait until 1802 when his peace with Britain assured safe passage across the Atlantic before he could transport his *Grande Armée* across it to realize his dreams of an American empire. As the first step in his design, French power was to be reinstalled in the colonies and established for good in Louisiana, retroceded to France by Spain in a secret treaty two years previously.

The great campaign for a French or French-Spanish empire in Central and South America was to be launched from two strongholds: Louisiana and San Domingo. The veterans of this campaign in the *Grande Armée* could look forward to rewards carved out of this empire in the New World.

Napoleon entrusted General Leclerc, his brother-in-law, with the reconquest of San Domingo for France. Leclerc was supplied with a day-to-day schedule specifying how to bribe Negro and mulatto leaders, ship them to France, or trap and force them to surrender. Leclerc distributed ranks of general and admiral among the island leaders and sent them to Paris where they would be out of harm's way. All honors due to their high ranks in Napoleon's army were carefully paid at their departure.

Toussaint, however—the most important leader—remained inaccessible to the French general. Rather than miss Napoleon's deadline for his campaign, Leclerc declared Toussaint and his deputy commanders outlaws and opened hostilities against them. The magnificently led, well-disciplined and equipped armies of the French would have certainly won quick control of the island, but for two circumstances.

News from Guadeloupe and other French possessions in the Caribbean reached the inhabitants of San Domingo to the effect that Napoleon's armies were reestablishing slavery in those islands. This was true; Leclerc was carrying similar orders, temporarily being kept secret, in regard to San Domingo. Upon the news of this treachery, the mulattoes and Negroes of the island despaired of any good will from the whites. Their bitterness turned them to resort to a furious fight to the death.

The second circumstance was more grave for Leclerc: with the coming of the rainy season in the spring of 1802, yellow fever devastated his army. In the single month of May, 3,000 French soldiers fell to the disease. Reinforcements arrived from France, only to fill the hospitals and cemeteries. But even with his troops weakened, Leclerc drove Toussaint's troops into the interior and eventually tricked the Negro leader into a meeting, arrested him, and shipped him to France, where he was jailed in a fortress and later died.

In November, however, the yellow fever shattered Leclerc's army for a second time, and Leclerc himself was one of the victims. His successor, General Rochambeau, had to deal with Toussaint's successor and chief-deputy, the Congolese blackguard, Jean J. Dessalines, dreaded even among the Negroes for his cruelty.

Meanwhile, at the peak of his military successes in Europe and with the peace treaty of Amiens concluded with Britain, Napoleon was equipping 15,000 fresh troops to reinforce the ranks of the campaign in San Domingo, and he planned to send even more troops after the ships bearing the first had re-

turned to France; he was determined not to let this disobe-
dient band of slaves stand between himself and his grandiose
plan for an American empire. However, an external event
did in fact frustrate his plans, though he thought only temporarily: the peace of Amiens was upset a year after it had
been concluded, and Napoleon decided that Britain would
first have to acknowledge defeat before he could embark on
transoceanic adventures in conquest.

British ships now blockaded San Domingo and halted all
communication with the island by sea. In other circumstances, Rochambeau would probably have crushed Dessalines' troops, but he was now left with only two alternatives: capitulate to Dessalines or to the British. He surrendered to the British with a few thousand men, the last
remnants of the *Grande Armée* which had lost 50,000 soldiers
to disease and to the fury of the colored natives of San
Domingo.

In the delirium of his victory, Dessalines raided the few
pockets of the island where white men still clung to their
native homes and lands and expelled or exterminated every
one of them, to the last white child. At the end of 1803, he
declared the island, under the name of Haiti, to be a pure
Negro community in which no such distinction as "mulatto"
would be tolerated. In 1804, he crowned himself emperor
of Haiti à la Napoleon and reigned until his assassination
two years later.

The North American continent and its islands were now
confronted with a defiant and permanently independent kingdom of black men in the Caribbean.

It was many years before the white countries accepted
Haiti. The South prevented its recognition by the United
States for a half-century after Haiti's independence. In-
tercourse with Haiti would "introduce a moral contagion,

compared with which physical pestilence, in the utmost imaginable degree of its horror, could be light and insignificant," Senator John McPherson Berrien of Georgia protested in Congress in 1825. The great southern rhetorical cannons had to be dragged out to the defense of the whole system when Haiti suddenly materialized.

Senator Thomas Hart Benton of Missouri pointed out the American diplomatic relations with a black Haiti would be a direct provocation for American slaves to revolt. He thundered:

> We receive no mulatto consuls or black ambassadors from her. And why? Because the peace of eleven states will not permit the fruits of a successful Negro insurrection to be exhibited among them. It will not permit black consuls and ambassadors to establish themselves in our cities, and to parade through our country, and give their fellow blacks in the United States, proof in hand of the honors which await them, for a like successful effort on their part. It will not permit the fact to be seen, and told, that for the murder of their masters and mistresses, they are to find friends among the white people of these United States.

We can now realize how the presence of black diplomats of a host of African states in Washington and New York has been instrumental in assisting the American Negro of our day to make his theoretical equality before the law a reality. The concern of the senator from Missouri in 1825 in protecting his interests must be seen in retrospect as legitimate.

The public temperament had been agitated in other American states besides Virginia at the end of the eighteenth century. The war between England and the France of the Revolution was raging along the American seashore and in the West Indies; one or the other of the two powers was intermittently putting American neutrality to strenuous tests. President Washington had proclaimed neutrality, but American citizens were divided in their loyalties and took stands passionately for the victory of one or the other of the two contestants. Each man insisted that his preference alone went to serve the interest or honor of America.

The preference for British or French victory in the struggle generally could be reduced to a preference for one or the other of two visions for America the two camps entertained: an America dominated by agriculture or by commerce. The domestic antagonism went so deep that a situation arose whereby no less a man than Alexander Hamilton, while secretary of the treasury, kept the British representative in America informed of state secrets; on the other side Jefferson while secretary of state, though never quite so carried away by partisan concerns, cultivated an intimacy with the French ministers that was hardly campatible with his position representing a neutral nation.

In general, Britain benefited from American neutrality more than she would have through an alliance. France, however, badly needed American support; thus she was committed to a program of activating American public opinion on her side by revolutionary propaganda.

American partisanship for the British or French cause became a dangerous internal split, a crisis that might have brought on civil war and a dissolution of the new Union. The ruling Federalists, who favored Britain, could not depend on being able to convince the majority to support them permanently; they had in mind for America an authoritative federal government and intended to maneuver the population into accepting it by discrediting their opposition. Since the opposition—the Jeffersonian Democrats—advocated a policy favorable to France, the Federalists charged them with putting the cause of the French Revolution before that of America, thus rendering the Jeffersonians suspect of treason and subversion. This antagonism reached its peak in the years 1798–99, when the Federalists attempted to crush the opposition through the Alien and Sedition laws.

Since this split generated passionate discussions, even within the sanctity of family circles, it could be assumed that its reverberations would be felt among the slaves. Indeed, the Federalists ascribed the slave unrests to the "American Jacobins' blabber of liberty."

Some later revolts did in fact reveal that the controversy had had its effect on the slaves; taking it for granted that the Frenchmen stood for liberty, when planning revolts the Negroes often resolved to spare the lives of the French.

However, the last years of the century had passed in relative calm, except for a series of large fires which had occurred in several states. These fires, from Georgia and South Carolina to New York and New Jersey, were believed to have been set by Negro arsonists, though without positive proof.

The presidential election year of 1800 brought to a vote the question of whether America would develop in the direction of a democratic or authoritative republic. The slaves may have sensed an opportunity to be seized in a dissension among the whites. The South was full of rumors of intended slave revolts.

In the last days of August of that year, a great conspiracy of slaves came to light near Richmond, Virginia. The conspiracy was by far the largest up to that time in the history of the nation.

On Saturday, August 30, 1800, in the late afternoon, two Negro slaves, Tom and Pharao, possessions of the wealthy plantation owner Mosby Sheppard, knocked on the door of his counting room. When the planter let them enter, they confided that the Negroes were to rise in the neighborhood of the Thomas Prosser plantation on the road to Richmond. The revolt was to begin with the killing of the Prosser family, the Mosby family, and another family in the area, about six miles outside of Richmond. The insurrectionists were then to proceed to Richmond, itself. When was the revolt to take place, Sheppard asked. "Tonight," was the answer. Who was the principal leader? Prosser's Gabriel.

Gabriel was a giant Negro who was known to wear his hair in a long black mane, in imitation of his Biblical hero, Samson. "His courage and intellect was above his rank of life," a contemporary wrote, though he added that the slave was also illiterate. Other sources insisted that the Negro had learned to read from the wife of his master, who had been impressed by the bright young boy and had found great satisfaction in teaching him. (This view might have been tendentiously spread to warn of the danger in instructing Negroes: since learning would either corrupt their minds or show the futility of being decent to a black slave, as he was an ingrate by nature.)

Gabriel's imagination had lent him a sense of Old Testament destiny. He thought himself a man of mission, put to a hard test by an exacting divinity. He spoke little and his words sounded like paraphrases of the Scriptures.

Upon hearing of the conspiracy from his two faithful slaves, Sheppard wrote a note hastily and forwarded it to Governor James Monroe. Monroe called up the militia all over the state, had a cannon set up in front of the capitol at Richmond and set guards at the penitentiary and the magazine at Richmond where arms had been stocked. Mounted patrols were ordered to search all roads leading to Richmond, and a strong cavalry unit was sent out to cover the area of the **Brook Swamp**. The swamp ran across the high road to Richmond from the Sheppard plantation and was spanned by a bridge. The blacks had to pass that bridge to get to Richmond from the region of the Prosser plantation.

Before dark on that Saturday a cloudburst let loose "the greatest rain perhaps ever known"; it swept away the bridge, and smashed the fords. The rising brook inundated field and road. The patrol surveyed the surrounding region from a nearby tavern, but failed to sight anyone suspicious. In the morning, Governor Monroe heard with relief that the notice of the conspiracy was probably a false alarm.

However, Sheppard had notified not only the Governor, but also Major Mosby. The planter Prosser, whose slaves seemed to have taken an initiative in the conspiracy, could not be notified as he had been absent from his plantation since August 7. A young man who had recently inherited his lands, he was little respected in the neighborhood and was said to treat his slaves barbarously. Gabriel had organized the Negroes of his plantation during the planter's absence to be the nucleus of the rising. The overseers of the plantation may in this instance have relaxed their customary vigilance: the brutality of their new master put the burden of disciplining the slaves on them, causing them to feel insecure in their position and bitter.

The planter Mosby, whose family was to be one of the first to be attacked in the alleged uprising, was one of the patrol who had gone to Brook Swamp to intercept the expected rebellion. He had taken shelter from the rain in the tavern and remained there until 8 A.M. the next morning. He had then gone home exhausted but rejoicing that the rumors of the plot were groundless. As he himself later testified, his joy was shortlived:

I had not been on the bed but a very little while before a Negro woman of my own came to me, and the first word she spoke was "you must not tell." Then she asked me if I had heard that the negroes were going to rise. I told her I had. I then asked her when they were to meet. She said somewhere about Mr. Prosser's and as they did not meet last night they would meet tonight. I asked her how many she understood were to meet. She answered 300 or 400, some from town some from the country, and that a number of them were to be mounted on horse-back, who were to go at a distance and kill and destroy all as they went—to take them, as I understood her, in their beds—and that the main body was to move on to Richmond.

Mosby's woman was well informed. When the storm of the evening before had broken, the leaders had decided to postpone the rising until the next night (Sunday). Many had originally argued for Sunday anyway, but Gabriel had resisted. In spite of the downpour, many slaves had come walking towards the assigned spot, but the leaders had sent out messengers to all group leaders, notifying them of the shift. Some slaves deemed the deluge a divine warning and would have stayed at home even without Gabriel's message.

Gabriel, who had indeed masterminded the plan for the revolt during his master's absence in August, had followed a carefully drawn up plan of action. This plan can be pieced together from various accounts of the conspiracy and its background.

For three weeks before the date set by him for the revolt, the tall Negro met on each Sunday with Negroes of local plantations at their barbecue parties or dances; on these occasions he would approach and initiate into the conspiracy men whom he had been told could be relied on. Each of these men was given a solemn mission. Some objections were raised

89

as to whether the rising would not need more than three weeks' preparation, but Gabriel and his brother, Martin, argued against delay. They pointed out the extraordinary advantages of the planned date: the country was at peace, its soldiers recently discharged, arms had been stored away, and the city of Richmond had abandoned its patrols. Such an opportunity was not to be missed. Even the Bible warned of delay, it was argued.

The organizer assigned to lead the rising in Carolina County, Ben Wolfolk, later one of the chief witnesses of the prosecution against the conspiracy and its originators in court, used Gabriel's sense of Biblical righteousness of his cause to inspire the Negroes of his county—though, he later admitted, he had been skeptical of the so-called "divine signals" Gabriel was using to justify the conspiracy:

> I had heard in the days of old when the Israelites were in service to King Pharoah, they were taken from him by the power of God, and were carried away by Moses. God had blessed him with an angel to go with him, but I could see nothing of that kind in these days.

Though Wolfolk may have been doubtful of Gabriel's Moses calling, he nevertheless was superstitious enough to be among those who interpreted the deluge of the day of the planned rising as a heavenly sign, warning against revolt.

Gabriel had a deadly answer to those who, like Wolfolk, may have doubted that the conspiracy was favored with divine inspiration: "Didn't God say that if we are to worship Him we should have peace in our land; five of you shall conquer an hundred, and a hundred a thousand of our enemies?"

Besides being influenced by the prophecies of the Bible, Gabriel also felt a spiritual kinship with the French Revolution (thereby, incidentally, justifying some of the arguments of Jefferson's critics); he was said to have planned to buy a piece of silk cloth and have the egalitarian slogan "Liberty or Death" printed on it.

As partisans of the cause were being recruited, a stock of arms was collected and placed in Gregory's Tavern—the very tavern where the white patrols gathered in the rain to survey the ground of the supposed revolt. The tavern was in easy walking distance of the three large plantations around which the revolt had been organized. For arms, Gabriel had been successful in procuring 500 bullets and 10 pounds of gunpowder; Jack Bowler, another giant, collected 50 bayonets mounted at the ends of crude sticks. Solomon, one of Gabriel's brothers, fashioned swords out of broken scythe blades—two swords to a blade—and Gabriel manufactured wooden handles. In addition to this arsenal, every member of the conspiracy had been ordered to bring along a knife or a club with him.

Altogether the array of weapons available was not impressive, and may appear to have been pitifully inadequate, given the projected scope of the rising; the whites of the time, however, thought differently realizing the very grave potential threat of such an organized and armed band: "they could hardly have failed of success; for after all we only could muster four or five hundred men, of whom not more than thirty had muskets." This was the more realistic evaluation of James Thomson Callender, writing to Thomas Jefferson of the revolt on September 13. (The democratic journalist was under imprisonment in Richmond at the time for a crime under the Sedition Law.)

Moreover, the strategy worked out between Gabriel, his brother Martin and Jack Bowler required few weapons in its initial phase. This phase called only for the murder of

their masters, their masters' families, and neighboring planters. Here, the element of surprise was the most powerful
weapon.

Only a hundred men were to be needed for the stand at
Brooks Swamp Bridge. Gabriel was to take another hundred
to Gregory's Tavern to pick up the arms hidden there. Fifty
men were to march quickly to Rockets, the lower section of
Richmond, to set it on fire; this would provide a diversion
to alarm the upper town and induce the townspeople to
gather there. While they were occupied with extinguishing
the fires, Gabriel's troops were to enter the upper town, one
contingent running to the penitentiary, where the stock of
arms would now be transferred. Two Negroes working there
had been primed by Gabriel several weeks earlier to open
the doors for the invaders. Another group of insurgents was
to storm and capture the Capitol, appropriating any arms
they found. All white men, women, and children were to be
killed, and town Negroes were to be forced to join the rebels
or die like the whites. With arms captured in the town, the
groups would then reunite and march to the lower town and
massacre the whites attending the fires. Sam Bird, a freed
Negro, was detailed to contact the Catawba Indians in the
region and persuade them to join the attack on the whites.
John Scott, another organizer, was to rouse the Negroes in
nearby Petersburg to similar violence.

The manpower Gabriel had calculated he would have at
his disposal was: 1,000 Negroes of Richmond, 600 in Caroline County, and an additional 500 recruited from the coal
pits.

It was later learned from Jack Bowler during the trials of
the conspirators that all Quakers, Methodists, and Frenchmen would have been spared in the fighting, and that it was
hoped that poor whites would join their ranks against the

wealthy classes. There was also a rumor current among the slaves at the time of the conspiracy that a French army had landed at South Key and would be ready to support the revolt. According to one version of the affair, Gabriel had also planned to appeal to the white men of Richmond for the emancipation of the slaves before swooping down on the town and annihilating them. Should they have accepted his conditions, he wished to celebrate the event—somewhat naively, it seems—with a stupendous banquet.

In all versions of the plan for the revolt, speedy action was indispensable to its success, if indeed there was ever any chance for its success. This necessity would have left little time to discriminate between the guilty and innocent citizens of Richmond during the massacre. Gabriel had not excluded the possibility of failure: he had resolved to retreat into the mountains of Virginia, build an eagle's nest there, and live or die a free Negro.

In actual fact, none of the phases of the revolt was ever put into action. After the planter Mosby had heard of its inception from his serving woman, the state militia was dispatched to arrest twenty Negro slaves on the Prosser estate. On the grounds of information received from them, further arrests were made in Richmond and Caroline counties, though Gabriel and Jack Bowler (also called "the Ditcher") had disappeared. The Court of Oyer and Terminer, held for the County of Henrico, prepared for trial of the principals on September 11. Governor Monroe promised pardons to those who assisted in the cause of justice.

The story of the conspiracy was reconstructed solely from confessions. Cooperating defendants received the death sentence on one day, deposed as witnesses against other participants the next, and were pardoned on the third. This procedure was irregular, but was perhaps the best and quickest way for the prosecution to ascertain the extent of the plot, its personnel, and leaders. There is no trace of any other pressure or inducement applied to slave witnesses to denounce others or confess, as had been the case in the prosecution of other conspiracies.

Governor Monroe obviously was motivated by a desire to finish with the judicial procedure as quickly as possible: the Federalist press was eager for the opportunity to develop the potential irony of the situation to the disadvantage of the Jeffersonians; it could be construed that the slogans of liberty being used by the gentlemen of the South in their election campaign for Jefferson had backfired and that they had provoked a slave rebellion against those very same gentlemen. Furthermore, Monroe had, as American ambassador to revolutionary Paris, been known for his enthusiastic public support of the principles of the French Revolution. This would have rendered him a particularly vulnerable target of abuse by the Federalist press and propagandists.

Thus, whereas the scope of previous conspiracies had been exaggerated by the authorities to alert the whites and intimidate the slaves, Monroe insisted on a great measure of secrecy in the Gabriel Conspiracy. The contemporary public received only vague reports of the trials, though there was widespread and keen interest in them; the official records have preserved only spotty accounts of the trials.

To Monroe and to other leaders at the time of the conspiracy, the time seemed ripe to whittle down slavery in Virginia. Cotton had not yet become king in the South, and the twenty years that the Constitution had left open for the slave trade still had eight years to run. The economic advantages of retaining slavery still had not become all-powerful. Under the impact of the revolt, Monroe corresponded with Jefferson concerning the possibility of making the terms of slave manumission easier and of settling freed Negroes "and the most spirited slaves" in the Louisiana Territory, the latter having just been acquired. Jefferson's own preference was to direct Virginia Negroes to the new state in Haiti; this proposition was to come up before the Virginia Assembly in 1806, but the majority would stand against strengthening what was to them the already subversive influence of San Domingo over sympathetic American slaves. At that time, the Assembly would resolve that free Negroes were to leave Virginia within the year from their receiving freedom; after that period, if found in the state, they were to be sold back into slavery.

The trials of the Gabriel Conspiracy leaders were conducted quickly: the Court of Henrico County condemned five of the principals on September 11, and they were executed on the following day. Five more defendants were sent to the gallows on September 15. All died unrepentant.

A reward of $300 was offered by the governor for assisting to bring Gabriel and Jack Bowler to justice. On September 25, the three-masted schooner *Mary* landed in Norfolk. An apprentice on the ship informed the town constable that Gabriel was a passenger. The Negro leader had boarded the ship on the previous Sunday, carrying with him a bayonet mounted on a stick which he had dropped in the river. He had been stowed away on the vessel for eleven days, presumably fed by the Negroes who eventually because of fear or the temptation of reward revealed his presence there. Gabriel was apprehended. The constable noted with annoyance that the skipper of the *Mary* had evinced no interest in the presence of the conspirator aboard his ship, nor in his delivery and arrest, nor in the reward.

News of the arrest spread quickly in Richmond. A large mass of people, white and black, gathered as two constables led the tall, dignified Negro to Governor Monroe. After a short interview, Monroe dismissed him, stating that Gabriel was ready to die and unwilling to reveal any facts of the conspiracy he had led.

He stood trial on October 3. "The behavior of Gabriel under his misfortunes was such as might be expected from a mind capable of forming the daring project which he had conceived," a Norfolk paper commented. The execution was carried out on October 7.

Jack Bowler, "the Ditcher," even taller than Gabriel with the same long hair and the strength of a bull (the court estimated his value at four times that of any other executed slave except Gabriel) was persuaded by a free Negro to surrender to the authorities. His betrayer accepted an abridgment of the reward set for his prize: $50 instead of $300.

The court also held trials in Caroline County by the end of October. Altogether, forty-five Negroes were executed. It was obvious that many more had been implicated in the conspiracy in several counties. But the prosecution had to be restricted for several reasons besides the political ones stated above. The state paid compensation to the owner for every executed slave.

A legend was inevitably woven around the figure of Gabriel. Perhaps the secrecy of the trials, which allowed so little of fact or personality to emerge into the light of public domain, contributed to the aura of mystery surrounding his character. It is surprising to note that the legend of his heroism survived as long as it did, and that accounts of the conspiracy were being reprinted thirty years after his death. Accounts have always differed wildly: it was said that he was a free Negro who had traveled all over the South to organize a general revolt, and had established connections, selected leaders, and hidden a large stock of arms to this end; the conspiracy was to have been discovered when three Negroes were seen "riding out of a yard together"; a prize of $10,000 had been put on his head; he escaped on a ship that was to sail to San Domingo; help had been sent to him by the Negro government of Haiti; he was found when his little nephew whom he had sent for a jug of rum innocently revealed his presence; he made a flaming speech before the court with shattering impact on the white men present. . . .

For the great avenger of enslaved humanity it painted him, the legend conjured up a more fitting vision of Gabriel's death than hanging: four wild horses were said to have been driven in opposite directions to tear his body apart.

V

THE FREED NEGRO:
A LEADER EMERGES

"The accused have exhibited a spirit which, if it becomes general, must deluge the Southern country in blood. They manifested a sense of their rights and contempt of danger, and a thirst of revenge which portend the most unhappy consequences."

(John Randolph of Roanoke, on Gabriel's Rebellion,
September 26, 1800)

G ABRIEL'S revolt had been effectively frustrated, but its memory continued to disturb the whites' peace of mind in the South. The fearlessness of the rebels while they faced death at Norfolk and Richmond evinced a determination that the white people did not expect of slaves. It made honest citizens tremble at the prospect of what other plans for their destruction the Negroes of the South had in mind—these same Negroes who were constantly around them and who seemed so meek and submissive in the day-to-day chores they were performing.

John Randolph, the eccentric gentleman of Roanoke, was as anxious as Governor Monroe that information concerning the conspiracy should be limited for political reasons. He gave a canny assessment of the scope of the rebellion and its repression, and he realized that its ramifications could provide the Federalist opponents the ammunition they needed during the election year against the democratic slogans of the Jeffersonians:

> It is now ascertained to have been partial and ill concerted, and has been quelled without any bloodshed, but that which streamed upon the scaffold. The executions have been not so numerous as might, under the circumstances, have been expected. You ... will not be surprised to learn that our Federalists have endeavored to make an electioneering engine of it.

Reports from Virginia in the wake of Gabriel's trial show that the whole state had been thrown into nervous tension. Townspeople became clairvoyants, predicting exact dates on which successive revolts were to occur, and when the slaves would strike again. If nothing should happen on the date fixed, the prophets were nonetheless given credit for anticipating the event.

Richmond expected a renewed revolt to break out on Christmas of 1800; Norfolk looked for it a few days before New Year's; Petersburg predicted it on New Year's Day. The report from Petersburg to the governor showed a sense of prophecy to which had been added a knack for detail:

> There does not remain a doubt but a general insurrection of the negroes is intended on the next Thursday night ... and assassination of all Petersburg's white inhabitants is intended; they do not intend to spare even the helpless infants.

Such holidays as Christmas and New Year's were considered particularly dangerous, because on those days the slaves were given a rest and thus had opportunities to get together without stirring suspicions—as, indeed, Gabriel had done on the three Sundays before his projected revolt.

The alarms continued to be sounded in 1801. On January 19, Williamsburg reported information that "leaves no doubt but that an insurrection of Negroes would shortly take place"; on January 22, Powhatan was no less sure of it. Southhampton set the date for February 14, and 500 armed white men were duly assembled there at night to face it.

In 1802, the suspicious white minds continued to manufacture Negro conspiracies. In both Richmond and Halifax County, white men were alleged to have been involved with them, either as instigators or as assistants.

At the same time in North Carolina, Negroes were widely suspected of mass poisonings of whites.

In the two decades following Gabriel's Rebellion, a series of events occurred which marked the establishment of the power and importance of the United States. These events were to determine the fate of slaves and of the institution of slavery in general.

Jefferson reaped the greatest windfall of history in the Louisiana Purchase. He would have been satisfied to receive from Napoleon a free harbor on the Mississippi at New Orleans; instead, Napoleon offered him for $15 million all of the Louisiana Territory from the mouth of the Mississippi north into what is now Montana—a vast area twice the size of the United States before the purchase in 1803. Napoleon accomplished a twofold aim in the transaction: he needed money for a new war with England, and, since he knew he could not prevent the British from seizing New Orleans in the war, he was dealing a blow to British ambitions in the North American continent by transferring it to American ownership.

The Mississippi River became a valuable asset to the

United States, a carrier for men and goods from the interior of the country to and from overseas ports; a road to the West, opening the virgin lands and forests there for exploitation. But the challenge also presented a grave problem: what sort of labor, slave or free, was to be recruited for the settlement and working of the vast new lands? Upon this question hinged the delicate balance of power between North and South as it had been set up by the Constitution. The problem had a pressing immediacy: the fateful date of January 1, 1808, was drawing near. After that day, as clearly stated in the Constitution, no more slaves could legally be imported to the United States.

The date had been set by the Constitutional Convention with the thought in mind that it would provide a beginning of the end, not only for the slave trade, but for slavery itself. The domestic situation had taken a turn favorable to the liquidation of slavery. The growing of tobacco had returned less and less profit while it exhausted the soil; slaves were becoming a burden in the upper South. Their market value decreased, despite the demand for them in the deep South, where cotton growing was becoming increasingly important. After the prohibition of slave importation, such states as Virginia, Maryland, and North Carolina hoped to sell their slaves at increased prices: for the prices were bound to rise when competition from foreign importation ceased entirely.

The halt of slave trade from abroad signaled the beginning of a massive slave trade within the country—a change that was accompanied with no less domestic turmoil and misfortune than the old slave trade had once provoked. Negroes who had been brought up in familiar surroundings among people they had much in common with lost all the security they had won. They were torn from their families, friends, and memories without notice or explanation, carted away, and sold into unknown distant places. New indignities and uncertainties plagued them as they became commodities to be transferred en masse from state to state.

The most propitious developments in theory turned out in practice to work against the slave and make his condition worse.

The cotton gin shortened the difficult and time-consuming process of removing the seeds from the fiber in the boll, making production more profitable than any other industry in the deep South. Production rose a thousand times in volume from 1791 to 1860. In the single year 1793–1794, the export of cotton rose from 187,000 lbs. to 1,601,760 lbs. Concomitantly, the slave population of the United States doubled between 1790 and 1820. With the help of the gin, more cotton was produced in a single day than had been previously done in six to seven weeks.

The labor of cotton picking under the fierce southern sun was hard work for the slave, but it did not impair his health as the cultivation of rice and indigo did. Under the cotton economy, slaves did not die so quickly. They became exploitable assets for many years—a change which was reflected in the rising prices they could command. The offspring of a slave mother had formerly meant a burden for the master. He had been obliged to feed the children as well as the mother and could have expected no earlier return than when the child reached the age of seven. That child might die soon afterwards in the rice swamps. But now, food for seven years proved an excellent investment in a working force that could be active and valuable for several decades.

These changes in the economy benefited neither the slaves nor the country. Border states were transformed into breeding farms for slaves. Human zoos appeared. They brought a new prosperity for the slaveholder, but were a source of moral degradation for himself and for his charges. At the same time, the prospects for a peaceful liquidation of the institution became fainter. In John Fiske's words: "after the abolition of slave trade in 1808 had increased the demand for Virginia-bred slaves in the states further south, the very idea of emancipation faded out."

"Slave rearing early became the source of the largest and often the only regular profit of nearly all slaveholding farmers and of many planters in the upper South, especially in Virginia," wrote the historian Frederic Bancroft. These farmers and planters relied on the "slow increase of capital from propagation." Henry Clay also held that slave labor would survive in the farming regions "if the proprietors were not tempted to raise slaves by the high price of the southern market."

In vain, decent Virginians like Thomas Jefferson Randolph indignantly scolded their fellow Virginians in the House of Delegates:

> How can an honorable mind, a patriot, and a lover of his country, bear to see this ancient dominion, rendered illustrious by the noble devotion and patriotism of her sons in the cause of liberty, converted into one grand menagerie where men are to be reared for market like oxen for the shambles?

Slaveholders customarily sent their surplus slaves in gangs to the South, usually to be sold in the slave market of New Orleans. Slaves were put in chains overnight to make sure they could not escape. A British traveler, J. S. Buckingham, met one such gang in Virginia and described it:

> The sun was shining very hot, and in turning an angle of the road, we encountered the following group: first, a little cart drawn by one horse, in which five or six half-naked black children were tumbled like pigs together. The cart had no cover-

ing, and they seemed to have been actually broiled to sleep. Behind the cart marched three black women, with head, neck and breasts uncovered, and without shoes or stockings; next came three men, bare-headed, half-naked, and chained together with an ox-chain. Last of all came a white man on horseback, carrying pistols in his belt.

This process, according to Buckingham, was known all over the South under the euphemism of "removal of slaves from one state to another." Farmers and traders from Kentucky and the West drove horses, mules, cattle, and swine to the Atlantic states and bought young black slaves in exchange, whom they either sold to a slave dealer or took home and sold directly to the farmers.

The extent of this new slave trade can be envisioned by the example of Virginia: in one decade (the 1830s) Virginia exported 118,000 slaves to the southwest; 67,000 to South Carolina; 23,000 to Kentucky.

Even such a state as Georgia, where slave plantations were flourishing, took up breeding for sale—for, as Bancroft asserts, "the greatest profit of all was what the master thought of and talked of all day long—the natural increase of his slaves, as he called it. His Negroes were far more for him than his land."

A new evil was added to further the corruption of the slave trade: illegal importation. The British also abolished slave trading, except within the West Indian islands. As a consequence, slave prices in Africa collapsed, but skyrocketed in the West Indies. American slavers flying the Spanish flag carried about 15,000 slaves a year under more appalling conditions than ever. Cuba and the Danish islands became the new centers of distribution.

At the height of this form of trade, at least one historian,

E. A. Andrews in *Slavery and the Domestic Slave-Trade in the U.S.* (Boston, 1836) sounded a note of wonderment at the contradictions it betrayed both in the human mind and in the value judgments of society. Some of these contradictions have not been explained to this day, and remain as problematical features of the character of southern whites of the United States. For Professor Andrews, the puzzle boiled down to one question: is it possible to departmentalize the human mind to the point that it can entertain in one segregated corner a moral code violently in warfare with all its other assumptions? (A more psychologically oriented age may now wonder in what ways a mind so distorted took its revenge for such abuse.)

Andrews considered it inconsistent with the laws of human nature that a rich slave trader should be held in respect by society. Slave traders acquired wealth, he wrote, "by trafficking in the miseries of the already wretched African"; he acted as though empowered by some higher authority to buy a husband torn from his wife and a wife who had been forcibly separated from her husband, and to sell these derelicts into hopeless slavery. Yet what astonished Andrews the most was that despite the "hardening influences, operating habitually on his character," the slave trader could endeavor to "cultivate at the same time, those gentle manners and kind affections which render him an object of attachment to his fellow men and even to his slaves themselves."

Apologists for the slave trade would have us believe that the Negro slave woman who had become a breeding animal under the new system lost all interest in her child, knowing that it would be taken away from her anyway. Some writers thought that such indifference was a defense mechanism against the painful consciousness of indignity. And there were incentives for the mothers, too—one method of prodding her to her "duty" was to promise her freedom after a certain number of childbirths.

But the English visitor Buckingham, after his travels throughout the South, would not accept these explanations without first exploring the problem at its source: "from informations I could obtain in this subject," he wrote, "the negroes feel these separations as acutely as any whites could do, and are unhappy for years afterwards." Other contemporary writers claimed that the slave mother, having been degraded to the role of a domestic animal, lost even the most elementary human feelings such as mother love.

New Orleans had been successively governed and transformed in character, language, and system of government by the Spanish, the French, and finally the Americans. Each rule had its own ways of adapting slavery to Christianity, enlightenment, or democracy. Each rule established different regulations and took different attitudes toward freeing slaves through will, deed, or purchase. Each change of power involved an interruption or diversion of authority affecting the slaves and cast them into moods alternating between fear and hope.

The unsettled situation of New Orleans exploded into at least one serious rebellion in 1811. In that year, the parish of Saint John the Baptist, about thirty-six miles from the city, experienced a rising of its slaves. The movement spread along the Mississippi. Negroes formed disciplined units of as many as 500 men and marched on New Orleans to the beating of drums. They were met and defeated by the troops before they reached the town.

The War of 1812 brought renewed opportunities for mass escape from bondage, and in the first year of the war about 1,000 slaves fled to the British in Norfolk, Virginia. The women and children were sent to the West Indies and the men enrolled in labor units of the army. This process of flight continued throughout the war. Two years later, a brigadier general reported the state of affairs in Westmoreland County, Virginia:

> Our Negroes are flocking to the enemy from all quarters, which they convert into troops, vindictive and rapacious. They leave us as spies upon our posts and our strength, and they return upon us as guides and soldiers and incendiaries.

In the series of campaigns known as the Seminole War, which were conducted over the years 1812 to 1818, former slaves from Georgia and South Carolina actually defended their freedom in small Florida communities they had set up in league with the Indian tribes which inhabited the area.

The Seminoles, a tribe that had broken with the Creeks of Georgia and Alabama, settled in Florida, and were being used by the Spanish to raid plantations of Georgia and South Carolina. The tribes were despised in the South for their vagrancy and for the lures they proffered to slaves to run away to join them. Andrew Jackson, in his *Memoirs,* reflected the opinion of whites everywhere on the virtues of these Indians:

> This desperate clan of outlaws, from civil, and even from savage society ... have drawn into their confederacy many runaway negroes, whose African sullenness, has been aroused to indiscriminate vengeance, by the more frantic fury of the American natives.

In 1812, Georgia patriots organized a campaign to conquer Florida, set up a government there, and requested annexation to the United States. A body of Georgia militia penetrated into the St. Augustine region, and met fierce resistance from the Seminoles, and particularly, from the

Negroes, who seem to have been living in a feudal arrangement subservient to the Seminoles but protected by them. Lieutenant Colonel Smith, reporting from camp near St. Augustine, gave a distressing picture of the patriot army after the clashes: "having dwindled away to nothing, it is doubtful whether it will revive ever again." The Georgian party withdrew, but the next year fresh troops arrived—including both Tennessee militia and U.S. troops, and commanded by Brigadier General Fleurnoy. Fleurnoy issued a firm order: "each Negro taken in arms will be put to death." But Indians and Negroes slowed the invasion long enough for Congress to demand a halt to the campaign.

Before this could happen, the Negroes had already paid a heavy price: one of their settlements near "Bollegg's Town" had been destroyed by U.S. soldiers, guided by seven Indian prisoners. The Negro settlement at the time of its demise was apparently a prosperous and well-provisioned one. Even though some of the Negroes had to deliver as many as ten bushels of corn per year to their Indian masters, they had ample stores and were good farmers, a fact that emerges from the report of Colonel Smith on February 24:

> Tuesday Febr 11 was employed in destroying the Negro Town shown us by the Prisoners. We burnt three hundred and eighty six houses; consumed and destroyed from fifteen hundred to two thousands bushels of corn; three hundred horses and about four hundred cattle. Two hundred deerskins were found.

The Negroes from this remarkable community fled to the Suwanee River and there built new villages. In 1814, General Jackson launched a new campaign led by General Gaines. Gaines built Fort Scott at the junction of the Seminole, Flint, and Chattahoochee Rivers "in order to overawe the negroes."

However, the British took a hand in the campaign and offered aid to the Negroes: a British warship, the *Orpheus,* landed at Apalachicola, and the commander, Major Edward Nicholls, called upon the Negroes to join him, promising them land in the West Indies after the war had been concluded. About 300 Negroes and 30 Seminoles heeded the call and established a new fort near St. Augustine, naming it "British Fort." When the Anglo-American conflict ended in the peace of 1814, the British troops evacuated the fort, but left guns and ammunition to the Indians and Negroes. American troops besieged the fort in 1816, and a direct hit by a cannon destroyed it entirely. Three hundred Indian and Negro defenders were killed.

In 1818, Andrew Jackson invaded Florida and put an end to the resistance there, overwhelming the Indians and Negroes on the Suwanee and burning the Negro forts and villages. Many of the surviving Negroes fled by boat to the Bahamas. Others became integrated with the Indian tribes.

The objective of the American armies was, of course, the annexation of Florida, but the incentive for action came from the Georgia and South Carolina planters, whose property had been periodically raided by intruders from Florida, and whose control of slaves was tenuous so long as Negro settlements and military forts in Florida were tempting them to join and be free.

The Negro slaves in the Florida territory may have become associated with the Indians when the shrinking lands of the latter became a refuge for slaves and their cause became a common one, to stem the advance of the whites. But when the Indian fought, he was defending a civilization and a way of life that the Negro could not share. The Negroes, when left to themselves, built up a pattern of life that was roughly the same as that of a freedman in the

South. The coexistence of the two races in Florida clearly demonstrated that the Indian and the Negro wanted to live in two different worlds; the Negro's image of a desirable society was one derived from his experience of the white man's habits of life, but with himself as a free member of it.

Yet the legions of abortive rebellions in the South must have suggested something to those Negroes who felt the urge to do something towards changing their own status and that of their kinsmen. For success, leadership from outside their own ranks was indispensable. Action had to be coordinated with events in white society favorable to it. The slave, no matter how intelligently he put together bits of information gathered from eavesdropping and conversations with other Negroes, could not do it. And white men could not fulfill the function of leadership needed; white men driven to the causes of the slaves were often motivated by an alien resentment. Between white and Negro discontents yawned a wide gap of tradition; only commonly lived experience over a long period of time could bridge the gap. The answer to leadership among Negroes lay in the free Negro.

The hysteria of the time brought forth a quixotic figure —an eccentric storekeeper and accused inciter of Negro sentiments—George Boxley, of Spotsylvania, Virginia.

Boxley had served as an ensign in the militia during the War of 1812, and had been considered a good drill officer. At the end of the war, he found he had been frustrated in his military ambitions, and made no secret of his dissatisfaction with the condition of society in the United States: he complained that the gap between the rich and poor was too wide, and that the government favored the rich, giving offices to wealth rather than to merit.

The town of Spotsylvania considered this soldier of fortune, this tall thin man with thick whiskers and voluble conversation, as a dangerous malcontent. The feeling was reinforced after Boxley opened up a general store in the town, selling not only his whiskey, but his ideas, to Negro customers. It was feared that his dangerous notions might infect the Negroes and incite them to rebellion. Some citizens held that this was Boxley's precise objective, that he maintained his store only to be in touch with Negroes whom he hoped to turn to conspiracy and uprising.

In March, 1816, a woman slave belonging to a Mr. Ptolemy Powell denounced Boxley, protesting that he had conspired with several Negroes, promising them liberty in a free state. She named several principals in the conspiracy, and they were arrested. In a letter to the magistrature, Boxley emphatically denied any part in a conspiracy or any knowledge of one; then he "armed himself with a musket, his sword and razor, and trembling in every limb and pale as death (he) mounted his horse and rode off." Fifteen minutes later, his horse returned to Spotsylvania, lacking its bridle and saddle. Boxley himself, however, was not lost sight of for long.

The next day, he was reported seen in the town of Louisa, trying to collect evidence that the Negroes arrested in Spotsylvania were innocent. In the meantime, the magistrature had ordered the arrest of thirty-one slaves from three townships who, according to the witness, had frequented Boxley's store and had conspired to raid Fredericksburg and Richmond: a day during harvest having been chosen, the slaves were to meet at Boxley's house, taking horses, guns, swords, and clubs along ready to follow him.

Hearing of this mass arrest, Boxley surrendered and was arrested. He did not deny his radical opinions, but stated that divine inspiration had dictated them to him as the truth about the imperfections of the Republic. He had, indeed, talked of his views with Negro customers, but had intended his words to have had a cheering or friendly effect, rather than to suggest that these views be acted upon.

Boxley's family insisted that he was insane. Whether this was true or not, he escaped from Spotsylvania with the help of his wife, and although a $1,000 reward was set for his recapture, the records do not reveal that he was ever apprehended. But for listening to the friendly white man's misplaced rhetoric, six Negroes were executed and another six were deported.

In the beginning of the nineteenth century, Virginia led the United States in the number of free Negroes living within her borders—one-eighth of the total for the country. In 1820, there were 36,000 free Negroes and mulattoes in the state as against 600,000 white men and 425,000 Negro slaves.

Under the impact of the Declaration of Independence, freedom was frequently given to individual slaves through deed and purchase. Manumissions increased towards the end of the eighteenth century when slavery appeared uneconomic.

Slaveowners, particularly planters, pointed out the wretched state of the free Negro, claiming that he had no security or protection when he was jobless, sick, or old. Most freed slaves did indeed have a hard life, since even apprenticeship in a craft was set by law to last much longer than that of a white applicant. On the other hand, the fact that he could be hired at low wages without any guarantee of steady work favored him in consideration for certain jobs. In Petersburg, Virginia, free Negroes were active in a number of occupations, as servants and unskilled workers, but also as carpenters, bricklayers, caterers, shoemakers, and fishermen. Many other towns had a similarly large field of opportunities for the skilled free Negro. Nevertheless, freedom meant no equality for him. He was discriminated against in various ways: even the penal code prescribed flogging for the free Negro when prison sufficed as punishment for the white.

The whites of the South must have sensed early that the free Negro was a potential leader for the rest of his race who were still slaves. In fact, whites believed that the mere presence of a free Negro was a kind of provocation. After all, he had access to information and knowledge which, if conveyed to the slaves, could implant ideas of freedom leading to revolt and bloodshed. Such whites were imbued with the American belief in the power of education and wanted to protect their slaves from its liberating influence. When rebellions occurred, manumissions were either limited by new regulations, or the freed Negroes were ordered to leave the state under penalty of forfeiting their freedom. Several states would not admit freed Negroes into their cities; some prohibited the instruction of Negroes in reading, and craftsmen who were obliged to educate their apprentices were relieved of this duty with respect to free Negroes. Communication between free and slave Negroes was prohibited, though such regulations were put into effect only during times of panic.

Henry Clay offered words of warning on the dangers of free Negroes: "Of all description of our population," he wrote, "the free persons of color are by far, as a class, the most corrupt, depraved and abandoned." John Randolph of Roanoke was speaking for many whites when he asserted that "it was notorious that the free Negroes were regarded by every slaveowner as one of the greatest sources of the insecurity and unprofitableness of slave property; that they excited discontent among their fellow beings; that they acted as channels of communication, not only between different slaves, but between slaves of different districts; and that they were depositaries of stolen goods."

It was found among planters in Maryland that the mortality of free Negroes was higher than that of the slaves, and that they did not enjoy a fair opportunity for the cultivation of their talents.

All of these arguments were used to counter the institution of freeing slaves. However, the historian E. A. Andrews, writing of them, dispassionately, found their conditions "in truth, proverbially wretched"—but he added that "none of the free Negroes manifest an inclination to return to slavery." It was better to suffer in freedom than to enjoy the securities of slavery.

Though the problem of the free Negro came under discussion at each new revolt or conspiracy, it turned into a national issue only after a proposal made by Virginia, following Gabriel's revolt, was taken up by the American Colonization Society in 1810. The proposal had originally suggested buying land outside the United States to be settled by Negroes who were free and for the use of others subsequently freed. The American Colonization Society dedicated itself to a program of returning to Africa all free Negroes and all other Negroes who desired to go there, the latter if their master was ready to manumit them.

The opening of the territories west of the Mississippi River in the wake of the Louisiana Purchase suddenly caused the problem of the free Negro—and, tangentially, the problem of slavery—to move to the center of passionate debates in and out of the Congress about whether the new territories should be slave or slave-free states. The question of whether the western population should strengthen the southern or northern representations in the Union had tremendous political and economic significance. If slavery could be established in the newly acquired territories, the position and power of the South would be enhanced.

When Missouri applied for statehood in 1818, these problems came to a head. The campaign of the American Colonization Society was losing popularity among the planters, who believed the resettlement of Negroes—free or would-be-free—in Africa would cause unrest among the slaves.

The movement also ran into strong opposition from the majority of free Negroes, who were the most immediately affected by the proposal. Their leaders issued a proclamation in January 1817, from Richmond, stating that free Negroes "prefer being colonized in the most remote corner of the land of our nativity, to being exiled to a foreign country."

A convention of free Negroes in Philadelphia in August 1817, resolved:

> Whereas our ancestors, (not of choice) were the first successful cultivators of wild America, we their descendants feel ourselves entitled to participate in the blessings of her luxuriant soil, which their blood and sweat enriched; and that any measure or system of measures, having a tendency to banish us from her bosom, would not only be cruel, but in direct violation of those principles which have been the boast of the republic."

The Missouri statehood problem ended in the Compromise of 1820. Missouri was given the right to slavery, but slavery was prohibited elsewhere in the Louisiana Territory north of latitude 36° 30'. To preserve the balance of North and South, Maine was admitted to the Union at the same time as Missouri.

The white man's arguments and newspaper articles were

passed on to slaves by educated free Negroes. Although the eloquence of the most outstanding speakers in Congress on the virtues and faults of the system caused some agitation in the South, nothing changed physically. Things went on as before; the Colonization Society pressed its campaign, and the number of slaves in the South kept growing.

Some of the young Negroes, however, thought that it was futile to expect liberation when the slaves themselves were not ready to present their claim for freedom. Local revolts might signal the burning wish of the slaves, but the protest would have to shake and threaten the whole South to be effective. Slaves with their movements, meetings, and conversations strictly limited could not organize such broad action. Leadership, as the whites rightly suspected and feared, had to come from free Negroes.

Charleston, South Carolina, eventually brought forth such a free Negro. His name was Denmark Vesey. He knew both the white and black worlds, but belonged to neither of them.

As a fourteen-year-old boy, Vesey had been among 390 slaves shipped from St. Thomas, the Danish possession in the Caribbean that had become a slave trading post. The group was crowded onto the deck of the vessel of Captain Joseph Vesey, sailing for Cap Français, chief port of the French colony of San Domingo.

Captain Vesey and his officers were struck by the four-teen-year-old's alertness, physical beauty, and intelligence. They made him the ship's mascot and gave him the name "Telemaque"—which English tongues corrupted to "Denmark," after the little European country on whose island he had been purchased with a shipload of other slaves.

Though the boy was his favorite among the slaves, Captain Vesey sold Denmark with the other Negroes when he reached San Domingo, loaded his ship with sugar and molasses, and sailed away.

At his next call in St. Thomas, the captain was officially informed that the sale of the Negro boy had been canceled; he had been found subject to epileptic fits. Captain Vesey took Denmark back in good grace—at least, he made no further attempt to sell him or get rid of him in any other way. For the next twenty years, Denmark was his trusted assistant on the sea and in his Charleston residence.

Denmark Vesey saw a great deal of the world in the twenty years of his apprenticeship. He assisted the slavers in herding and guarding kidnapped Negroes, driving them on the ship, putting manacles on their hands or feet, and keeping watch that they did not break loose to kill him and the other members of the crew. On land, Denmark assisted in fitting the Negroes for sale. Obviously he was very efficient at all these operations, because he managed to maintain his master's favor for twenty years. Opportunities for his escape must have been legion, but he resisted temptation. He may have witnessed with his own eyes the revolts of San Domingo; in any case he was an avid reader of any newspaper or pamphlet that fell into his hands, either in English or French. He knew of the continued waves of revolts in the French island; he knew of the eventual victory of the blacks there and the subsequent extermination of whites. The lesson of Haiti was to loom large in his thoughts and plans later, but while assisting Captain Joseph Vesey in his slave trade he had shown no active sympathy with its victims.

A sort of divine intervention changed the course of Denmark Vesey's life in 1800. In that year, he drew a $1500 prize in the East Bay Street lottery of Charleston. He bought his freedom for $600, his master having shown his good will by setting a very moderate price for a thirty-three-year-old

Negro endowed with such exceptional intelligence and application. With the rest of the money, Denmark set himself up as a carpenter. Entering Charleston as a free Negro, he joined a large community that numbered over 3,000, who were active as unskilled workers, but also as coal and wood dealers, merchants, and contractors. Denmark became a prosperous and well-established member of the community. He had several wives, and children by each of them, and it was said that he displayed towards them "the haughty and capricious cruelty of an eastern Basha." The rules of the time dictated that if a free Negro married a slave girl, his wife and the children that she gave birth to would remain slave unless the husband was able to buy them out of bondage. Even if he was able to do so, there was a drawback to freeing one's family: regulations and practices continually changing under the impact of slave scares and rebellions often obliged the newly freed Negro to leave the state. It was a painful matter to leave one's community for the unknown; it was difficult to find a new place to live, for several states did not admit free Negroes. Should one enter another state illegally, he could be sold back into slavery. Thus, though Vesey may have been a bad father, his children's curious fate as slave progeny of a free parent may have weighed heavily on his gradual decision to dedicate his life to freedom of the slaves gained through their own action. "All my children were slaves and I wished to see what I could do for them," he later said.

In Charleston, Denmark Vesey seems to have become a man broiling under a repressed burden of hatred—a hatred concealed as he had learned to conceal his emotions for his race while faithfully serving his slaver captain.

He was consumed with self-disgust for his former status as the eager henchman of a trader who had handled members of his race, at times with less consideration than would be given to an animal or lifeless cargo. Vesey also hated his own race: a race mishandled, maltreated, dehumanized, and largely resigned to its fate and enduring it stoically, except for sporadic outbreaks as the years, decades, and centuries passed. He was marred by the bitterness and desperation of this hatred.

He hated most the Negro chieftains who had raided peaceful tribes to sell their people for a miserable return of brandy, firearms, or tawdry rags. These savage peddlers of his homeland were more brutal than white men; they hunted and delivered their kin, trussed up and secure like wild beasts. Without their greed and stupidity through the centuries, white men would never have been able to carry the millions of Negroes over the oceans as if they had been born to be slaves of other peoples on another continent. These chieftains had organized the tribal wars to make prisoners and sell them to the white man; they had contributed through their jungle hunts to the debasement and destruction of civilization; they had deprived their fellow Negroes of their places as free men in a world their ancestors fashioned to the nature around them and to their habits of living in it. Denmark despised these gravediggers of his race.

How could he avoid also despising himself—for had he not given himself with efficient devotion to the ugly trade in his own kinsmen?

At one point around 1818, this twisted child of the slave trade must have decided to make good for the way he had sinned against his brethren and against his own children. Then he turned all his dedication, relentless energy, secretiveness, and hatred towards organizing revolt. He eagerly sought news of Haiti and listened to black sailors at the Charleston Battery and the wharfs in search for a clue to the success of the black nation in retaining its independence. He learned about the unsuccessful rebellions that flared up sporadically in the southern states and shared a melancholy sense of failure for their insufficient leadership, organization, or realistic purpose.

Vesey resolved to take his time and proceed systematically. He would organize his revolt with the utmost precaution. He would plan every minute detail, take into consideration all eventualities, and, above all, select the most capable men, those of the firmest character, for his leaders and subalterns.

Vesey's personality and position in Charleston was marvelously suited to organize a Negro rising. He was a first-class carpenter, and his shop flourished. His unusual knowledge of the events of the world and his interest in public affairs attracted white men and Negroes to his shop. In his discussions with them he imperceptibly steered the subject towards slavery. Negroes who heard him talking with white men must have admired his courage and his evident superiority in intelligence and information over many of the white men who had read nothing and knew little about events that occurred beyond their beautiful city of Charleston.

As a Negro himself, although free, Vesey could associate on equal terms with slaves. He used such meetings in his shop to strengthen their self-confidence and stir pride or hope in them.

Vesey fascinated the slaves, but he also frightened them, and disturbed their peace of mind and their moral torpor. He assailed them unsparingly: he once told a slave that the life of slaves was so abominable that they ought to rise against it. The slave remarked that, as far as he was concerned, his own life was fine, and he was satisfied. Thereupon Vesey became enraged and scolded the complacent Negro: because of fools such as he, who cared nothing but for themselves, and would not sacrifice for the sake of others who lived in shame and misery, nothing was being done to change the abject state of the Negro. This very slave, as a trial witness against Vesey later, testified that in this outburst Vesey had threatened him: "after all things were well done, he would mark him."

Vesey had nothing but contempt for those slaves who accepted their conditions. "Why do you bow to a white man?" Vesey asked a Negro while they were walking in the street. "But I am a slave," the man replied, astonished and baffled. "You deserve to be one," Vesey replied. "What can we do?" the slave asked. "Listen to the story of the demigod Hercules and the wagoner: the wagoner's cart was stuck at the bottom of a hill. He began to cry and pray. Hercules came and advised him to put the whip to the team and his shoulder to the wheel. You, yourself have to work and take risks for your freedom."

He had equal contempt for those slaves who humiliated themselves more than their state required, and for those who served the slaveholder in keeping down his race: the Negro overseers, domestic servants, and—in the nightmare of his past—his memory of himself. He too had given the best years of his life to aid a white slave trader whose name he still bore. Even more than the African chieftains, his dull indifference to the sufferings and humiliations of his own race had made him the most execrable traitor.

Vesey found an ideal place to look for leaders: the African Methodist Episcopal Church of Charleston. There he could examine character and aptitude for the functions of revolt. At the same time, he could use the pulpit to stir hope, desire for betterment, and courage for action. The church had organized its congregation into classes led by the most intelligent Negroes.

Vesey became a favorite preacher of the church. In one way or another, his sermons always were concerned with slavery. Nothing was nearer to the hearts of his listeners than the stories of God liberating the Israelites from slavery in Egypt. In the enchanting words of the Bible, the Negro slaves identified themselves with the Israelites and confidently came to expect God's intervention for their freedom.

Vesey also read the words of Genesis, of how the world was created by God, and God had created men equal, Negro as well as white. Knowing how sensitive Negroes were to all Scriptures, he quoted passages to prove that slavery was contrary to the laws of God, and suggested that the slaves should do something to assure their liberty. God helps those who help themselves. Again referring to the Bible, he insisted that God had imposed on his listeners the duty to change the state of things that offend His will. It was their bounden duty to act, no matter what sacrifice that action demanded. To strengthen their resolution, he assured the Negroes that the Scriptures vouchsafed success once they submitted to God's instruction.

At these meetings, Vesey also used the words of secular authority. He quoted the eloquent speeches against slavery of Rufus King of Massachusetts and the other congressmen, and watched the effects of the words on his hearers. Impetuous and domineering as he was, he possessed unusual self-discipline; he could quietly work on men to soothe their reluctance and dispel their scruples.

The Bible may have inspired their hopes, but what particularly inflamed the passions of his audiences was the story of San Domingo, the island where all had been won for the Negro: freedom, power, and wealth. And though the more cautious hesitated for fear of bloodshed and the wrath of the white men, many responded to another argument Vesey interpolated in his discourses: the North had already liberated the slaves. The federal government favored it. White people in the South alone opposed emancipation. Action by slaves would be a legal measure, lending force to the lawmakers' will; rebellion would be directed at eradicating illegal local resistance to the will of the nation.

Vesey spent the four years after 1818 preparing the revolt. He mapped Charleston and the counties around it, traveled within an eighty-mile radius learning the size of the plantations, the kind of slaves working on them, and the most alert individuals. In Charleston, he surveyed the magazines, the distribution of the militia, their force, arms, times of change, and commanders; he also marked every store selling guns and ammunition and catalogued the approximate stock they held.

Slowly, he came to a choice of his closest associates who would share the responsibility of the plan with him. With these leaders, he could select another body of sub-lieutenants and divide authority for the plan and the troops among them. Information concerning the master plan and its highest executants would be withheld from the sub-lieutenants; even less would be revealed to men commissioned for certain particular functions. The mass of people who enlisted would be initiated into the plot in vague terms, given only the facts of what must be the individual concern of each. It would be suggested that help might be forthcoming from Haiti or other foreign powers to create the impression that those in authority would not act before success was insured.

These were to be the leaders of the rebellion:

Peter Poyas was slated to be commander in the field. Witnesses deposed later that the slaves respected and feared Vesey more than they did their God, but that Peter was said to have had a magnetism in his eyes: once he set his eyes on a man, there was no resisting his power. Poyas scrutinized candidates, swore them to secrecy, and threatened those who broke it with death. He had volunteered to the most daring task of the plot—he would attack and disarm the main guard at the governor's office in Charleston, himself.

Monday Gell, a Charleston harness-maker of excellent standing. He had an uncommon facility in writing and acted as secretary to the top leadership.

Gullah Jack, known as a sorcerer. A sorcerer was held indispensable to the success of the plot. Gullah Jack's power rested on his reputation of being invulnerable. The Angola Negroes firmly believed that he was endowed with the power of making others immune from death; but he intimated that his power had limitations: his charms could not protect the Negro conspirators from treachery by their own kind.

A host of sub-lieutenants: Tom Russell, charged with manufacturing small pikes "on a very improved model"; Polydor Faber, who would fit the weapons with handles; Bacchus Hamelt, the arsenal keeper who would collect and hide firearms and ammunition; William Garner and Mungo Harth, leaders of the mounted companies; Lot Forrester to enlist country Negroes, who would be commanded by Ned Bennett, a personal servant to the Governor of South Carolina, Thomas Bennett.

No detail of the revolt was left to improvisation. Vesey had taken his lesson not only from San Domingo, but also from the futile rebellions that sputtered in the South, the latest having been one at Camden, South Carolina, in 1816.

Enlistments were made with caution; any man willing to join the plot was screened first by a group of middlemen, then allowed to meet with the local leader authorized to admit him.

Slaves who eventually refused to enlist, after making overtures to the group, were threatened with death, whether the rising took place or not.

Vesey was always in direct touch with the free Negroes who had not joined the snobbish free men's circles where solidarity with slaves was considered taboo. He also had access to slaves whose masters had lent them to the craftsmen of Charleston. These slaves worked for a salary paid to their masters, part of which went towards payment for their own food and board. They lived like free help, with the substantial difference that the master could take them back or sell them if he found a more remunerative arrangement for their use. While they enjoyed relative freedom, it was easy to contact them, and easier still to enlist their help.

Peter Poyas had one rule of thumb for the plot: "Don't mention it to those waiting-men who receive presents of old coats from their masters, or they'll betray us." Most previous conspiracies had been betrayed by domestic servants. As part of the white man's household, they had a special function. They had shed the anonymity of the field slaves, assumed individuality, and entered into a human relationship with the master's family. They were, of course, anxious to keep the privileged position they enjoyed by gaining the trust of white families. In most cases, a genuine feeling of warmth grew between white families and their household servants.

Still, the domestics preferred to spend their hours of relaxation on Sundays and holidays with their own people. Unlike the free Negroes, who could easily take on the roles of desperados or bandits, they were torn by a crisis of loyalties. A conspiracy in preparation put before them a terrible choice. They hesitated, terrified by the bloody implications. Should they join the insurgents or denounce them? Some who joined and were accepted asked Vesey whether ministers, women, and children should not be spared. He vehemently protested against any such measure, insisting that on the precedent of San Domingo, Negroes could not sustain power while "one white skin" remained intact. This, Vesey scrupulously pointed out, was the command of the Scriptures in sundry passages:

> Behold, the day of the Lord cometh, and thy spoil shall be divided in the midst of thee.
> For I will gather all nations against Jerusalem to battle; and the city shall be taken, and the houses rifled, and the women ravished; and half of the city shall go forth into captivity, and the residue of the people shall not be cut off from the city.
> (Zechariah, 14:1-2)

> ... And they utterly destroyed all that *was* in the city, both man and woman, young and old, and ox, and sheep, and ass, with the edge of the sword.
> (Joshua 6:21)

In general, when domestic slaves learned of such plots, they sped to their masters to tell all they knew or guessed of conspiracies. Through such confidences they could at least salvage the trust their masters had placed in them. Fear—the fear of being wrongly accused of complicity in resistance to slavery—fostered a hypersensitivity to normal expressions of resentment in the slave quarters. Curses, empty threats, and meaningless imprecations could be magnified into the ominous rumblings of rebellion. The fanatical alertness of

the trusted servant could precipitate the loss of many innocent lives.

A domestic slave did, in fact, betray the conspiracy of
Denmark Vesey. Peter Poyas was right to warn every confederate to keep vigilance against the "waiting-men" of the
white folk. He was wrong in another prophecy he made.
"God has a hand in it," he said. It did seem so. After four
years of planning for the conspiracy since 1818, the project
had still not been betrayed in the slightest detail.

One fine day in the spring of 1822, a slave named William,
"slave of Mrs. Paul," forgot Peter Poyas' warning. While
he was looking at ships in the Charleston harbor, he met
another slave, Devany, owned by a Colonel Prioleau. Encouraged by his master's absence from the city, Devany
had been relaxing while on an errand for his master's wife.
After approaching Devany and engaging him in conversation, William gained the impression that the man would
readily join the conspiracy. "We are determined to shake off
our bondage," he intimated. "We stand on good foundation;
many have joined, and if you will go with me I will show
you the man who has the list of names and who will take
yours down."

William had misjudged the reliability of his confidant.
Devany, frightened by the unsolicited information, went to
a free Negro friend, seeking advice about what to do. He
was urged to make a clean breast of it to his master's family
or risk being numbered among the conspirators and share
in their fate. Devany complied, alerting his master, Colonel
Prioleau, on the latter's return in the afternoon. The mayor
of Charleston, Mr. Hamilton, was informed of the plot, and
William was arrested.

Since William denied having revealed any such plot to

Devany, he was subjected to solitary confinement "in the black hole of the Work-House." There he mulled over his indiscretion for two weeks, trying to repress his terror. Finally, he broke down, confessed, and named the two organizers of the revolt known to him: Peter Poyas and Mungo Harth. These two were arrested immediately.

An incredible stroke of temporary good fortune favored Poyas and Harth. So well had they hidden their activities, and so many had been the rumors of conspiracies reported by creditable people and subsequently proved to be without substance, that the authorities did not regard the talk of revolt seriously. Peter Poyas and Mungo Harth enjoyed the complete confidence of their masters. Their mien must have convinced Mayor Hamilton of their innocence. The record states that "these men behaved with such great assurance; trunks and premises when searched innocent of any suspicious content." Their owners vouched so steadfastly for their characters that they were discharged.

A letter was found in Peter Poyas' trunk which should have increased the suspicions of the authorities, had his behavior not dispelled it so effectively. It ran:

> Dear Sir:
> With pleasure I give you an answer. I will endeavor to do it. Hoping that God will be in the midst to help his own. Be particular and make a sure remark. Fear not, the Lord God that delivered Daniel is able to deliver us. All that I inform agreed. I am gone to Beach Hill. (Signed) Abraham Poyas.

The sketchy contemporary sources fail to mention whether Peter was asked to explain this letter, nor does it state who wrote it. His master, Poyas, did have a slave named Abraham, but he was most probably illiterate and had not been to "Beach Hill." Commentators on the Vesey conspiracy have always been intrigued by the puzzling language of the letter. Peter was not incriminated by its cryptic contents.

There was no one to corroborate the denunciation by William, who seemed to be suffering from solitary confinement and would understandably be ready to accuse anyone of anything. On the contrary, Ned Bennett, slave to Governor Bennett, whom William had also mentioned but who had not been arrested due to the Governor's absolute trust in him, came voluntarily to the mayor asking to be examined if he was suspect in any way.

And so, in spite of William's defection, the whites stayed ignorant of the design. The revolt was scheduled to take place as planned on Saturday, June 16, 1822, after the fifth stroke of the clock at midnight.

On Friday the 15th, Mr. John Wilson came to see Mayor Hamilton. He told the official that his wife's slave, George, had communicated to her rumors he had heard, the gist of which was that a revolt was planned for the next evening at midnight.

On the same day, another gentleman came to the mayor (most of the names of informers were deleted from the record from fear of reprisals by slaves). This man gave an account of what his own faithful slave, a class leader in the African Methodist Episcopal Church, had heard from a friend. The friend had been approached by Rolla, another of Governor Bennett's servants, three months previously, saying that the night of June 16 had been fixed for the rising and that "people from San Domingo and Africa would assist them in obtaining their liberty, if they only made the motion first themselves."

Furthermore, William, who had been put back into solitary confinement, became frightened for his life after he was told of Peter Poyas and Mungo Harth's discharge. He began to name more alleged conspirators.

Mobilization by the whites of Charleston was begun. The city guard was put in readiness. Sentinels and patrols armed with muskets searched the streets while arrests of suspected slaves took place. The white population spent Saturday night close to the main guard at the governor's office, not daring to go home. On Sunday the 17th, a body of "hussars, light infantry, Neck rangers, and the Charleston riflemen" strengthened the guard to assure for any eventuality. But the leaders of the conspiracy, seeing that their plan had been leaked, had given it up at the last moment.

The trial, conducted before a jury, began on June 19. Except for the owners of slaves who were standing trial and their counsel, the public was excluded. However, the court published a carefully-edited account of the trials later, revealing that the greatest consternation of the judges, jurors, and all white men at the trial had been elicited by the proceedings. All the accused, without exception, had been liked and respected by their owners, whom they had served faithfully for a great many years. The discovery of the conspiracy was a great blow to the morale of the white community; it meant that slaves in their possession could no longer be trusted in the slightest degree. What caused most concern was that the revolt could easily have succeeded in Charleston, and could have spread rapidly over the whole state of South Carolina. The depositions of the accused disclosed that practically no slave approached by the leaders had refused to join. Those who had hesitated had done so only doubting their strength in the face of the white peoples' power.

Once the revolt had begun, these doubtful would also surely have taken the field. "We will not want men; they'll fall in behind us," the leaders had assured the parties to the plot. Gullah Jack allegedly had reported to Vesey that Monday Gell had made contacts with *6,600* men in the country around Charleston. All these were ready to join; he had advised not to wait much longer, but had urged fixing an early date for the rising. The date had been set to coincide with the influx of the thousands of slaves who customarily came to town on Sundays, paddling their canoes along the Ashley, Cooper, and Dwandos rivers and into Charleston Bay to enjoy the hustle and bustle of the market. These Negroes, idle and in a holiday mood, were expected to join the rebels in town.

One of the leaders of the conspiracy, Rolla, confessed in the course of the trial. The rest remained tight-lipped to the end, obeying the instructions of Peter Poyas. The latter was lying on the floor of the Charleston prison, chained to a companion, when investigators entered and, using threats and promises, tried to persuade the two prisoners to inform on the rest of the conspirators. He rose from the floor with a superhuman effort and shouted to his companion, who had begun to waver: "Die like a man, silent, as you see me do."

On the opening day of the trial, Denmark Vesey had still not been found, although he had managed to meet Monday Gell shortly before Gell's arrest. Vesey was witnessing the collapse of the enterprise that he had prepared with so much care for four patient years. According to Gell, who finally betrayed his chief, Vesey was still scheming a last attempt "to rescue those who might be condemned, by rushing on the people and saving the prisoners, or by all dying together."

Finally, after it was feared that he might have escaped for good, Vesey was found in one of his wives' houses, where he had hidden from Monday June 17 until the following Saturday. On that day, June 22, "during a perfect tempest" in the night, guards acting on Gell's information came and arrested him.

"What infatuation could have prompted you to attempt an enterprise so wild and visionary? You were a free man, comparatively wealthy, and enjoyed every comfort compatible with your situation." Thus, during his trial, Judge Lionel H. Kennedy wonderingly questioned Denmark Vesey, the would-be angel of death for the black peoples.

In his great shock at Vesey's audacious intentions, the judge could only refer to the Christian tenets of humility for a scale on which to measure the enormity of Vesey's defiance:

> It was to reconcile us to our destiny on earth, and to enable us to discharge with fidelity all our duties, whether as master or servant, that those inspired precepts were imparted by Heaven to fallen man.

Vesey listened to the judge, "his arms tightly folded, his eyes fixed on the floor," but he said nothing. During the trial, he carefully followed every item of the testimony. And his defense counsel later made use of the judge's astonishment at Vesey's "infatuation" in risking his life for motives that were other than egotistical. It was asked, ironically, that the favor of the argument's full logic be bestowed upon the defendant:

> If the court held it incredible that a man in his (Vesey's) position of freedom and prosperity should sacrifice every thing to free other people, why not give him the benefit of the incredibility? The act being, as they stated, one of infatuation, why convict him on the bare word of men who, by their own showing, had not only shared the infatuation, but proved traitors to it?

* * *

San Domingo had loomed large in the conspiracy, and as a factor in the trial as well.

It was testified that Monday Gell had written two letters in April to President Boyer of Haiti. Another slave had carried the letters to Vanderhorst's Wharf in Charleston and had given them into the charge of a Negro cook on board a schooner bound for that island. In the letters, the leaders had asked assistance after the initial success of the rising. The plan provided for the seizure of all ships in the harbor, the murder of officers and crews, excepting the captains, who would be needed to navigate the ships.

Vesey had considered it to be unsafe for the victorious rebels to remain in South Carolina. The white people of the Union could be expected to organize a large-scale counter thrust against them soon afterwards. So the former slaves were to leave America for freedom in Haiti aboard these ships and others they hoped would be sent from the island. Haiti's government had allegedly already promised to receive and protect them. All money confiscated in the banks of Charleston and all goods stocked in its stores would be loaded onto the ships. Wild rumors had been circulated among the slaves to encourage them to rebel. The whites intended to massacre the blacks on the Fourth of July, before the troops of San Domingo, said to be ploughing the sea towards Charleston, could arrive. This would make it seem expedient to launch the rising before that date and also would serve to spark hopes among the doubtful that well-armed, battle-tested Negro brethren of another country would strengthen their ranks.

Despite the information that emerged from the trial attesting to the high degree of the conspiracy's organization and propaganda efforts, Governor Bennett later admitted that the really essential features of Vesey's plot would never be known: the informers had never known them, and the leaders, who did, could not be induced to disclose them.

The trial lasted until August 3. Thirty-five defendants were condemned to death. Thirty-four were ordered deported, twenty-seven were acquitted, and twenty-five discharged without trial.

During the trial, Denmark Vesey showed signs of emotion only once, when Judge Kennedy reproached him for the destruction he had brought on his followers. Tears came to his eyes, but he said nothing.

All the leaders of the conspiracy, it was reported, died like brave men—except the sorcerer, Gullah Jack, who lost his composure and implored the court for weeks, or days, of delay before his execution.

"Never were an entire people more thoroughly alarmed than were the people of Charleston at that time," a contemporary writer noted.

Charleston—and the South—had narrowly averted disaster at the hands of an avenger who would, "with the edge of the sword," have gladly wreaked the Biblical wrath of his race upon her citadels.

VI

THE ISLANDS REVOLT

AFTER the collapse of the conspiracy of Denmark Vesey there were reports of unrest, of fires, and the suspicion of arson, of the hanging of Negroes, but the number was not extraordinary for the times.

In 1826, the *Decatur,* owned by the well-known slave trader, Austin Woolfolk, was bound with a transport of twenty-nine slaves from Maryland to Georgia. The slaves on board rebelled and killed two members of the crew, intimidated the rest and commanded the boat to make way to Haiti. The ship was intercepted, and conducted to New York. There, all the slaves escaped. One of them was recaptured, however, and was executed for his crimes on December 16, 1826.

In 1830, there was a rash of fires. Camden, North Carolina; New Orleans; and Cambridge, Maryland all were devastated by blazes. Arson was suspected, and each occurrence held the usual tragic consequences for the Negro population of the town. In Virginia, Governor Giles ordered the distribution of arms throughout the state as they were requested. Restlessness prompted by the fear of slave rebellions required reassuring measures.

The Vesey conspiracy shook the complacency of the white man. Even if the planters were determined not to give an inch on the matter of freedom for their slaves they did not relish the idea that they were sitting on a powder keg. It was shocking to think that their Negroes, physically so close and so obedient, harbored thoughts of the cold-blooded murder of planters and their families. It was far easier to believe that faithful servants would mind their own business if it were not for the wicked strangers in their midst who sowed the seeds of hatred and rebellion among them. Denmark Vesey was a free Negro, wasn't he? Free Negroes were public enemies. They should be sent to Africa.

In this system of reasoning, the colonization movement that had started as a pro-Negro act turned ever more transparently into a method of getting rid of those Negroes who had won some measure of freedom. It was easier to advocate such a program than to carry it through, however. Free Negroes performed services for which there was no substitution. Skilled workers among the whites did not settle in the South where they would have to compete or work with free Negroes.

The planters could only resort to the old familiar medicine: limit the freedom of Negroes, limit their effectiveness as subversive agents. South Carolina ordered guardians to be assigned to each free Negro after the age of fifteen, and required probationary reports on his conduct periodically. An unfavorable report resulted in the free Negro being sold into slavery.

The Vesey revolt called attention once again to the fact that speeches of northern congressmen against slavery, newspaper commentary on the excesses of slaveholders in the

South, and reports of rebellions could be read and introduced to the Negro grapevine by free Negroes with education. The public demanded the discouragement of Negro teaching. Pastors were warned and kindly masters reprimanded. Laws were urged to prohibit the spread of literacy and limit contact between free Negroes and slaves.

On many plantations the Negro slaves were given less consideration than domestic animals, and no white man could expect human sympathy from slaves who might gain the upper hand. Whites realized that not even the harshest protective measures could be relied upon to bring security to the system in which they lived. "You may place the slave where you please," said James McDowell, later to be governor of Virginia, "you may put him under any process, without destroying his value as a slave, debase and crush him as a rational being—you may do all this, and the idea that he was born to be free will survive it all." Adam Hodgson, traveling in the South, listened to the complaints of the slave-holding families he met while watching their slaves working in the fields and about their houses, remarking their bursts of vitality and gaiety. He sounded a warning: "Habit and example led the planter to believe that he must render the Negro industrious by the use of the lash, and obedient by shooting the refractory, which puts the Negroes so low, so distant from him as to exclude him from their sympathy."

Even with the slaves safe from the influence of free Negroes, the whites still had to deal with events outside their control. No peace was assured on the plantations while revolutionary ideas were loose in the Western Hemisphere. In Latin America, revolutionary movements established the principle that abolition of slavery should come with independence. These new opportunities for haven to the south brought new memories of the fate of the whites in Haiti. Had not Denmark Vesey sought the aid of President Boyer there? Masters and slaves pondered on the significance of these events.

South Carolina forbade the entry of Negroes from the Caribbean and the disembarkation of any Negro crewmen, under the threat of severe punishment to any captain who disregarded the prohibition. International protest ensued, the British holding that such a local rule was a breach against established customs of foreign ships in domestic ports. The U.S. State Department tried to convince the governor of South Carolina that the State Department alone had jurisdiction in international affairs; the governor stood stoutly in defense of "state sovereignty."

The Caribbean colonies of most European powers had their own slave revolts in the 1830s. The South inevitably became involved in these conflagrations, for, despite legal prohibition, slave trade from Africa and from the West Indies was continuing, under more outrageous circumstances than ever. This trade could compete with the legal domestic breeding trade only because of the advantage of cheaper prices.

The events of the Caribbean had only an indirect impact on the South, but they involved Cuba and a future territory of the United States, Puerto Rico. There were more free Negroes in Puerto Rico in the 1830s than in all French and English islands in the Caribbean, where the total slave populations were twenty times that of Puerto Rico.

The proximity of Cuba and Puerto Rico to the United States and to British colonies in the Caribbean was a hindrance to revolution and independence in these two colonies. Although the United States and Great Britain had recognized the independence of the South American states, all of which except Brazil had emancipated their slaves, they refused to countenance such revolutions in Cuba and Puerto Rico for a long time because of the fear that emancipation in these islands would endanger slaveholding interests elsewhere. The U.S. envoy to Russia clarified the predominant American view in a note to the Tsarist government:

> The United States have seen with satisfaction the efforts of the nations of the American continent to withdraw themselves from the yoke of Spanish domination. This is not so with regards to the islands of Cuba and Puerto Rico ... A premature declaration would probably result only in the afflicting repetition of the disastrous scenes of St. Domingo.

The Americas were in ferment, with revolts occurring in Antigua, Tortuga, and Caracas, as well as in French Martinique. Newspaper reports of the revolts that rocked Jamaica in 1831 and the tales told by refugees landing in the United States froze the hearts of the whites of the plantation states.

There were 300,000 slaves on the island of Jamaica. A rumor had spread among them that the King had ordered their freedom. The local colonial authority denied it in strong terms, but the slaves decided to take matters into their own hands and to eradicate those who stood between them and their King, or between them and their freedom.

The majority of the slaves on the island broke into small firing parties of about fifty men each and dispersed to set fire to plantations. More than 150 plantations were destroyed in this way. The roofs of the buildings were wood, and the fire quickly spread from them into the ripe cane standing in the field and over large areas where sugar and rum were fed to the flames.

The governor of the island called out the militia, consisting of 18,000 men, including free Negroes. As the slave parties moved on, carrying devastation in all directions these defensive forces were joined by military troops. Warships made surprise landings of armed troops, but were frustrated by the hit-and-run tactics of the slaves who had an advantage in their knowledge of the island's immense woods, narrow defiles, and almost inaccessible mountains.

All commercial vessels were asked to join in the fight against the slaves. At Kingston, ships were moored so that their guns could fire up the streets of the town. American and Spanish ships helped the British to suppress the rebellion. "When the shades of the nights descended, and the buildings on the side of those beautiful mountains, which form the splendid panorama around Montego Bay, were burning the spectacle was awfully grand," gushed one onlooker. Major General Sir Willoughby Cotton ordered retaliatory measures; every Negro house, all Negro hogs, poultry, and provision-grounds on property where fires broke out should be destroyed.

The regular army and the island militia, in cooperation with His Majesty's ships *Blanche, Sparrowhawk,* and *Blossom* finally forced the slaves into open battle, when the superior power of the whites prevailed. Without a mopping-up action by Jamaica maroons the victory would not have been so decisive. The British had learned to rely on the help of descendants of Spanish slaves, who, when the British had conquered Jamaica, had retired into the interior. Years afterwards they had made an agreement with the colonists nearby to take possession of tracts of land on which to build their towns. The maroons had become loyal subjects, and in such disturbances the authorities armed them with muskets and cutlasses and used them against rebels.

Theodore Foulks, an eyewitness to the Jamaican revolt,

ended his account of it with these words, "Like the heavings of the ocean after a storm, they gradually subsided, and full tranquility was eventually restored." Indeed, the curse of slavery was soon to end itself, with the passage of the emancipation law by Parliament in 1833.

VII

DAVID WALKER AND HIS *APPEAL*

Visitors to the South were keenly interested in the slave economy. Antislavery campaigns in Europe and the North had made people sensitive to the issue and curious as to how slavery worked out in reality. What were the attitudes of master and slaves? Did the slave accept the institution as stolidly as the southern whites assured outsiders, or was he ready at all times to murder his master, as the abolitionists purported?

Frederick Law Olmsted, the landscape architect, studied slavery and wrote books about it. As an institution for the production of wealth, he found it to be wanting. "In failing to proportion reward to effort, and offering little incentive to labor except fear, it was unfavorable to productive work and imputed no motive in the slave to economize in consumption or in handling tools with care."

While the nonslave states prospered on free labor, slavery destroyed most industries in the South except agriculture, and the land itself became exhausted and less profitable. Pine brush encroached upon former fruitful fields. "Even the wolf," a Virginian was quoted as saying, who "was driven back long since by the approach of man, now returns, after the lapse of a hundred years, to howl over the desolation of slavery."

"Hatred and revenge on the one hand; fear and suspicion on the other; these are sorry elements of such a social system," a traveler commented.

Out of necessity, some planters did offer incentives to a few of their slaves. There were no craftsmen on the plantations, and Negro slaves were trained to be blacksmiths, wheelwrights, coopers, and cobblers. They repaired furniture, erected buildings, and made the plantations almost self-sufficient in the crudest industrial needs. Selected slaves also worked in tobacco factories, sawmills, sugar mills, and in the production of turpentine. The nature of their jobs lifted their status, woke their ambitions, and in general provided them with more freedom.

Although such opportunities were given to a few slaves, the great majority of them had to endure the endless monotony of work in the fields. Olmsted remarked on the deadening influence this sort of labor had:

> Field Negroes had very little contact with whites. They were handled in groups, and did not receive individual attention. Most of the work assigned to them was simple and monotonous, exacting little intelligence or expert skill. At the height of the crop season, the labor was long and severe, inducing great weariness. The inevitable tendency of these conditions was to deaden intellectual activity. This was particularly true on the immense plantations in the rice, cotton and sugar growing sections. A certain amount of this dullness of mind and clumsiness of movement is seen among all agricultural laborers, but the absence of independent will, the subjection to forcible pressure, and the original density of ignorance greatly emphasize the characteristics.

Adam Hodgson visited the little dwellings of Negroes on a South Carolina plantation in 1823, and found them "generally grouped around something like a farmyard; and behind each of them was a little garden, which they cultivate on their own account." Hodgson described the huts not unlike the hovels of the poor Irish, but with the luxurious addition of a chimney:

> The bedding of the Negroes consists simply of blankets, and their clothing is generally confined to a sort of flannel garments. Those whom I saw at home were cowering over a fire, although the day was oppressively hot, and the little Negroes were running themselves with great satisfaction about the door. Twice a day they had as much as they asked for of Indian corn, sweet potato, and broth, with the occasional addition of a little meat. On many plantations it is usual to give out these allowances once a week to let them cook it for themselves. The field hands worked severely from sunrise and finish at 3 or 4 P.M. in large gangs and rigidly held in a monotonous routine which caused them to become depressed and stolid.

Sundays were reserved for the Negroes' own enjoyment. There were three free days at Christmas, one day in spring for sowing their own gardens, and another in the fall for reaping.

Because the slaves saw no connection between their labor and what they received, they were wasteful and destructive. Hodgson was shocked at the dirtiness and raggedness of Negroes on plantations near Charleston; he found them in better shape in Virginia and Georgia. He asserted:

> Humanity may mitigate the suffering of the wretched victims of the slave system, and habit renders them less sensible to their degradation; but no tenderness can eradicate from slavery the evils inherent in its very nature.

Travelers in the South were quick to see that the Negro's interest in his work was not dulled by nature, but by circumstance. On the Louisiana sugar plantations, Olmsted saw Negroes looking forward with pleasure to the "grinding season." They preferred it to any other, despite the fact that it involved the hardest labor of the year, and required at its height eighteen hours of work a day. When he asked why this was so, the Negroes answered: "because things were lively, strong coffee was given without stint, and there was abundant noise and 'go' about everything done." A slight release of pressure, and spirits soared. All visitors found that Negro slaves quickly recovered their good humor when music and dance transformed them into frolicking crowds. The group, rather than the family, bound the Negro community together.

Although education for the Negro was either forbidden or discouraged in the South, visitors were impressed by the number of intelligent slaves they met. These slaves seemed to have resisted the institutionalized campaign to reduce their understanding to that of brutes.

The American convention of antislavery societies resolved to launch a nationwide campaign to repeal state laws prohibiting the education of Negroes. Their petitions made little headway in the South, but their arguments were remarkably similar to some present-day Negro proposals for reparations due them for the past offenses and omissions of the whites; in the words of the Convention: "The colored people claim more than freedom in return for the injuries they have suffered, and for that reason special attention was recommended to both the literary and industrial education of the children."

In the crystallizing Negro thought, one voice stood out above all the rest. It was a voice of the biblical prophet and

European revolutionary. It quivered with eighteenth century satirical rhetoric and the attuned transcendentalism of the Boston preacher. It was a voice that brought for a moment an alien note of violence and discord to a happily expanding America. It was a Negro voice, uncommonly broad in scale, and richly modulated, heralding bloody vengeance on the white man and defying his standards, even his God. It shook in anger, implored, thundered, cursed. In its cadence the white man was lashed and lashed again, his hypocrisy reproached, his character unmasked, his history ridiculed, and his civilization abominated.

The same voice turned with bitterness on the black race and bewailed its dullness and subservience. It was the voice of a scholar, quoting unquestionable authorities, yet suddenly calling them to account for their discrepancies between word and fact. It was a voice of encouragement, giving the Negro to understand that he was as strong as the white and would be stronger. The same voice roared for the merciless destruction of the whites, and softened to hope that there would be change in the whites; then it would rise again to give no quarter. Whether rising or falling, the voice seemed to be that of a Great Soul.

The voice was that of David Walker, son of a slave father and a free Negro mother. His vehicle was an *Appeal in Four Articles,* "Together with a Preamble to the Colored Citizens of the World, but in Particular, and Very Expressly, to those of the United States of America," published in Boston, September 28, 1828.

David Walker was born in North Carolina in 1785. According to the laws of that state, the child inherited the status of his mother, so that Walker was born free to the extent a Negro could be free. In 1827, Walker moved to Boston, where he ran a secondhand clothing store on Brattle Street.

His pamphlet, the *Appeal*, published soon after, reveals not only his robust talent for rhetoric and argument, but an extraordinary knowledge of ancient and modern history, and an intense study of the Bible. The pamphlet was republished in two later editions, with Walker's own ever more vehement additions.

In December, 1829, copies of the pamphlet were received by a Negro preacher in Savannah, Ga. The steward of a vessel that landed in the harbor delivered a package of fifty copies to his home. Upon reading a few lines of its "Preamble," the preacher became frightened and hastened to the police, to report the unsolicited receipt of subversive booklets. They were seized by the police. When it was seen that they advocated a general slave insurrection, they were immediately forwarded to the governor of the state.

Upon reading the *Appeal*, Governor George R. Gilmer was thunderstruck. In a brutal tone, the leaflet practically declared war against white America. Governor Gilmer informed the Georgia legislature of the seizure of printed material and issued an order that the vessel whose steward had delivered it be put in quarantine for forty days.

The legislature began deliberating measures to be taken to prevent the further circulation of the pamphlets.

It was found that a Mr. E. A. Burritt had come into possession of copies of the same pamphlet. He was summoned before the Superior Court of Baldwin County and accused of distributing subversive literature. He was acquitted, after claiming an interest in antislavery publications with no sympathy for their position. He had acquired the pamphlet, read it, and out of carelessness had allowed some of his friends to read it. He had not meant to serve the cause of publicizing the pamphlet.

Under the impact of the *Appeal,* Georgia made it punishable by death to circulate incendiary literature tending to incite the slaves to rebellion or conspiracy.

The mayor of Savannah requested Mayor Otis of Boston to punish the author of the seditious pamphlet and its publishers; but Mayor Otis issued a public statement in which he denied the request, finding nothing incriminating in the *Appeal.*

The mayor of Richmond, Virginia, seized two copies found in the possession of two Indians, and one with a Negro man. In Fayetteville, Georgia, the police received information that the pamphlet had been circulating among Negroes.

Rumors that the leaflet was being clandestinely distributed stirred such excitement in Virginia that the House resolved to forbid the education of free Negroes. (The bill did not pass the Senate, however.)

Louisiana ordered all free Negroes who had settled there since 1825 to be expelled, after the leaflet had been discovered in several communities.

In North Carolina, Governor John Owen sent a copy of the *Appeal,* one of many that had been found throughout the state, to the legislature, with the comment that free Negroes had been found distributing literature that "awfully distorted the peaceful doctrines of the Bible ... but these people make systematic attempts to sow sedition among the slaves."

On reading the *Appeal* many people who were otherwise slow to take alarm, were panic-stricken. They felt that insurrection was imminent. Petitions from the counties of Sampson, Bladen, New Hanover, and Duplin (N.C.) poured into the governor's office, reporting that "their slaves are become almost uncontrollable. They go to the woods and there continue for months and years, committing grievous depredations on our cattle, hogs and sheep." Militia patrols were requested.

When the town of Washington, North Carolina, discovered copies of the pamphlet, it doubled its night watch and searched its free Negroes for hidden arms. For a show of force the local militia was called out. Additional supplies of arms and ammunition were requested of Governor Owen in Raleigh.

The pamphlet continued to pop up and was found in the possession of Negroes throughout the upper South.

What was the gist of Walker's message that so alarmed the white brethren of the South?

Walker was grieved by Thomas Jefferson's often reiterated statement in his "Notes on Virginia" that the black race was inferior to the white in the endowments of mind and body. In this conviction, Jefferson had hailed the colonization plan in 1811 as "the most desirable measure which could be adopted for gradually drawing off this part of our population; most advantageous for themselves as well as for us." Walker deeply respected Jefferson, and was therefore all the more hurt by the statesman's ingrained view of the inferiority of the black race.

> It is indeed surprising, that a man of such great learning, combined with such excellent natural parts should speak so of a set of men in chains. I do not know what to compare it to, like putting one wild deer in an iron cage where it will be secured, and hold another by the side of the same, then let it go, and expect the one in the cage to run as fast as the one in liberty. So far, my brethren, were the Egyptians from heaping these insults upon their slaves, that Pharaoh's daughter took Moses, a son of Israel for her own.

If Jefferson, the best of white men, had refused to apply to Negroes the principle of equality he so eloquently upheld in the Declaration of Independence, how could the colored people expect fair treatment from other white people?

Of course, Walker wrote, the Negroes had not had the opportunity to develop as the whites had, but this was the result of the Negro's oppression. "We will have a chance to develop . . . by and by. God will not suffer us always to be oppressed. Our sufferings will come to an end, in spite of all the Americans this side of eternity. Every dog must have its day, the Americans' is coming to an end."

Walker was especially enraged by the servility Negroes displayed to whites, and the implied conviction that the white race possessed a natural superiority over blacks and a God- or nature-given commission to rule over men of colored skin. This feeling had to be destroyed first, Walker thought. True liberation was not only a matter of hypothetical freedoms achieved through action, it was also getting rid of the Negro's own doubts as to his worthiness.

> The whites are of the firm conviction that Heaven has de- signed us and our children to be slaves and beasts of burden to them and their children. They think because they hold us in their infernal chains of slavery, that we wish to be white, or of their color—but they are dreadfully deceived—we wish to be just as it pleased our Creator to have made us, and no avaricious and unmerciful wretches, have any business to make slaves of, or hold us in slavery.

Walker used vicious sarcasm to prick the American whites' "liberal" but sentimental sympathy for persecuted peoples in distant places:

> I saw a paragraph . . . in a South Carolina paper, which, speak- ing of the barbarity of the Turks, it said: "The Turks are the

most barbarous people in the world—they treat the Greeks more like brutes than human beings." And in the same paper was an advertisement, which said: "Eight well-built Virginia and Maryland Negro fellows and four wenches will positively be sold this day, to the highest bidder." I declare, it is really so amusing to hear the Southerners and Westerners of this country talk about barbarity.

Walker asked by what right do the men of the South and West call others "barbarians"?

Christians, Americans, not only hinder their fellow creatures, the Africans, but thousands of them will absolutely beat a colored person nearly to death, if they catch him on his knees, supplicating the throne of grace.

Walker refused to accept the theory of the innate inferiority of the black race. In a cursory review of history, he insisted that the white race had its own defects, such as cruelty, throughout its history:

The white race has always been an unjust, jealous, unmerciful, avaricious and bloodthirsty set of beings, always seeking power and authority, view them in Greece, in Rome, in Spain, and in Gaul, in Europe and in Asia, and everywhere we see them acting more like devils than accountable men.

Walker contended that Christianity made the whites a more vicious race, though the arguments he lent to support his case were, perhaps, unconvincing:

As heathens, the whites were cruel enough, but as Christians they were ten times more so. For as pagans, they were not quite so audacious as to go and take vessel loads of men, women and children and in cold blood, through devilishness, throw them into the sea, and murder them in all kinds of ways, but being Christians, enlightened and sensible, they are complete, prepared for such hellish cruelties. Therefore, I advance my suspicions of them whether they are as good by nature as we or not.

There was no more urgent task than awakening the self-respect of the Negro slave. Walker relied on an effective sense of rhetoric to rouse his fellow blacks to an attempt at self-appraisal:

> Are we men? I ask you O! my brothers, are we men? ... Have we any other master than Jesus Christ? Is he not their master as well as ours? What right then have we to obey and call any man master but Himself? How we could be so submissive to a gang of men, whom we cannot tell whether they are as good as ourselves, or not, I never could conceive.
>
> Do you suppose any man of good sense and education would submit himself, his father, his mother, his wife and children to be slaves to a wretched man like himself, who, instead of compensating him for his labors, chaines, handcuffs, beats him, his family almost to death, leaving enough life in them however, to work for and call him master? No! No! No! he would cut his devilish throat from ear to ear.

The *Appeal* reached out to stimulate a sense of responsibility, to shake the Negro out of the apathy and degradation caused, Walker thought, by the heavy repression of the white man:

> I know that there are many swell-bellied fellows among us, whose greatest object is to fill their stomachs. Such I do not mean—I am after those who know and feel, that we are men as well as other people; to them I say, that unless we try to refute Mr. Jefferson's arguments respecting us, we will only establish them.

As for the colonization plans, they were swept away with one blunt statement:

> This country is as much ours as it is the whites, whether they will admit it or not.

Self-confidence was needed for the struggle. Yet what can be accomplished when the whites have all the powder and the guns to support their dominion? The answer lay in the Negroes' advantage in man-to-man fighting:

> Let twelve good black men get armed for battle and they will kill and put to flight fifty whites. . . . If you commence, make sure work: don't trifle, for they will not trifle with you. Kill or be killed. . . . Look upon your wife and children, and mother and answer God Almighty, and believe this that it is not more harm to kill a man who is trying to kill you than to take a drink of water when you are thirsty.

The black man should be ashamed, Walker thought. Only the will to risk and sacrifice everything for freedom counts in the ultimate reckoning.

> Why do they not bring the inhabitants of Asia to be body servants to them? They know they would get their bodies rent and torn from head to foot. . . . The Indians would not rest day or night, they would be up all times of night, cutting their cruel throats. But my colour (some, not all) are willing to stand still and be murdered by the cruel whites.

God will be for the slave; and if God be for him, who can be against him? questioned Walker.

> I believe it is the will of the Lord that our greatest happiness shall consist in working for the salvation of our whole body. . . . Do any of you say this never will be done? I assure you that God will accomplish it—if nothing else will answer, he will hurt tyrants and devils into atoms and make way for his people.

Walker had been in Boston long enough to absorb the idea of self help:

> O my brethren! I say unto you again, you must go to work to prepare the way of the Lord.

To those who might ask whether murder of whites by blacks would be a sin against the commandments of God, he had a ready answer:

> The fear of the Lord does not consist of protecting devils. Should the lives of such creatures be spared? Are God and Mammon in league? What has the Lord to do with a gang of desperate wretches who go sneaking about the country like robbers? They should be killed like rattlesnakes. Are they not the Lord's enemies?

Walker felt that anyone who doubts that God will be on the side of the black slaves in the Good Fight doubts the justice of God:

> God Almighty is the sole proprietor and master of the whole human family . . . who can dispense with prejudice long enough to admit that we are men, notwithstanding our improminent noses and woolly heads, and believe that we feel for our fathers, mothers, wives, and children, as well as the whites do for theirs. I ask you O Ye Christians!!! who hold us and our children in the most abject ignorance and degradation, that ever a people were afflicted with since the world began—I say if God gives you peace and tranquillity, and suffers you thus to go on afflicting us and our children, who have never given you the least provocation—would he be to us a God of Justice?

Although David Walker foresaw a merciless struggle on a darkling plain between the races, and absolved the slaves from any scruples concerning the murder of their oppressors, he offered a last chance to the white men. He implored them in moving words to grasp the chance:

> Remember, Americans, that we must and shall be free and enlightened as you are. Will you wait until we shall, under God, obtain our liberty by the crushing arm of force? Will it not be dreadful for you? I speak, Americans, for your good. We must and shall be free, I say, in spite of you. You may do your best to keep us in wretchedness and misery, to enrich you and your children, but God will deliver us from under you. And woe, woe will be unto you if we have to obtain our freedom by fighting. Throw away your fear and prejudice, then, and enlighten us and treat us like men, and we will like you more than we do now hate you.

To seal the pact with his race, Walker was ready to sacrifice his own life for the cause: "I want my life not dear unto me, but I am ready to be offered at any moment. For what is the use of living when in fact I am dead?"

The *Appeal* stunned the South. Its savage hatred had never been measured or measurable before. There had been no suitable rhetoric to fill the void of abuse. But how could the whites be genuinely surprised, when they justified their own harsh rule over Negro slaves on the grounds that they might otherwise massacre the white people? True, they enjoyed believing their own stories about the happiness of the slaves. But confrontation with the opposite side of the story toppled their peaceful illusions.

What frightened them most in this particular instance was Walker's brilliant articulation of his hatred, and the religious and historical arguments supporting it. It was disturbing to be branded as cruel, hypocritical, and un-Christian in such eloquent terms. Fortunately, Walker's fury caused him to exaggerate. The mirror he held up so rudely to the whites was so very ghastly that it could be dismissed as false and distorted.

There was a lurking horror that the *Appeal* might, indeed, accurately voice the hatred of the mass of slaves, or that its powerful cadences might create that hatred and fan it to a general revolt. The printed word of the *Appeal* could infiltrate the entire South; it could break down the limitations imposed on free Negroes, and penetrate the isolation of plantation regulations. It did not have the size and shape of the usual agitator. An insurrectionist had to walk or ride from county to county, state to state; a pamphlet could easily be slipped into a pocket and passed about clandestinely.

Not long after the *Appeal* was circulated, a revolt broke out in Southampton County, Virginia, the savagery of which eclipsed even the brutal shock of the *Appeal,* making its effectiveness hard to gauge. The revolt was Nat Turner's. And the *Appeal* may have had a direct influence on the events in Southampton County, where Turner exerted his mystical force. It was later discovered that Walker had visited Richmond, Virginia, in January, 1830, bearing a bundle of thirty copies of his pamphlet, to be delivered to a certain Thomas Seivis, a free Negro. Knocking at the door of Seivis' house, Walker was told that the other Negro had died a short time before. Walker began to distribute the pamphlet himself, but was arrested by the police after having passed out ten copies. The undelivered copies were confiscated.

The Mayor of Richmond, oddly enough, either impressed by David Walker's strength of character, or in deference to the Negro's learning, did not feel the confiscation of the pamphlet justified. Instead, he himself bought up the extra copies, perhaps hoping to avoid making an issue out of the *Appeal* that might gain it added publicity. Walker was allowed to return home, where he died in obscurity a few months later before his name became a familiar one in the South. Many believed that suspicious circumstances were associated with his death.

VIII

THE NAT TURNER AFFAIR

N AT TURNER was born on the plantation of Benjamin
Turner, Esq. in Southampton, Virginia, close to the
border of North Carolina, on October 2, 1800. His father
was a "highly spirited" slave who ran away when Nat was
a young boy. His mother, Nancy, had come directly from
Africa as a slave and was said to have gone raving mad at
Nat's birth so that she had to be tied up to prevent killing
her new baby.

The fit of rage on the part of the mother apparently never
reoccurred. Nancy raised Nat; but his grandmother, a superstitious old woman, undertook the boy's spiritual education,
and told him that a birthmark he bore on his body was a
sign that he would grow up to be a great man.

Nat Turner was evidently a talented and intelligent man;
but such capabilities had no normal channels in which to be
developed or realized in a Negro slave. Instead, they were
to seep out from their repressed hiding places in peculiar
and sinister ways. Though he may have awed his playmates
and neighbors with his intelligence, it probably went un-
noticed among the white Turners, who paid little attention

158

to the gossip of their domestic slaves on Nat's exceptional traits. The boy learned to read so fast that he later could not recall how he did it. He told the story that once, when he was crying, his mother Nancy gave him a spelling book to quiet him; in no time he distinguished the letters, discovered the secret of how to decipher their combinations, and immediately knew how to read and write.

As a boy, Nat assisted his master, a coach-maker, in his shop. The older man found the boy neat, handy, and inventive. On his own initiative, Nat began experimenting with pottery, making paper and gunpowder, probably after having read something about the processes. These tasks he took on both to satisfy his own inner restlessness and to provoke and sustain admiration for his cleverness. Such adulation he sought not out of vanity but out of a desire to find something powerful in himself, and to confirm and articulate it. For Nat Turner was a puzzle to himself, and was exhilarated by his own mysteriousness.

He lived in a kind of haze, unable to indulge in true introspection, hemmed in by a confusion as to his own motives, yet prodded by the admiration of family and friends. He was an isolated mystic, stranded without counsel and without the tools or signs or symbols to help him understand himself or interpret the meaning of the world outside of him.

Nat always attended Sunday meetings. Once when he was praying, a quotation read by the preacher struck him like an electric shock: "Seek ye the kingdom of heaven," the voice said, "and all things shall be added unto you."

This quotation rang in his ears even while he was at work. Once again, while praying, he heard the same words, in a voice from afar, which seemed strange but familiar, warm but imperious.

These curious details and other information on his life

Nat Turner later gave to Thomas A. Gray, who was assigned to defend him in the Court of Southampton County. The lawyer published the confidence under the title *Confessions of Nat Turner*. The pamphlet was bought by an avid public in both the North and the South, which regarded it as something of a thriller. Its sale reached 50,000 copies, an unprecedented figure for the sale of a booklet at the time. Six judges and a clerk stated in a preface to the *Confessions* that the details had been read back to Turner at his trial, that he recognized them as true, and wished to add nothing to the text.

Turner described the spirit that had spoken to him as the same one that had exhorted the prophets of old. "For two years," he confided, "I prayed continually, whenever my duty would permit; and then again I had the same revelation, which fully confirmed me in the impression that I was ordained for some great purpose in the hands of the Almighty."

He prayed to the spirit voice that he heard to enlighten him as to the purpose he was called on to serve. And at the same time, he practically withdrew from the world, doing his duties as slave, attending Sunday services, but talking to other people as if in a dream.

A new overseer was assigned to Nat's group on the plantation. This man knew nothing about the exceptional abilities of this small flat-nosed, thin-haired slave of light color, who, though strong, did not move quickly enough when ordered. He cared less for him. Nat Turner was given lashes, scars of which stayed with him to be seen six years later, when, in 1831, he was brought to stand trial.

Nat ran away, as his father had done before him. Thirty days passed and he had not been caught. The incident brought the usual inconveniences to Nat's fellow workers among the slaves, when one of their number became a fugitive and succeeded in going north, but they did not mind it. Such successes elated them; they meant frustration for the whites and victory for the slave over the master and his world.

There was general outrage among Nat's comrades when, unexpectedly, after the thirty days had elapsed, he suddenly returned to the plantation and gave himself up. The defeat and frustration of the master was turned into a spectacular triumph. A recaptured fugitive could be held up to the slaves as proof that they could not escape the white man's power, but a fugitive who returned of his own volition proved further that life on the plantation was the best a black could hope for. Nat was received back with bitterness and anger by his fellows. They insulted him, called him cowardly and servile, saying that, "if they had Nat's sense they would not serve any master in the world."

Nat Turner took the insults and reproaches in his stride. He had waited undisturbed in his hideout in the woods for a call, and after thirty days of prayer and meditation, it had come: Nat, as he later related in his *Confessions,* was rebuked: "I had my wishes directed to the things of the world, and not to the kingdom of heaven ... I should return to the service of my earthly master. For he who knoweth his Master's will, and doeth it not, shall be beaten with many stripes, and thus have I chastened you."

So while he was despised in the outer world, Nat experienced within himself the serene satisfaction of living with God.

Yet he was not able to become indifferent to his reputation among men. Did he act from vanity or sinful pride? Did he need the approval and recognition of his extraordinary character by others, and the sanctity of their respect?

In any case, clearly, he felt he had been ordered to act in fulfillment of a command. In his own words, he saw the challenge: "Having soon discovered to be great, I must appear so"; therefore he "studiously avoided mixing in society, and wrapped myself in mystery, devoting my time to fasting and praying."

Nat's spirit voice finally revealed its complete design: He was elected for great purposes. What were these to be? In frightful scenes, they were revealed to him. He saw a vision of white spirits and black spirits contending in battle: "The sun darkened, the thunders tolling in the heavens and blood flowing in streams, and a voice spoke: 'Such is your luck, such are you called to see, and let it come rough or smooth, you must surely bear it."

Nat understood. It was to come to a bloody accounting between the white and black peoples. He was to be the leader of the black forces in the conflict.

Before the voice would announce to Nat Turner the time to accomplish his calling, he sought enlightenment concerning some natural phenomena, the secret of which he had vainly sought. He burnt with curiosity to know the laws of the revolutions of the planets, the operations of tides and changes in the seasons. The black tribes from which he was descended in Africa had surely had myths that most vividly covered and explained these natural events, but the myths had gotten lost without trace in the sober, thin, toil-worn atmosphere of this alien and northern continent. The new mother country refused to give to the descendants of the children of Africa the new scientific lore of the white man.

While Nat Turner was buried in fast, prayer, and hard work, the spirit voice spoke to him more often, and revealed more of events to come. It stretched like the hand of the Saviour from east to west, and said: "Behold me in the heavens." And straightway, Nat saw a human-like body of light "in different attitudes." Working in the fields, he discovered hieroglyphic characters on leaves and branches. There were numbers and figures in the heavens; everything dripped with blood. The voice spoke again, heralding the news that "the Serpent was loosened and Christ had laid down the yoke he had borne for the sins of men, and that I should take it on and fight against the serpent, for the time was fast approaching when the first should be last and the last should be the first."

Turner did not fail to sketch out his visions in rough outline to his fellow slaves. He knew it was not enough to be great. To lead those who had not been granted the privilege of divine message, one must be recognized as an anointed leader.

One of the overseers, Ethelred T. Brantley, was a sick man and had been told by the slaves about the mystic powers residing in Nat Turner. Brantley began to talk with the slave. Nat advised nine days of praying and fasting. The overseer heeded the advice. After the days of repentance passed, blood oozed from the pores of the sick white man's skin, and he was healed. He also "ceased from his wickedness."

Nat then asked one favor of Brantley: before he took over Christ's yoke he felt he ought to be baptized, yet no church was allowed to baptize a Negro slave. Perhaps Brantley would wade into Person's Mill Pond with him and baptize him? Brantley accepted. Many slaves gathered and stared at them as the two stepped into the water to perform the rite of immersion. They were jeered and derided. Months later, after the revolt, Brantley was dismissed from the Turner plantation and left the state for good.

Time went on, and the voice had not completed its messages. Nat and the other Turner slaves were transferred through inheritance and marriage to the estate of Mr. Joseph Travis at Cross Keys. It was only in 1830 that Nat heard the voice promise to reveal to him the secrets of nature, so that he felt perfected and ready to receive commands to act in the great bloody struggle he was born to precipitate.

Nat told one of his comrades of the directions given to him by the spirit voice. The man was Hark Travis, described later by one of the arresting officers as "the most perfectly built Apollo." Hark had probably talked of revolt to Nat Turner, and thus inspired Nat to confide in him. But Nat could not be pressed as to the timing of his plan. He merely prayed and waited for the voice to announce the time by some unmistakable sign.

The sign appeared in February, 1831. An eclipse of the sun occurred, spreading terror among the Negroes. Nat wasted no time, once his sign was received. He communicated to Hark Travis that the celestial phenomenon was the sign he expected. Hark Travis and four friends from a neighboring plantation, who had been plotting together, immediately recognized in Nat the authority, energy, and optimism needed for leadership. The date of July 4 was set for a revolt. When the others urged arranging further details of the undertaking, however, Nat withdrew inscrutably, complaining of mental confusion, immersed himself in prayer, and refused to enter into preliminary talks with his potential co-conspirators.

July 4 passed. It would have been a very inauspicious day for a revolt, when white people were gathered together and would have been ready to strike down any suspicious gathering of slaves. Nat probably had begun to doubt the meaning of his eclipse and awaited another sign to confirm the message.

A second sign appeared on August 13, even more flamboyant than the eclipse. The sun appeared as if in a fog; the Raleigh *Register* described its appearance as "of intensely blue and a greatly obscured radiance":

It changed from the usual brilliant golden color to a pale greenish tinge, which soon gave place to a cerulian blue, and this also to a silvery white. In the afternoon it appeared like an immense circular plane of polished silver, and by the naked eye a spot could be seen.

The newspaper report then went on to say that:

"A similar phenomenon may never have come under observation of anyone now living, yet ... it is related by Plutarch in the first year of the reign of Augustus, the sun's light was so faint and obscure that one might look steadily at it with the naked eye."

Whatever the explanation for the phenomenon, it was explained locally according to whatever fear, fantasy, knowledge of optics, or observation suggested. Fear generally played the largest part in the interpretation of its cause and meaning.

Nat Turner saw the strange light as a sign of victory. "As the black spot passed over the sun, so shall the blacks pass over the earth," he explained to Hark. Both held that there should be no further delay in their plan for revolt. The crops had been gathered in, and an almost festive mood prevailed in Southampton County. It was known among the blacks that most of the white men of the vicinity were planning to go on the next Saturday to a camp meeting in Gates County, North Carolina. Nat and Hark determined to hold a barbecue on Sunday, August 21, in the large forest in the southern part of Southampton County. Mr. Porter's slave Henry was initiated into the plan and the three laid down a strategy.

The barbecue proceeded according to plan. A pig was roasted, and brandy was prepared. Henry Porter, Mark Travis, Samuel Francis, and Nelson Williams arrived at about noon, bringing along two young men with them, one Jack Reese, a friend to Hark, and the other a six-foot-tall man named Will, or Big Will, whose face was disfigured by an ugly scar extending from his right eye to the tip of his chin. This man had a fresh grudge against the white people: his wife had been sold by his master to traders.

Nat came to the meeting late, at 3 P.M. Perhaps he had been absorbed in prayer before embarking on the venture. He disliked having Will, a complete stranger, at the most intimate conference; but Big Will said that "his life was worth no more than the others and his liberty as dear to him," and the dark determination that emanated from his towering figure reassured Nat. A discussion began about all foreseeable details, lasting until 2 A.M. Monday morning, at which time the group set out on their mission.

One hatchet and one broad axe were all the weapons the slaves could count on. So, the revolt was to start at the Travis plantation in the dead of night and on that very same night. It was a quiet evening. Windows and doors had been left open to admit the cool night breezes. Nat and Hark both knew where there was a collection of guns and muskets hanging in the Travis house, and enough powder to supply them. They were to steal the arms and proceed from one mansion to another, killing every white person and calling on the slaves to join them in a march on the county seat, Jerusalem, Virginia. There they would attack the county magazine, divide the town between their forces, and kill. Once the town was in their possession, they agreed, there would be charity extended to the surviving white men. The taking of Jerusalem might prove the spark to light a general uprising. If it did not, the rebels could withdraw, carrying arms, food, and general supplies to the Dismal Swamp, which traditionally had been a place of refuge. From the Dismal Swamp they could gradually take over the State of Virginia by guerrilla warfare, "as the Americans had in the Revolutionary War. By so doing they would call the attention of the civilized world to the condition of the Negro race," and seek for help from outside the country.

With a hatchet and a broad axe and home-made clubs, these six men thus began the biggest slave uprising in the United States.

The Travis home was first on the list. All was quiet there. Nat related the motions of the intruders in his *Confessions*:

> Hark went to the door with an ax for the purpose of breaking it open ... but reflecting that it might create an alarm in the neighborhood we determined to enter the house secretly and murder them whilst sleeping. Hark got a ladder and set it against the chimney, on which I ascended, and hoisting a window entered and came down-stairs, unbarred the doors, and removed the guns from their places.

It had been decided that Nat was to execute the first act of retribution. On trial he admitted that his master had, perhaps, been unusually indulgent, but that it made no difference: no man can be master of another man.

> Accompanied by Will, I entered my master's chamber. It being dark I could not give the death blow. The hatchet glanced from his head; he sprang from his bed and called his wife. It was his last word. Will laid him dead with a blow of his ax.

They then went to the stable, saddled the horses, proceeded to the next house, and killed all of its occupants. Murdering people as they lay in their beds or took panic-stricken flight, they moved from house to house, though at great distances from one another. In some places the black slaves joined them, armed with scythes and clubs; in others the servants, faithful to their masters or frightened for their own safety, fled into the woods. When the rebels found uncooperative slaves, they forced them to go along, fearing their defection to the whites.

The party soon consisted of mounted Negroes at the front of a column, followed by a pedestrian rabble, Nat Turner himself marching behind the column. The rear guard arrived generally after the men in front had finished the killings, and indulged in collecting guns and loot. A boarding school lay in the path of the rebels; all the children were killed there. The number of the insurgents grew to sixty, and never exceeded that number during the whole of the revolt, despite the fact that twelve thousand Negroes lived in the county, and only eight thousand whites. Were the slaves ignorant of the rising, or did they refuse to be a part of it? A Negro girl testified at the trial that they had known of the rising six weeks before it occurred. Was it true that Nat Turner announced the date as the last Sunday in August, meaning the 21st, unaware that there was another Sunday that August, and consequently the slaves were unprepared to rise?

When his troops numbered about sixty, Nat decided to strike at Jerusalem. It was still early Monday morning, and the county seat was about three miles away.

The troops had to pass through the plantation of a Mr. Parker to get to Jerusalem. Relatives of some of the slaves in the party worked on that plantation and it was thought they would be anxious to join the uprising. The buildings of the plantation were quite far from the gate. Nat was opposed to losing time, for the alarm might reach the white men before they themselves penetrated Jerusalem, and an armed meeting might result. But the men concerned would not listen. They were stoked with brandy which they had stolen from the houses looted. Nat should have resisted and given orders, but he yielded instead and stayed at the gate to the Parker plantation with six or eight men, while the rest proceeded the half mile to the house. Time passed, and these men did not return. Nat became impatient and went to fetch them. In his absence, a party of white men appeared at the gate and, seeing the slaves there, moved in to attack them. These remaining Negroes ran off into the woods, but at that moment the rest of the rebel band approached, returning to the gate from the Parker plantation. The white men fired on them, never thinking that these could return their fire. When fire was returned, the white men, uncertain of the size of the Negro troop, decided to withdraw; on their retreat they met a party of armed white men coming from Jerusalem, having heard the news of a slave uprising at Cross Keys. The two groups merged and returned to the scene of the shots. The Negroes fled in disorder.

Nat Turner knew of a private road to Jerusalem, and resolved to wait until his men could gather again, hoping to resume the march at dawn on Tuesday. But this delay was fatal to the revolt. Though many of the rebels found their way back to Nat, others tried to run away, or returned home as if they had never joined the rising. It was estimated at the trials that there had never been more than ten real fighters in the group; the rest joined the rebels for the excitement of it or were forced into service by the rebels at gunpoint so they would not betray the conspiracy.

The road that Nat knew about passed through Dr. Samuel Blunt's estate. Dr. Blunt, his son, and three other people at the house were forewarned of the arrival of the insurgents.

The Blunts had six guns ready, held their fire until both mounted and foot contingents of the rebel force were in firing distance, and then blazed a volley at the mob. This dispersed the Negroes in panic; they fled again, only to be cut off by another group of white men armed with shotguns near the home of Captain Harris. With this final engagement, the entire Negro troop was dissolved. Nat spent the night of Tuesday in the woods, waiting for fellow rebels to contact him, but none did; he waited there two nights and two days without meeting a single man of his group.

He concluded the revolt had failed. Walking through a field, he saw a pile of fence rails, dug a hole under it with his sword, the only weapon he carried, and hid under it. At night he returned to the Harris plantation, which had been abandoned by its inhabitants in terror of the slaves, and collected food in quantity. He discovered a well with fresh water, and resolved not to move away until he could find a Negro who might inform him of the situation in the county.

In the meantime, messengers from Southampton County had reached all military posts in the area with the news of the revolt. Its extent was wildly exaggerated. Refugees poured into Jerusalem, including no less than four hundred women and children, in every sort of conveyance. Panic was fanned by rumors that 300 heavily armed slaves had crossed the bridge between Cross Keys and Jerusalem. It was even said that two or three white men were the leaders of the revolt.

The U.S. Army moved into the situation quickly. Colonel House of Fort Monroe embarked on the steamer *Hampton* with three companies of men. A corps of marines from the sloops *Natchez* and *Warren* sped to Southampton. Volunteers from Norfolk rushed toward Jerusalem, and the Richmond artillery and a troop of horse guard from Petersburg had left for the scene by Monday afternoon. A hundred men from Murfreesboro, North Carolina, sixty from Winston, North Carolina, set out for the border; three to four hundred men in Hertford County, North Carolina, were awaiting orders to march.

Soon General Epps, commander of the forces at Jerusalem, had far more soldiers than he could use or handle. He wrote to the governor of the state on August 24 that "twenty resolute men could at any time have overcome the insurgents"; General Broadnax, who arrived at the first alarm with two regiments of the Mecklenburg militia, expressed the same opinion.

General Epps soon became aroused over the lawlessness of the situation. The white militiamen arrived in Jerusalem burning with wrath, and finding no rebels, began an indiscriminate slaughter of the Negroes. The Richmond horse guard came resolved to kill all Negroes in Southampton County. The massacre of the whites was over, the massacre of the blacks began and continued until General Epps, "aroused by the revolting acts of atrocity," threatened the entire county with martial law should the bloody chaos continue.

The victims of the uprising were slowly counted. Fifty-five people had been butchered by the slaves on the twenty-mile journey they had made from the Travis plantation toward Jerusalem: thirteen men, eighteen women, and twenty-four children.

It was estimated the white militia had taken a retaliatory toll of "several hundred" victims.

Rebels and huge crowds of suspects filled the jails to the bursting point, but the leader, Nat Turner, was not among them. There were rumors and reports: he had been seen in Botetourt County, he was drowned in the New River while trying to escape to Ohio, he was arrested in Baltimore. A reward of $1,100 was promised for his apprehension. There were offers of troops from as far away as New York.

The whites of Southampton County had to find Nat Turner, punish all Negroes who had taken part or had knowledge of the revolt, and seek compensation for slaves lost in the punitive campaign by the white militiamen and by court action.

Patrols, posses, and individuals scoured the woods; U.S. troops searched Dismal Swamp, where Turner's rebels had planned to retreat; and it was alleged that there were several hundred fugitives hiding there. The Court of Southampton County began to try the arraigned slaves, fearful of an attack on the prisons. Quick convictions and executions followed. Freed Negroes were transferred to the State Supreme Court for trial; a few of the slaves thought to be leaders were held to be witnesses against Turner in the event he was arrested.

Several times Nat crawled out from under his fence poles, and began stealthy night walks to Jerusalem. He never got farther than three miles down the road. At dawn, one day, he hid in a haystack in a field on Nathanial Francis' plantation. A white man with a gun passed by and, seeing something moving in the hay, fired a volley of buckshot that pierced Nat's hat, but left him unscathed.

The Negro mystic returned to his hole at the Travis plantation. Not once did a Negro man or woman pass by who could inform him of what was going on in Jerusalem. Tormented by loneliness, he was kept from surrendering by ignorance of the complete failure of his revolt and its consequences. His uncertainty left straws to grasp: his closest confederates might have found a refuge somewhere, were waiting until the excitement had died down, would try to locate him, draw up a plan of how to escape.

During his seclusion he was seized with visions of miraculous interventions and was lulled by dreams, alternately dreadful and glorious. Finally he lost the ability to distinguish between dream and thought.

One day a dog, scenting meat from the direction of the rail heap, stole a piece of it from the stock in the hole. The same night, two Negroes passed nearby to go hunting with the dog. The dog ran toward the hole and began to bark. Nat, elated by the sight of fellow human beings, climbed out of the hole and told the two Negroes who he was; they ran away as if the devil had appeared to them.

Nat had been in his hiding place for more than two months when, on October 30, a Benjamin Phipps noticed some motion around the fallen fence poles. Soon Nat's head emerged. Phipps raised his gun and aimed at the Negro, but Nat Turner shouted that he was ready to surrender. The emaciated, ragged figure, still wearing the hat perforated by the buckshot, crawled out and lay flat on the earth. The man bound him and drove him toward the house. Nat Turner's revolt was finished.

Mr. Gray, to whom Nat made his confessions, wondered whether Nat still believed in the spirit voice and the mission it conferred on him, even when all had turned wrong.

"Wasn't Christ crucified?" was Turner's answer.

The lawyer described the black rebel who now accepted his fate as a kind of martyrdom: "Clothed with rags, and covered with chains, yet daring to raise his manacled hands to heaven with a spirit soaring above the attributes of men . . ."

On November 5, 1831 Nat Turner was tried. In contrast to the debacle following the collapse of the Negro uprising, the trial was fair and free from outside interference, although there was great interest in it all over the United States.

Nat Turner confessed that he had committed the acts of which he was accused as his attorney set it down in his *Confessions;* but he pleaded not guilty, causing stirs and murmurs of surprise among jury and judges of the court.

His attorney explained that Turner pleaded not guilty because he had no feeling of guilt.

Was this conviction of innocence a result of his belief in the rightness of the cause of his spirit voice? Nat denied complicity in other plots; when asked whether he had conspired with slaves in North Carolina who had allegedly risen about the same time, he merely indicated that they must have read the signs as he had done.

Or was the absence of guilt feeling a result of his own belief that extreme means—even mass murders—were justified if they served to foster liberation from slavery?

Since these questions were never asked at the trial, the ambiguity of Turner's motives remains; the problem cannot be resolved. Did he lead the slaves toward insurrections in response to what he deemed the command of the spirit voice, or did his alleged communication with this mysterious spirit serve only to enhance his prestige among the blacks, and serve as a convenient and powerful point of mystique around which to organize his revolt?

> ... Borne down by the load of guilt, your only justification is that you were borne away by fanaticism. If this be true, from my soul I pity you; and while you have my sympathies, I am, nevertheless, called upon to pass the sentence of the court.

So declared the presiding judge, the Hon. Jeremiah Cobb, as he sentenced Nat Turner to death, brushing away forever the question of his motivation under the name of "fanaticism."

On November 11, Nat Turner was hanged with three of his associates, Hark, Nelson, and Sam, whose execution had been deferred until Turner himself could be tried. It was said that the Negro leader met his doom quietly, eagerly urging the executioner to perform his duty.

By the end of the affair, fifty-three Negroes had been brought before the court on charges; of these, seventeen were executed, and twelve were transported out of state. The Superior Circuit Court had tried four free Negroes and sentenced three to hanging, acquitting one.

One single woman was among the executed: Lucy, slave of Mr. John T. Barrow, who had attempted to block the escape of Mrs. Barrow from the rebel murderers. On September 26, Lucy had been taken from jail and, "riding upon her coffin to the place of execution, was hanged and buried in the well-known burying ground of the insurgents."

After the defeat of Nat Turner's plot, the massive deployment of white armed forces and the resulting indiscriminate murders, mass arrests, and restrictions on their precarious freedoms, the Negroes of Virginia walked light and talked small for some time.

"At the time of the Old Prophet Nat the colored folk was afraid to pray loud," an old Negro woman told Thomas Wentworth Higginson,

> for the whites threatened to punish 'em dreadfully, if the least noise was heard. The patrols was low drunken Whites; and in Nat's time, if they heard one of the colored folks praying, or singing a hymn, they would fall upon 'em and abuse 'em, and sometimes kill 'em, afore master or missis could get to 'em. The brightest and best was killed in Nat's time. The

whites always suspect such ones...the patrols would tie up the free colored people, flog 'em, and try to make 'em lie against one another and often killed 'em before anybody could interfere.

Many hundreds of Negroes were murdered, and the slaughter abated only when the County of Southampton, which had acknowledged its duty to compensate masters for slaves executed on court orders, refused to do so when slaves were killed by mobs who had taken the law into their own hands.

Of the many tragic scenes involving conflict of the interracial loyalties which resulted from the tensions of that time, one related in the Richmond *Enquirer* may be taken as pathetically typical:

> Rev. M. B. Cox, a Liberian missionary, then in Virginia, told this story: In the hunt for the insurgents, a slaveholder went into the woods, accompanied by a faithful slave, who had been the means of saving his life during the insurrection. When they had reached a retired place in the forest, the man handed his gun to his master, informing him that he could not live a slave any longer, and requesting him either to free him or shoot him on the spot. The master took the gun, in some trepidation, levelled it at the faithful negro, and shot him through the heart.

"If this be true," the *Enquirer* commented editorially, "great will be the desert of these noble-minded Africans."

Oddly enough, after the first shocked horror at the news and distorted rumors of the revolt had waned in the South, a new and surprising conviction circulated briefly among the white population of the slave states: that, due to the continuous protection of the U.S. military forces and the massive solidarity of the white population in the slave counties, and of the states neighboring Virginia, the slaves could never again pose a serious threat to the system of the whites. Nat Turner had been put down; so equally would any new troublesome wretch, no matter how dangerously he glowered.

Such overconfidence melted away soon, however, for the majority of the white population; the slave system often brought on violent alternation in popular sentiment, and such was again the case at this time. The relief could only be permanent in the hearts of slaveholders somehow removed from the daily fact of black slaves as a necessity intertwined in the lives of their families. The great majority of southerners owned not more than a dozen slaves, active in the nursery, in children's care, household chores, and in the field. Yet should these few harbor a murderous hatred for white men in their hearts—and who, under the circumstances, could say that they did not—there could not be a day or night secure for the planter or slaveholder.

Frederick Law Olmsted talked with a Negro couple in Louisiana more than twenty years after the Nat Turner affair and received a vivid description of just how violent the fright of some whites could be and the extent to which they would insure themselves against the remotest possibility of disorder and surprise attack:

"When I used to live [in Alabama], I remember when I was a boy—must ha' been about twenty years ago," said the men, "... folks has dredful frightened about the niggers. I remember they built pens in the woods where they could hide, and Christmas time they went and got into the pens, 'fraid the Niggers was rising." "I remember the same time where we was in South Carolina," his wife said, "we had all our things put up in bags, so we could tote 'em, if we heard they was coming."

A Georgia lady related that in the time of the scare after Turner's revolt "there was not a person on her plantation she dared trust her life with; and ... she never retired at night without an axe so near her pillow she could lay her hand upon it instantly."

Among the hundreds of slave rebellions recorded in all kinds of contemporary documents, the accusation of rape was raised in but an insignificant number of cases, whereas miscegenation by the master race with Negro women was an accepted fact of life. In the United States, unlike other countries, law and custom made no distinction between a full-blooded Negro and one so far removed from Negro ancestors that only a drop of Negro blood remained in his veins. It is now impossible to ascertain how many full-blooded Negroes still exist here, and indeed, how many pure-blooded whites.

North Carolina, at the same time that Turner was setting out to strike his blow in neighboring Southampton County, was busy setting up safeguards against such incitements as those in the tracts of David Walker. The death penalty was to be imposed on any individual who might publish, distribute, or import into the state printed matter "tending to incite the Negroes to conspiracy or resistance." The same severe punishment was to be dealt to persons who would incite in a Negro the spirit of insurrection, conspiracy, or rebellion.

On October 4, 1831, rumors spread that a general slave rising was taking place in the eastern part of North Carolina.

Mr. Usher, a citizen of Washington, North Carolina, was informed by a free mulatto that the alleged leader of the conspiracy was a slave who went by the name David, property of the sheriff of Sampson County, and that the action was to involve slaves in three counties. David was arrested, tried, and convicted. Subsequently, probably to save his own life, he confessed to the charge and named associates: the group, he explained, had planned to attack Wilmington in a two-pronged advance, and had expected to be joined by about 2,000 slaves, seizing arms and ammunition in much the same manner that Nat Turner had.

This David and another Negro were immediately executed to prevent them from being lynched. In the weeks after the news of the Turner uprising had reached the eastern part of the state, thirty Negroes had been jailed in Duplin County, twenty-five in Sampson County, and fifteen in New Hanover County. The militia was in arms throughout the state; yet the Fayetteville (N.C.) *Observer* stated on September 21 that "not a single party of negroes, nay, not a single individual, has been found in arms or in rebellion in any of the counties."

These incidents were lumped together as the "revolt" which Turner later was questioned about when he was finally apprehended; he had replied that the individuals involved must have read his own "celestial signs."

North Carolina was seized with another hysterical reaction in the wake of Turner's trial at the beginning of November. An alleged plot in Onslow, North Carolina, led to the hanging of two more Negroes and the murder of about fifteen others by an angry mob; rumor had it that Wilmington and Clinton had been seized by rebel slaves. According to the Raleigh *Register*, a "plot of meditated insurrection" was discovered among the slaves working in the gold mines in Rutherford and Burke. "Fortunately for the accused," wrote the author of a history of North Carolina, Guion Griffis Johnson, "in Sampson, Duplin and New Hanover their trial, under the act of 1816, had to await the regular term of superior court. The feelings of the whites cooled meanwhile considerably."

The situation was the same throughout the South: alleged plots brought misfortunes to Negroes in Laurens County, South Carolina, in Macon, Georgia, in Fayetteville, Tennessee; in Northampton, North Carolina, partial justice saved some: the Attorney General ordered the release of Negroes held in prison in connection with a rumored plot because of insufficient evidence of their guilt, but about fifteen other Negroes had died previously at the hand of the citizens.

One restrictive law after another was passed until, in the words of John Spencer Basset, the slave "was bound hand, foot and brain in the power of his master. Moreover, public feeling became inflamed. Slavery could no longer be discussed as a public policy and there arose with most people ...a fervent intolerance of all views advanced against the system."

As if to shatter any complacency on the part of southerners, and to strengthen their determination to hold tighter to what they possessed, in January of 1832 some 50,000 slaves in Jamaica set fires and clashed with armed bands of white men. The casualty list was typically disproportionate: three or four whites were burnt in their houses and ten killed in the fighting; of the Negroes, 400 were killed and about 100 were subsequently executed.

Meanwhile, another ugly manifestation of the unease of the time which seemed to have been sparked by the Turner revolt was growing in the South. It was duly noted that Turner, as well as being a kind of natural mystic, had some religious education and was a lay preacher of sorts. Preaching itself might be dangerous, and, certainly, missionaries among the blacks were to be feared; therefore, such unwitting accomplices of subversion through the Christian faith also became scapegoats of the recurrent unrest.

Preachers were arrested and expelled from the British islands in the Caribbean. Measures were introduced to limit preaching to Negroes by white men, or preaching by Negroes in any place except where a white person was present.

The essence of the problem was not whether the Christian religion suggested either the submission of slave servant to master or the rising of the just against unjust submission. On these points the Scriptures and their interpretations remained ambiguous. The real danger lay in educating the slave to *make a choice* between such ambiguities as were inherent in religion, *i.e.*, whether to develop a conscious sense of his humanity and soul in a slave rather than letting him languish in a black underworld of ignorance in which, conveniently, no alternative to slavery was suggested.

The very deep impression that the bloody Nat Turner revolt made on Virginia emerges from the character of the debates in the Virginia House of Delegates in December of 1831 and January of 1832. Here was the white conscience at work on measures to be taken and lessons to be drawn.

Debate was initiated by petitions to emancipate the slaves in America by removing them from the state to Africa. As in Maryland, Virginian funds should be made available from the public till for the expenses of a fare to Liberia. Since compensation to the master for the slave was not contemplated, the transfer should concern only free Negroes and such slaves as the master intended to free.

The radical nature of the petition itself, the reaction of the Virginian delegates to it, and the discussion of the whole question of slavery that ensued in the House of Delegates are significant. Both the moral and economic arguments against slavery were eloquently stated.

"Let me ask," Mr. Bodnax stated in support of the petition, "is there one man in Virginia who does not lament that there was ever a slave in the State? And is there a man, who considers the decay of our prosperity, and the retrograde movement of this once flourishing Commonwealth, who does not attribute them to the pregnant cause of slavery?"

In his support, Mr. Moore produced the following moral argument: Ignorance is the safeguard of slavery. Yet ignorance is incompatible with moral feeling, and renders the slave incapable of distinguishing right from wrong. He is accustomed to sacrifice truth without remorse, as the only means to escape punishment. The slave perceives that he can never attain the least distinction in society, however fair and unexceptionable his conduct may be. The impulses of passion are never restrained in him by that dread of infamy and disgrace, which operates so powerfully, in deterring freemen from the commission of acts, criminal or dishonorable. He looks upon the whole white population as participating in the wrong he endures. "The demoralizing influence of the indiscriminate intercourse of the sexes among the slave population, need only be hinted at to be understood," the delegate said, and he went further in stating that slavery itself had a demoralizing effect on the white community. He asked: "Can it be expected that where so large a mass of the population of the county is corrupt, that the other classes can entirely escape the contagion? Sir, it is impossible."

Mr. Randolph sounded a warning: "The hour of eradication of the end is advancing.—It must come—Whether it is effected by the energy of our own minds, or by the bloody scenes of Southampton and St. Domingo, is a tale for future history."

Mr. Brown, however, came to the defense: slavery was an evil, "the greatest, perhaps, that an angry Providence could inflict on a sinning people," but "it was too late to correct it. It was now so interwoven with our habits and interests, that it was impossible to free ourselves from it."

Against the veto implicit in the word "impossible," another delegate vainly offered the last, simplest objection to continuation of slavery: "slavery interferes with our means of enjoying life, liberty, prosperity, happiness and safety."

The use of that final, proud, pragmatic "impossible" was going to replace the traditional arguments—moral, historical, and economic—for the retention of slavery in the South. Slavery was, plain and simple, a way of life that could not be changed, evil or not, without destroying the foundations of southern society.

The emancipation bill received strong support in the House of Delegates, but the state Senate defeated an even less radical bill which would have allowed the State of Virginia to finance the colonization of free Negroes.

Developments, indeed, were running counter to emancipation. Within a few years the success of cotton growing in the Deep South and the prohibition of slave trade from foreign countries raised the financial value of the slaves as property. What state or nation is able to forego a capital investment of millions of dollars in property? So the slaveholders asked those who would argue that slavery was immoral.

Such events as Nat Turner's revolt and the debates and repressive measures it sparked in the United States ran a counterpoint to similar events in Cuba and Brazil.

In Brazil, the slaves had risen repeatedly since 1807, and their inevitable defeats did not subdue them for long. In Bahia, Muslim Negroes from the Gold Coast and Benin plotted in their mosques with equal ferocity against whites and such Negroes as would not join them. These Moslem

Africans clung tenaciously to their religion and spoke Arabic even after they had been carried across the ocean. They maintained secret organizations and allegedly had a secret writing known only to them, probably Arabic. In 1835, these slaves stormed the prison in Aguda, fired on the soldiers, attacked the police and army posts. There was much difficulty in subduing them.

In the spring of 1833, Africans who landed in Cuba started another revolt that threatened to engulf huge masses of slaves. According to press reports, about 600 Africans were landed on the coast who had heard rumors of a contagious disease devastating the blacks on the plantations. The newcomers attributed the source of death to their new white masters, who, they believed, poisoned the Negroes; an attempt to break out of camp was made. The guards were killed and, as the military was being summoned, slaves of nearby plantations joined the rebels and together they attacked the vanguard of the force that arrived to quell the disturbance. Only when reinforcements were added could the soldiery master the situation; 400 to 500 blacks were allegedly killed in this incident.

But Nat Turner and his legion of unnamed associates among the blacks of this continent ultimately did nothing to hasten the prospects of emancipation. While emancipation was occurring elsewhere throughout the Western Hemisphere, with the exception of Cuba and Brazil, hopes of freedom grew even dimmer for the slaves of the United States.

The Age of Reason flourished while slavery and slave trade were expanding into global proportions. How, then, we might now ask, did the nineteenth century, the "century of progress," affect these institutions that had been bred from the greed by which the West had been possessed since the discovery of the masterless continents of the world? In this period, a long series of struggles occurred among the western countries for a larger share in the trade in human lives. Africa became corrupted to the extent that her tribes began to prey upon one another and involved themselves in continuous warfare for the purpose of capturing human game for the trade; "they became ruthless where before they had been peaceable; they became predatory where before they had been mild," as W. L. Mathieson wrote. The first half of the century of progress saw a peak in traffic in Negro lives. The volume of this trade can only be estimated, for, as Lord John Russell rightly perceived, "no record exists of the multitudes who perish on the overland journey to the African coast, or in the passage across the Atlantic, or of the still greater number who fall a sacrifice to the warfare, pillage, and cruelties by which slave trade is fed."

Slave trade may still have been experiencing growth, but it was now running into ever more formidable legal and physical obstacles. Every new obstacle resulted in rising prices on the slave market, and encouraged the greediest and most ruthless speculators, ready to take risks in order to reap their prize. So no matter which set of conditions prevailed, the slave was locked in a vicious circle.

The Act of 1807 in the United States prohibited the importation of slaves from abroad. It led to an upsurge of the domestic slave trade and caused Cuba and Brazil to become huge markets for the entire Western Hemisphere. The demand for slaves received a new stimulus in the United States when growing cotton spread throughout the Deep South after the War of 1812, and the belief became established that the cotton economy could be profitable only in a slave labor system. Obviously, then, slave trade would continue as long as slavery existed. Slavery had survived the Enlightenment and was stubbornly resisting the sweep of the century of progress.

The U.S. Navy patrolled the seas in search of slavers, but only half-heartedly. In spite of the existence of legal prohibition since 1808, there was no record of any forfeiture incurred under the law, though it was common knowledge in the South at the time that an entire fleet of armed slavers had its headquarters in Galveston, Texas. In 1820, slave trade was declared to be piracy, a capital crime, but still there were no convictions until 1862. On February 7 of that year, Nathaniel Gordon, master of the *Eirie* was sentenced to be hanged. In the meantime, illicit slave traffic amounted to an estimated 14,000 bodies yearly.

Great Britain, once the leading slave-trading nation, now pioneered in antislavery and slave-trade legislation, and exerted tremendous effort and financial sacrifice to make it effective. After the fall of Napoleon, Britain dominated the seas of the world and the commerce on them. Her ships carried goods with less risk and higher profits than those that human cargo had brought. Her campaign against slavery, waged through several decades, culminated with Parliamentary prohibition of slavery in 1833. At the same time, however, care was exerted that ships of other nations should not take advantage of this law. Britain brought tremendous pressures to bear on seafaring countries to prohibit slave trade and to sign treaties with her stipulating the right of mutual search and confiscation of slaves aboard ship. In practice, this empowered the British Navy to conduct searches on all foreign ships for slaves, who were then conducted to Sierra Leone and set free in that colony, called with slight justification the "cradle of African civilization."

The British cruisers pursued and captured slavers vigorously; 116,800 slaves were caught and freed between the years of 1810 and 1840. They perfected their action by seizing empty slavers in harbor and preventing loaded ones from leaving Africa. But despite this vigilance, Brazil still imported more than 20,000 slaves a year and Cuba, about 30,000, under Spanish and Portuguese flags until British pressure and bribery resulted in treaties giving power to the British to search and confiscate. France and the United States, however, refused to allow this right to the British cruisers. In 1820, slavers transported and distributed under French colors no less than 60,000 Negroes to Cuba, Guadeloupe, and Martinique. In 1821, about 200,000 Negroes were carried off from the western part of Africa.

The United States long opposed the search of her ships by British vessels, though the American flag often flew from vessels masking the interests of foreign traders. But in 1819, American warships were stationed on African shores to intercept the traders carrying slaves for the American market. Slaves taken in transit were to be returned to Africa. Congress allotted $100,000 to allow President Monroe to settle such slaves in Liberia. In 1824, a treaty of mutual right of search and confiscation was negotiated with Britain, but the U.S. Senate refused to ratify it. Still, the blockade on slave trade became tighter, and the risks of the trade were thus increased. The profits attainable remained attractive enough to keep the most determined traders in business. If a slaver spotted a British or American warship on the horizon, he could always get rid of incriminating evidence by efficiently disposing of his slaves in the sea; such losses were provided for in the high insurance rates, and a slaver received compensation for those lost by "accident." As a rule, inferior slaves were thrown into the sea anyway: for every ten Negroes who left Africa, three would reach America; the other seven died, or were murdered.

The trade did fall into disrepute, however. International commerce was growing at a huge pace; cotton and other raw materials were being shipped to England where they were processed in newly-mechanized industries. A highly profitable business in more conventional goods made many merchants anxious to shed the stain of slave trade. Those who took it over were all the more ruthless.

In 1829, a British captain who had intercepted a slaver at the moment it was about to sail in safety into a Brazilian harbor, described the sensation among the slaves when they realized they were saved:

> Their dark and melancholy visages lightened up. They perceived something of sympathy and kindness in our looks, which they had not been accustomed to, and feeling, instinctively, that we were friends, they immediately began to shout and clasp their hands. The women were particularly excited ... Some, however, hung down their heads in apparently hopeless dejection; some were greatly emaciated, and some, particularly children, seemed dying ...

The British officers in this case insisted that the slaves be admitted to air and water on the deck of the slaver, but her captain protested that all the whites would be killed by the slaves when liberated. The British would not desist, and all slaves were released on the deck:

> It is impossible to conceive the effect of this eruption—507 fellow creatures of all ages and sexes, some children, all in a

state of total nudity, scrambling out together to taste the luxury of a little fresh air and water. They came swarming up like bees from the aperture of a hive, till the whole deck was crowded to suffocation. The children were lying in a torpid state, indifferent to life or death, many of them could not stand on their legs. It was when some water was brought that the extent of their sufferings was exposed. They all rushed like maniacs towards it. No entreaties, or threats, or blows, could restrain them; they shrieked and struggled, and fought with one another for a drop of this precious liquid, as if they grew rabid at the sight of it.

At other times, interceptors of slaving vessels had to relinquish the idea of letting slaves out to breathe fresh air when they were liberated, because they would refuse to return below deck. When it was attempted to force them, many threw themselves into the sea, locked in each other's arms, rather than endure more of the poisonous atmosphere there.

The profits involved were still too large not to tempt some adventurers to undertake the risks. In the 1830s, for example, a good slave fetched approximately $20 on the African coast, but could be sold for $500 in Georgia. As long as ships sailing under the American colors exercised their right not to be searched by the British, under the guise of freedom of the seas, the trade could not be stopped.

Very fast ships were used by the traders to escape pursuit when chased by British warships. Many slavers chose to return fire if there was any chance for them to damage the warship and escape. To be sunk and surrender in the lifeboats was preferable to letting British or American vessels confiscate the slaves as evidence and bring them before a court of justice. Some slavers were sailing as floating arsenals: the *Velos Passagero* carried 20 guns and a crew of 150 men to transport its 1,555 slaves. It fell in with the British sloop-in-war *Primrose* in 1830; the slaver surrendered after forty-six of her crew had been killed and twenty wounded.

The British cruiser *Black Joke* under Captain Ramsey pursued two Spanish slaving brigs, the *Rapido* and the *Regulo* during 1831. In the chase, the slavers heaved their slaves into the sea by twos, shackled together at the ankles, leaving them to sink or swim as best they could. Men, women, and children struggled in the water. "Dreadful to relate, upward one hundred and fifty of these wretched creatures perished in this way," Captain Ramsey reported. Similar chases regularly took place with varying success, both on the high seas and close to the shore of Africa.

When Andrew Jackson took office as President in 1829, all protest against slavery died down in Congress. There was but one antislavery congressman in the Capitol.

In the North, however, the protest took on the proportions of a fast-growing social movement, motivated by a quasi-religious zeal, and concentrated on a single issue: the abolition of slavery. In 1830, abolitionists in the North launched a campaign to shower Congress with petitions to abolish slavery in the District of Columbia (which stood under direct federal rule and was not protected by state rights from such action). In January, 1831, William Lloyd Garrison founded in Boston the New England Abolition Society, and launched his fighting newspaper, *The Liberator*. Two years later, the American Anti-Slavery Society began its nationwide movement for the immediate end of slavery.

At the same time, England took legislative action against slavery, passing in 1833 the law abolishing slavery in British possessions within a period of seven years, and indemnifying slaveholders for their losses. Lord Palmerston gave voice

to the sentiment which brought about this change in a speech
in the House of Commons:

> I will venture to say that if all the crimes which the human
> race has committed from the creation down to the present day
> were added together in one vast aggregate, they would scarcely
> equal, I am sure they could not exceed, the amount of guilt
> which has been incurred by mankind in connection with this
> diabolical slave trade.

IX

ABOLITIONISM:
A NEW VOICE OF DISSENSION

IT was the bloody Turner insurrection that made the whites more receptive to the idea of financing removal to Africa of free Negroes and those slaves who could buy their freedom. Although a majority of free Negroes were determined not to emigrate, some had lost faith in their ability to improve their lot and that of their descendants and chose to return to Africa.

The American Colonization Society conducted a two-sided emigration campaign: to the North, it presented its program as an antislavery mission, to the South, as a vehicle by which to rid herself of undesirable free Negroes and others.

Suspicions of the colonization program were expressed by distinguished white men of true antislavery sentiments. John Quincy Adams wrote to President Monroe that there were many humane members of the colonization movement, but also "cunning slaveholders ... who see that the plan may be carried far enough to produce the effect of raising the market price of their slaves." Such fears were groundless; the colonization society never raised enough funds to transport one-fifth of the normal yearly population growth of the Negroes to Africa.

As to the response of free Negroes, the most influential clergymen agitated against the society. Bishop Richard Allen of the African Methodist Episcopalian Church stated: "this land which we have watered with our tears and our blood is now our mother country, and we are well satisfied to stay where wisdom abounds and the gospel is free." Strangely enough, the growing Negro sense of being American coincided with a movement in the state legislatures of the South to establish the principle that Negroes, even if free, were not citizens of the United States.

The controversy between those in favor and those opposed to colonization projects had an important result. Negro opinion no longer echoed white slogans and sentiments, but, through organized bodies with the direct purpose of presenting a corporate resolution, voiced specifically Negro aspirations. A distinct Negro stand was taken in regard to social and political action of national concern, expressed and directed by Negroes.

The North American slave had completely lost his tribal associations. Though he was excluded from the benefits of his new American environment it was his only world.

Frederick Law Olmsted, while traveling through the South talked with a slave on a Louisiana plantation who had been sold out of Virginia. There he had been treated less harshly than by the French overseers in his new home of Louisiana. Olmsted reminded the slave that he was still better off than he might be in Africa. The slave asked anxiously if the "brack folks were better off to be here"; Olmsted replied in the affirmative, excepting Liberia. The slave then inquired:

Why is it, massa, when the brack people is free, dey wants to send 'em away out of dis country?

193

The slave opined he would not go, even if it were better somewhere else. He had grown used to this country, and didn't even wish to go back to Virginia from Louisiana, though Virginia was more pleasant. Olmsted asked him what he would do if free:

> If I was free, the man replied with great animation, if I was free I would, well, sar, de fust thing I would do, if I was free, I would go to work for a year, and get some money for myself —den—den—den, massa, dis is what I do—I buy me, fus place, a little house, and little lot of land, and den—no; I would like to do dat fus thing; den, when I come back, de fus thing I'd do, I'd get me a wife; den, I'd take her to my house, and I would live with her dar; and I would raise things in my garden, and take 'em to New Orleans, and sell 'em dar, in the market. Dat's de way I would live if I was free.

The Negroes may not have entirely forgotten the old kinship, language, and taboos of Africa according to Stanley Elkin in his book, *Slavery*, but, even for the first generation in this country, the memories had ceased to mean anything. "The old values, the sanctions, the standards, already unreal, could no longer furnish him guides for conduct, for adjusting to the expectations of a complete new life."

The idea of resettling the Negroes in Africa had originated with the British, for exclusively practical considerations. They had carried many slaves away with them from America in the Revolution; these had joined them on the assumption of becoming free. After the war was over, the British were at a loss as to what to do with them. Nova Scotia had no use for slaves. Planters of the West Indies protested their immigration as free Negroes. Then the British purchased territory in West Africa, Sierra Leone. In 1787, they shipped about 400 former slaves to settle the strip of land. Malaria wreaked havoc in the group, and they were plagued by the natives who tried to capture and sell them as slaves again. The venture appeared rather futile until in 1800, when about 500 maroons from the West Indies, immune from fever and accustomed to fighting, were resettled there.

The American colonization plan strove to find for free Negroes "an asylum from the oppression they suffered here, and by their means to extend to Africa the blessings of Christianity and civilization," but also to create a landing place for slaves confiscated when the American Navy captured slavers or smugglers. The federal government supported this part of the colonization program, which was otherwise run by the colonization societies.

The first American ship landed eighty-six emigrants in the highlands of Cape Montserado in 1820. Although the spot had been chosen for its elevation as a supposed protection against malaria, the colony was almost wiped out by that disease immediately. The survivors fled to neighboring Sierra Leone. In 1822, another expedition, well prepared to meet the hazards of the venture, arrived and settled near the coast of what is now Liberia. If the organizers ever seriously contemplated that the American Negroes would be reintegrated in Africa, they were sadly mistaken. Africa did not assimilate her children. The old traditions were not revived. Instead, the American ex-slaves dutifully established copies of the institutions of their masters' society.

The United States refused to assume sovereignty over the Liberian state; but the colony needed the authority to negotiate with foreign states and to exercise its rights, so the Colonization Society advised independence. In 1847, Liberia became independent, with its own Declaration of Independence. A year later, it was established as a republic, with a Constitution on the American model, with division

195

of powers in the government and the direct election of the president. Even the flag was a reflection of United States custom: a lone white star in a blue field, with six red and five black stripes, a reference to the eleven signers of the Liberian Declaration of Independence.

The Maryland Colonization Society had its own colonizing project. A group of settlers left Baltimore in 1826 under the auspices of the Society, leaving as a parting shot a bitter message to the whites: "We reside among you, and yet are strangers; natives, and yet no citizens; surrounded by the freest people and most republican institutions in the world, and yet enjoying none of the immunities of freedom."

This settlers' colony in Liberia received from the mother state true colonial standing. In 1847, it granted a Declaration of Rights and a Constitution as the State of Maryland in Liberia.

The Negroes brought with them to Liberia not only social and legal organization, but also a belief in "a will and impulse to improvement." Unhappily, they also imitated their former American masters by excluding the natives of the land from the rights established in their Constitution.

In the 1850s, Liberia received so many grants that she was able to equip her own ships and support immigration and settlement. But opposition in the United States was growing. Slaveholders feared a rise in the price of slaves if too many free Negroes left the country. Conventions of free Negroes stubbornly continued to oppose eviction from their native land, though life was made miserable for them in the free states in many places. Although the whites in the North hated slavery, it did not keep them from a cold discrimination against Negroes. Even Lincoln, during his campaign for the Senate in 1858, had echoed Jefferson's doubts on the possibilities of cohabitation of the races: "I am not in favor of Negro citizenship, or bringing about in any way the social and political equality of the white and black races."

Actually, the colonization of Liberia failed for another reason: the American Negroes living there did not wish to farm their new lands. They recoiled from agriculture, perhaps because of its distasteful association with their former slavery. Americans who visited Liberia in her early years saw this tendency with misgivings, but found no easy incentives with which to solve the problem. There was one fantastic suggestion worthy of note: Captain Edward F. Kennedy of the U.S. frigate *Java* advised tying the settlers to their ancestral continent by teaching them to raise orangoutangs from the Malay Archipelago to do their work for them in the rice and corn fields: "As long as they are not considered human beings," he wrote, "I see no reason why they should not be made to work as well as a horse or an ox."

The American Negroes were discouraged to find themselves in the position of having to defend themselves against new enslavement in Africa. Some Liberian tribes and chieftains would not willingly give up the benefits from the slave trade. In 1824, Monrovian settlers discovered fifteen slavers loading Negroes bought from black chiefs. Indignantly, they attacked the slave pen and freed its occupants. A further step was made to put an end to the trade in the region by the attack and invasion of Tradetown where three slave "factories" were located. The American Negroes opened fire on two armored slavers in the harbor on April 10, 1824, kept up a barrage for two days, and eventually forced the evacuation of the emplacement.

Liberia changed little in the following decades, though after the Civil War new attempts were made at colonization. The country occupied 350 miles of the African coastline, ran

300 miles into the interior, and numbered in its population about 20,000 "civilized people"—for so descendants of American Negroes distinguished themselves from the native Negroes. These latter in 1900 numbered about one million.

Benjamin Lundy, a New Jersey Quaker, campaigned in the South from 1815 to 1818 and tried to convince southerners that emancipation of the slaves was in their own interest. He ridiculed the scheme of colonization, holding that the cost of colonizing merely the annual natural increase of the Negro population would exhaust the wealth of a Croesus. As he explained it, "We might as well dry old Ocean with a thimble." Yet Lundy himself tried his hand at colonization of freed Negroes, and had negotiated on the subject with the governor of Haiti. As a result of his efforts a group left from Virginia in 1828, and another from Maryland the next year. Their experiences discouraged continuation of the scheme.

Lundy was too early a prophet. He ran into trouble even with antislavery audiences. It was easy for slave traders and lobbyists to convince his listeners that Lundy advocated equality for Negroes with the white men. Once in Baltimore, he was assailed and almost killed for his troubles.

Abolitionism became an act of a revived faith through the agency of William Lloyd Garrison and the appearance in Boston of his weekly newspaper, the *Liberator*. Son of a sailor who had deserted his family, Garrison was described as a man of "beautiful countenance and clear eagle eye, that resolute spirit which makes the martyr." He did not initiate American abolitionism as such, and was not the only leader of antislavery groups, but he was the most effective opponent of slavery on moral grounds. Slavery was a "heinous crime in the sight of God." He believed that if he could persuade the slaveholders of his opinion that they were inviting damnation, they would set their slaves free in a hurry to save their own souls. Garrison therefore opposed repayment to slaveholders who gave up their slaves; there was, he held, no indemnity to be paid for a crime. "Let the Southern oppressors tremble—let their secret abettors tremble—let their Northern apologists tremble," he thundered. Garrison caught the ear of the country; in 1835 there were 200 antislavery societies of his inspiration, and by 1840 these had increased to 2,000, animated by his spirit of uncompromise—for, to Garrison, there could be no compromise with the devil.

Garrison's radicalism alienated a great many people friendly to antislavery ideas in the North. His societies adopted resolutions to the effect that all laws admitting slavery were, before God at least, null and void. On this principle, the U.S. Constitution was worthless. Garrison's logical mind did not flinch at this stand, or from eventually declaring that the Union with the slaveholders of the South was immoral and should be liquidated.

Garrison's furious campaign against sin developed further into the realm of political ideas; he favored refusing allegiance to any government and denying preference for any country or nation, at the same time rejecting violence as an alternative. He became a kind of Christian anarchist advocating civil disobedience and direct action. He urged Negroes to send their children to school, to learn and practice a trade, to protect fugitive slaves, to register on the voting lists, and "in every way make themselves part of the community."

Garrison's abolitionists burned a copy of the Constitution in the streets of Boston in protest against "compromise with tyranny"; through such acts of radicalism they alienated more realistic but no less determined northern opponents to slavery, among them the indefatigable orator, Theodore Dwight Weld, and John Quincy Adams. Adams himself was convinced that the influence of British emancipation of the slaves in the West Indies in 1833 "may prove an earthquake on the continent" and deal the death-blow to slavery in the South.

When the revivalism had exhausted itself, the North reacted to it with violence. Meetings were broken up, Negro quarters attacked and murders were committed. The North was impatient with abolitionism. Elijah Lovejoy, who published an abolitionist paper in Illinois, was killed. Miss Prudence Crandall of Canterbury, Connecticut, was arrested, convicted, and imprisoned because she had taught Negroes from outside the state in her boarding school.

The northern reaction to the abolitionist discontent restored southern self-confidence. In 1831, two southern states had extended the right to vote to free Negroes. The abolitionist campaign stirred such strong reactions in its opponents and such fears of Negroes being integrated into white men's society, that the six northern states in which free Negroes had been given the right to vote tacitly canceled the privilege. The same thing happened, of course, in the two southern states.

An immense literature of controversy rolled off the printing presses and inundated the reading public. Today, the arguments for slavery in the books and pamphlets of the period sound forced, mutually exclusive, transparently sophistical, rather than seeking out a profession of truth through disinterested search. Yet those who argued for slavery expressed in all seriousness the conviction that it must be accepted no matter what reason or expediency, the alternative being the dissolution of the Union or war.

Proslavery writers used the Bible to prove that the Holy Scriptures accepted slavery. They pointed out in historical justification that slavery had always existed. Socially, the system was less cruel, less degrading even, than industrialism. They argued that slaves in the South lived better lives than the workers of the slums in English factory towns, who were starving in filthy holes and alleys. The American slave also lived on a much higher level than the peasants in Ireland or, in fact, those on the European continent at the time.

The alleged cruelty of the slave system was contrasted with the cruelty of the English punishments for crimes against property. To protect the interests of the slaveholder the courts of slave states often spared the slave who had infringed the law and code of the land. Proslavery writers referred to the conditions of the worker in England not only because of his wretched life, his lack of legal protection and the callousness of the community to his plight, but because British abolitionists actively supported the abolitionists in this country.

American slavery had existed before the Union, the southerners agreed. The Constitution sanctioned slavery by limiting only the trade in slaves from foreign countries. It had not removed or limited the power of the states to regulate the institution.

Southerners contended the country would not be served by abolishing slavery. On the contrary, the whole civilized world benefited from its presence in the South. It was taken for granted that cotton could not be grown in this country without slave labor. The failure of British attempts to expand cotton production in the West Indies, India and Egypt had proved this. Cotton imported from the American South gave bread to one million workers in America in 1840 and four to five million in English factories, mills, and workshops and supplied the civilized world with inexpensive cloth. Thus, the South reasoned, the world depended on black slavery of the southern plantations for its prosperity. This state of affairs may have been detrimental to the welfare of a number of Negroes—perhaps it was even morally wrong—but it conferred great benefits upon the mass of the home population and the world at large. It even was a godsend to the Negro here for, as everyone knew, if left to his own devices he fell into barbarism, as in Haiti and Liberia.

In one respect, however, the West Indies tarnished the South's image of Negro irresponsibility. The sugar plantations there had gone out of production after slavery had been abolished. The free Negroes, rather than accepting the pittance offered by their former masters as wages, had settled on unoccupied land in the mountains in Jamaica. In 1860 there were more than 50,000 small landholders farming there, producing yams, breadfruit, and other plants for local consumption.

Although the issue of slavery roused passions in this country, it was but a part of a broader controversy. Slavery had been chosen, as it were, by the contestants as the field of battle on which to draw up all the ranks of dissension.

Ever since the deliberations over the future Constitution of the Union, representatives of the several states had faced the same issue: whether agricultural or commercial interests should dominate the policies of the Union. The issue divided the country into sections. In a federal state, this tendency bore the seeds of a schism. The split first came to light at the Louisiana Purchase. Then, the prospect of an unexplored and fabulously wealthy western territory opening for settlement and exploitation put into motion competition between North and South for the organization of these territories. One or the other would be strengthened politically.

The virgin lands in the West invited farmers whose produce would be floated down the Mississippi to the Gulf of Mexico; the type and character of cultivation would be dictated by the climate, soil, and distance from favorable markets. In this respect westerners would oppose policies favorable to the East and eastern creditors; their interests would parallel those of the South. But if the West did not adopt slavery, it would go against a plantation-dominated domestic policy. The question of whether the West would support the North or South hinged ultimately on whether it would establish its economy on principles of slave or free labor. The choice between the two alternatives was to determine the future of the United States.

Garrison's abolitionism loaded the controversy with moral and religious dynamite, reducing the chances for a compromise. When he mobilized public opinion behind him, reconciliation was impossible. The South prepared for a struggle; looked for its northern allies in political realists, exporters, and shippers; and relied on those anxious to preserve the Union, workers fearful of competition, and the efficacy of prejudice.

In this manner, emancipation of the slaves moved into the forefront of the controversy between white Americans.

Garrison's propaganda was restricted in two ways. He was harassed by outside interference, and by his own refusal to admit Negro groups into his fold. This he did partly because many of his followers, though execrating slavery, would not associate with Negroes. He took a negative stand to keep the moral character of abolitionism intact. "... The anti-slavery cause," he wrote, "both religiously and politically, has transcended the ability of the sufferers from American slavery and prejudice ... to keep pace with it."

With Garrison's figure on the scene, the conspiracies of

slaves discovered by the planters of the South had a new villain—the abolitionist. In fact, abolitionist propaganda did activate white sympathies with the slaves, and some white men were found active in Negro plots.

Louisiana reported several conspiracies and rebellions in which whites were involved. On Christmas Eve of 1836, a plot was discovered in Jackson in which forty Negroes and two white men, one of them an overseer, were said to have participated. The white men were promptly hanged.

In July of 1835, in Livingston, Mississippi, two Negroes had been arrested on suspicion of plotting an insurrection, but had been discharged. The next day they were rearrested; they had allegedly acknowledged their part in a conspiracy. How much truth there was in the charge could never be found out because the mob took them out of prison and hanged them. Meanwhile, a rumor spread around Livingston that a nationwide conspiracy had taken place. It was claimed that white men had incited the slaves to revolt. Some implicated white men fled and others were forced to leave, but a certain Mitchell, a blacksmith in Livingston, was hanged. In Vicksburg, Mississippi, the populace sought out several gamblers and suspicious men who were said to have been involved in slave plots. Five of them barricaded themselves in a house, but the mob stormed it and captured them. They swore to leave the county for good, and were released except for the Earl brothers. The mob tortured one of the Earls so cruelly that he committed suicide. His brother was found guilty the next day and executed.

The New York *Evening Star*, relating these rather confused events, added: "Some excesses have been committed, but it is only necessary to visit Mississippi to be of the opinion that they are enterprising, intelligent, magnanimous and as chivalric, as any within the United States . . ."

John Vindover, a white carpenter, stood before the court of Fairfax County, Virginia, in 1833, suspected of inciting Negroes to revolt. He was told to quit the town.

Near Lynchburg, in the same state, a white man was seized in 1835. He had attempted to incite Negroes to revolt and was hanged. Another white man suspected of the same crime was arrested in the neighborhood of Charleston, South Carolina.

A huge conspiracy was detected in Iberville, Louisiana, in 1840. It was alleged that four hundred slaves had taken part in it. Twenty slaves were sentenced and executed. According to the report, "four white abolitionists" were implicated. Their fate has not been recorded.

In St. Martin and St. Landry parishes of Louisiana, 1840, the militia arrested two white men in the same year. Negroes denounced them as having approached them with plots. Since only Negro witnesses sustained the accusation, the two suspects were lashed and released upon the promise to leave the place forever.

In Augusta, Georgia, a white teacher by the name of Hawes was found to have been involved in a conspiracy for which one Negro slave was executed in February, 1841.

And so on, the contemporary press bears report after report of frustrated plots all over the South, and strict retribution to the unfortunate suspects.

However, neither the number of plots and rebellions nor their alleged size exhibit any spectacular growth of the spirit of revolt among the slaves because of the antislavery movements in the North.

On the sea, it was different. There, the changing times left their mark on the treatment of mutinous slaves. Haiti, and the islands of the British West Indies, received mutineers with cheers and heroes' welcome instead of with the hangman's noose, as had been the case before abolition.

Yet, while at sea, the seamen's laws still applied to slaves who were mutineers. The conflict between what was right on shore and right at sea in several cases had national and international implications.

On October 15, 1841, the United States brig *Creole* of Richmond, Virginia, commanded by Captain Ensor, set sail from Hampton Roads to New Orleans, loaded with tobacco and a shipment of 150 slaves. The slaves were the property of a certain McCargo, a trader, whose men were in charge of handling and guarding the slaves on board. On Sunday night, November 7, nineteen slaves rebelled, killing one of the trader's henchmen, wounding the captain, seizing all the arms, and subduing the rest of the crew. These slaves ordered officers and crew of the *Creole* to steer the vessel to a British port or else be thrown overboard. The ship was landed at Nassau. The American consul there was informed by customs officials of the arrival. He promptly requested the arrest and extradition of the Negroes on charges of mutiny and murder. He also insisted that the slaves were cargo, and as such should be handled according to the requirements of the bill of lading; that is, they should be turned over to the trader's commissioners in the port. News of the event having spread in Nassau, large demonstrations were held demanding the release of the Negroes. The British authorities yielded and freed all but the nineteen defendants, since slavery was not recognized in the territory. Furthermore, the authorities refused to extradite the nineteen mutineers. Because British law prohibited slave trade and had made it a punishable offense, it was held that the nineteen Negroes had acted in rightful self-defense.

Another case of mutiny on the high seas brought on diplomatic complications and became a controversial political issue, resulting in several years of political wrangling. This was the so-called *Amistad* case.

On August 29, 1839, Captain Thomas R. Gidney, on patrol along the shore of Long Island with his brig *Washington*, found a ship at anchor between Montauk Point and Gardiners Island in Block Island Sound. He dispatched Lieutenant Richard W. Meade with six armed men in a boat to examine the ship's papers and cargo. Climbing on board, the sailors were met by a grotesque scene: the crew of Negroes was dressed in colored silk material, which was also lying around the deck shredded in some quantity, obviously part of the ship's cargo. A large number of other Negroes were lying on deck, wasted away to mere skeletons.

The ship was of Spanish entry, hailing from Havana. She had originally set sail under the command of Captain Ramon Ferrar for Guanaja, a small island in the Caribbean. Her cargo was slaves, belonging to the captain.

The slaves mutinied, killed the captain and cook, and ordered the sailors to set sail for Africa. The sailors steered southeast by daylight, but changed the course at night. After several days the *Amistad* landed to lay in food and water, on what the sailors knew must have been American soil.

Lieutenant Meade signaled Captain Gidney to plough alongside the *Amistad*. Hearing the story, the Captain decided to escort the ship to New London. There the Negroes were promptly jailed to await trial. The local abolitionists raised a clamor against the possibility of the federal courts delivering the defendants to foreign slave traders. Information was received that the papers of the ships had been falsified to show that the Negroes had been born slaves in Cuba, or imported before slave trade there was officially prohibited.

The truth was that a Portuguese slaver had landed them a short time before in Havana. If they had been enslaved contrary to the laws of Spain, then they must be considered free and liberated.

Outrage and excitement prevailed in Connecticut over the prospect that the U.S. government might conceivably be lending its laws and military forces to the enslavement of free men. It was possible that the violence of the Negroes was an act of self-defense, an act of protest against being kept unlawfully enslaved.

A public subscription was begun to collect funds for a lawyer's fee so that the Negroes might have a fair trial. News of the case seeped to Washington.

Señor A. Calderon, minister of Spain to Washington, demanded the immediate release of ship and cargo, including the slaves. He referred to the treaty of 1795: under its terms, all ships rescued out of the hands of pirates on the high seas ought to be restored entirely to the proprietors. The minister also asked for extradition, for the ship had been sailing between two Spanish harbors, and murder had been committed on board under the sovereignty of Spain.

The District Court of Connecticut ordered all the *Amistad* slaves born in Africa to be freed. One slave was born in Cuba, and was therefore "kidnapped" to safety by local Negroes. The *Amistad* was subsequently sold for salvage.

In 1841, the U.S. Supreme Court stated that the Negroes on board the *Amistad* had never been lawfully slaves, and consequently could not be considered pirates.

The Spanish government changed its claim to one of indemnification, and in 1858, President Buchanan recommended to Congress that indemnification be paid to the owners of the vessel. No payment was ever made.

Though the abolitionist trend was not responsible for any

broad increase in the number of revolts in the South, escape attempts became more frequent.

In Virginia, slaveowners asked for state intervention, because slaves jumped ships in northern ports and disappeared. In Georgia, Negroes planned to overpower the crew of a British steamship, the *William Gatson,* upon her arrival in St. Mary's. Unfortunately, the ship was delayed, and because the Negroes had no jobs to do in the harbor, there was an inquiry which led to the discovery of the plot and the arrest of its participants.

In July, 1845, a long column of black people gathered from the Maryland counties of Charles, Prince George, and St. Mary's, setting out to "march to free Pennsylvania." The group of about seventy-five was led by one huge Negro armed with a long sword. Another had a gun, a third a pistol, and the rest carried clubs. They were still fifty miles from the Pennsylvania border when an alerted white posse caught up with them, arriving from several directions; the whites set on the Negroes, massacred many of them, and jailed thirty-one in Rochester, Virginia. One of the slaves was sentenced to be hanged, the rest to be sold out of the state by their masters.

Another large-scale attempt at escape to freedom was organized in 1849 by Lew Cheney, an intelligent young slave in Louisiana. This time, Mexico was the destination of the expedition. Cheney visited many plantations in Rapides and Avoyelles parishes, near Alexandria, Louisiana, and exhorted the slaves to run away. A large number of blacks assembled in the depths of a swamp and brought with them corn gathered from the fields and bacon filched from smokehouses.

Cheney, who had conceived the plot, then changed his mind and betrayed it, making it seem worse than it was: he informed the planters that the plan provided for an armed attack on them and their families and on all whites in the area. The whites surrounded the swamp, captured the blacks, and drove them in chains to Alexandria, where they were hanged. The aroused whites then went on to attack peaceful Negroes sleeping in their cabins and carried them off to prison to hang them too. However, the military on the Texan border were notified and opened the prison, demolishing the gallows. Lew Cheney assumed another name and disappeared from Louisiana.

The organized escape of slaves from the states of the upper South to the North and eventually to Canada soon developed into a very effective form of harassment by the northern abolitionists. By draining the ranks of slaves and providing exile for the boldest of the Negroes, the escapes caused a decrease in rebellions and were said to have become the "safety valve of the South."

Levi Coffin, a young white merchant of Newport, Indiana, organized an escape route from Virginia to assist relatives of Negroes freed by Quakers to join their families in Indiana. Coffin put a sportsman's zeal into his efforts and was later called informally the "president of the Underground Railroad." Quaker groups assisted fugitives once they arrived in a free state by pointing out their route from station to station towards Canada. Such fugitives were not secure from being kidnapped by agents of slaveholders working in the free states. Care also had to be taken not to arouse the hostility of prejudiced northern whites, particularly workingmen, to the practice of importing Negroes. Many Quakers were hesitant about lending their help to this system of escape, because they did not wish to become accomplices in breaking the laws of the land to further what was morally right.

The crucial section of the escape route lay in the South. There, the risks were undertaken by Negroes, slave and free. Fugitives moved in the dead of night and hid during the day. Hiding places had to be spaced a night's walking distance from each other. The way had to be cleared to ferries across rivers, cooperative ferrymen had to be found, food given or sold. The fugitive had to be sure he could rely on the men to whom he was entrusting his life and freedom. Such information was collected and conveyed by free Negroes to slaves ready to undertake the venture. Steady escape routes were established from Kentucky and Virginia across the Ohio River; from Maryland through Pennsylvania and New York to Canada; on the Atlantic Coast, from Florida to Delaware and further North via ships in which slaves were concealed.

For a time, there was no massive sympathy in the North for organized slave escapes. The same groups who opposed the abolitionists also disapproved of this method of attacking southern slaveholders. Disrespect for the laws of the land could not be supported by law-abiding citizens; slavery was a fact of life and should be altered only through constitutional means. Then there was the matter of the inviolability of rights of property. The slaves were the property of the people of the South. Those who helped them became accomplices in theft. Hostility to slavery was mollified by a distrust of Negroes, but so long as these Negro fugitives proceeded to Canada, no strong prejudice was formed against them.

The South could not let such assaults on its private property pass without resolute action. A law of 1793 had empowered the slaveholder to bring back fugitive slaves, and to seek the assistance of the local authority in this legal aim; but it contained no provision for punishment of those who helped slaves escape or interfered with the owners' attempts to apprehend him. Congress could not deny protection for the right of property. In 1850 it passed legislation providing severe punishment, and liability for damages, for those individuals who promoted the breach of property rights in slaves. It gave power to the owner of slaves or his agent to seek assistance of the local federal authority in the return of the escapee, once the identity of the escaped slave had been certified.

The new federal law supporting slavery caused widespread resentment. It imposed on the authorities of free states the duty of giving assistance in hunting out and carrying off its residents. The law was held immoral by many, and consequently null and void or unenforceable against the will of the citizenry.

Rumors spread that slave hunters were roaming the countryside and giving false affidavits leading to the reenslavement of free Negroes and Negroes long residents of the northern states. Alarm grew to hostility to slaveholders among respectable citizens: the law of 1850 represented for them but one stage in the thrust of the South for supremacy over the states of the North. The law of 1850 had another disturbing provision: it stipulated that new states could be admitted to the Union in the future with or without slavery, as their constitutions might provide at the time of admission. This clause practically invalidated the Missouri Compromise. Indeed, another law in 1854 expressly repealed the Compromise. It described the rule of thumb for organizing the Kansas and Nebraska territories, referring the question of slavery within their borders to the citizens themselves. Despite the excitement that these measures provoked, and the fear of southern predominance current in the North, the majority of the United States approved the developments.

Democratic candidates were elected president in 1852 and 1856.

On top of this series of measures strengthening the voice of the South in the Union, the Supreme Court in 1857 struck down the provisions of the Missouri Compromise in the Dred Scott case, ruling that it had been unconstitutional since its inception.

If law cannot rely on a substantial mass of citizens for its execution, its power fails. Disapproval of law becomes respectable and may in the end become shared by even those who are called on to execute it. Lawlessness is thus tolerated. If public disapproval stems from a sectional conviction that the law is wrong, then the unity of the country may be imperiled.

So the North began to reason in the 1850s. The practice of slave hunting with official assistance in its territories provoked riotous protest.

In many cases, through subscription among both whites and Negroes, communities bought slaves from their rightful owners to save their return into slavery, especially if the slave had a family or job. At times, public outrage united a whole town against the enforcement of the law, as in Boston in May, 1854.

The U.S. marshal in that town arrested one Anthony Burns, a Negro of about thirty-seven working for Coffin Pitts, a clothing dealer. Charles I. Suttle of Alexandria, Virginia, claimed the Negro as a fugitive slave. Suttle had found the slave through an agent. The agent vouched for Burns' identity before a federal judge, and was thereupon given the legal right to take the Negro man back to Virginia.

Anthony Burns insisted that he had not run away, but had overslept in a ship that had landed him in Boston. He had immediately been willing to return to his master, but had been told that Mr. Suttle would have first to prove the slave's identity before he could return.

A rumor spread in Boston that a slave hunter had kidnapped a Negro resident, and was to carry him back to slavery. "Shall he be plunged into hell of Virginia slavery by a Massachusetts judge of probate?" the abolitionists asked the people of Boston.

The appeal was responded to by the most respectable and highly placed citizens of Boston. Thomas Wentworth Higginson headed the effort. Peaceful ladies in town alarmed friends outside of Boston to join in the protest. "Do stir up Weymouth, for if this man is allowed to go back, there is no antislavery in Massachusetts. We may as well disband at once if our meetings and papers are all talk," so wrote Mrs. Wendell Phillips to Anne and Deborah Weston of Weymouth.

The abolitionists began a legal fight, filing a lawsuit for $10,000 damages, charging conspiracy of the slaveowner and his agent in the arrest of a free citizen of the state of Massachusetts. While the court was in session, public meetings were held demanding the release of Burns. A mob stormed the prison to free him. The windows of the courthouse were stoned and broken and in the scuffle, a pistol was fired, and a man was stabbed and died. The Mayor of Boston asked the military commander to protect the court building, and troops hastily surrounded the building.

Meanwhile, men of practical sense were busy with the owner's agent negotiating to buy Anthony Burns. The price was set at $1,200 and a collection started. Time was short, the court having set a deadline of midnight for the freeing of Burns; otherwise he would be escorted to a ship in the harbor and returned to Virginia. At midnight the collection was still $400 short. Burns was returned to his master in Alexandria.

Northerners collected passengers for the "Underground Railroad" in states where gradual emancipation was fairly popular. The planters stated that they lost $200,000 worth of slaves yearly, and that on a single day, fifty-five slaves had been estimated to have crossed the Ohio River.

Miss Delia Webster of Vermont was accustomed to recruiting passengers with blatant lack of secrecy in Kentucky. In 1852, she was arrested for these activities. Gallant Kentuckians intervened with the governor of the state for her pardon. Her companion, Calvin Fairbanks, did not fare so well. He was sentenced to fifteen years in prison. Undaunted, Miss Webster did not refrain from abusing this gallantry. Two years later, in 1854, she appeared again in Kentucky for the same purposes, but was promptly detected and forced to leave the state.

Kentucky ran into serious trouble with the free state of Michigan, when Kentucky agents entered the latter state to retrieve fugitive slaves. In one case, six runaways were captured in Marshall, Michigan, and led to the local magistrate. A mob of free Negroes formed, assisted by some runaway slaves and white people, and intercepted the Kentucky agents with guns, clubs, and other weapons. The mob staged an open-air meeting, debating what to do with the captives. The resolve was to send the Kentucky slaveowners home without their slaves.

"The master finds himself a prisoner and the servant set free," complained one of the planters, back in his home state.

Escape of slaves became popular among whites in the North, with such tales as these to fire a sense of bravado. It became a matter of good citizenship or Christian charity to be active in the movement.

Many free Negroes risked their own enslavement while

guiding fugitives through the South. Cases of real heroism were common. Most famous among them was Harriet Tubman, herself a fugitive from Maryland. Born in 1820 in Maryland, Harriet Tubman had almost killed an overseer on her plantation who had struck her in the head with a two-pound weight. She then flew the state, returning to lead her sister and two children to freedom. On a subsequent trip, she brought out her brother and took along other slaves as well. From then on, she made the trip back and forth regularly, bringing slaves out of the South and accompanying them to Canada. Her spirit was indomitable and her physical energy endless. If she found a slave lagging on the strenuous night walks, endangering the lives and freedom of all the other fugitives, she would raise a pistol, shouting "you go or die." It was said that she led about 300 Negroes out of the South in nineteen trips.

The "Underground Railroad" became legendary. There is no way of estimating the number of slaves who traveled it to freedom. The slaveholders exaggerated their losses, claiming that 100,000 slaves had deserted between 1810 and 1850, amounting to a value of 300 million dollars.

Ohio abolitionists boasted that they alone had helped 40,000 Negro slaves to escape. These slaves came from the states of the upper South; the census for this period shows a decrease in their number. However, these were also the states that supplied Negroes to the Deep South, and there is no way of telling how many went this way to freedom or that way to slavery.

The drain of slaves from the South was responsible for lively political activity there. Mass escape contributed to a scarcity of slaves, but the expansion of cotton growing also required more slave labor than, as one southern paper wrote, "can now possibly be acquired by natural increase or from those home sources which have hitherto yielded but a scarce supply." The "home sources" meant the Virginia and Maryland breeding grounds.

The problem was a serious one for the South. A solution had often been proposed, even in Thomas Jefferson's time, and by him: the acquisition of Cuba. President Buchanan liked the idea, for it could easily be presented as the best means of halting the clandestine trade in slaves, of which Cuba was the center. Feelers sent out to Spain determined the price was $100 million.

The shortage of slaves and a rising demand caused their prices to soar. A strong Negro sold for $1,835, a Negro fresh from Africa for $1,000. Small planters could not afford to pay these prices. They became the most vocal exponents in urging a revival of the old plan of setting up a plantation empire including Central America and even Brazil. Large planters had a more modest plan: the acquisition of huge fields for plantations in the territory bordering on the Caribbean and the Gulf of Mexico. These new lands would supply the world with cotton, rice, coffee, sugar, and other staples, produced by slave labor "for the benefit of the whole world."

Planters and merchants in the South held frequent meetings to deliberate on the best means of solidifying the influence of the South on federal policy-making against the increasing aggressiveness of the North. Appeals went to northern merchants who made profits on southern exports. They were asked to support the various schemes for territorial acquisition and the reopening of the slave trade. "Southern Wealth-Northern Profit," ran one of the slogans of the South.

It now seems an almost insane abuse of political realities for the South to have advocated the cancellation of the prohibition on foreign slave trade, considering how close the time was to the actual abolition of slavery in the United States. In the 1850s, however, slavery was actually experiencing its second boom. On the other hand, a new political entity appeared in the North and was grouping powerful interests behind it, with the program of halting expansion of slavery: the Republican Party. Its candidate in 1856 was a famed explorer of California; its campaign slogan was "free labor, free Kansas, and Fremont."

In the late '50s, convention after convention gathered in the southern states, made up of all sorts of professional and business interests. They all strongly endorsed the admission of slavery to the new states. Several delegates stressed that such resolutions made sense only if there were Negro slaves to settle there. Without reviving slave trade the extension of slavery to the West would remain a dead-letter issue not worth fighting for. Thus the Southern Commercial Convention, meeting at Vicksburg in 1859, voted a request for the repeal of laws that prohibited foreign slave trade.

Jefferson Davis took a stand for repeal at the Democratic State Convention at Jackson, Mississippi.

But the question of slave trade split the delegates at all these conventions. An Arkansan delegate went on record that she would "rather suffer herself to be torn by wild horses before trading again in African Negroes."

In fact, the governments and courts in the South took no action to enforce the ban on the import of slaves from abroad. This attitude amounted to the actual nullification of the federal law.

X

SLAVERY: THE DIVIDING ISSUE

"The Southern states very seriously contemplate to annex Cuba, Mexico, and some Caribbean islands and reduce their population to slavery."

So the British envoy to Washington reported to his superiors in 1856.

The annexation of Mexico was often in the minds of American explorers and adventurers of that time. They were flamboyant imperialists at heart, but they dignified their spirit under the glorious title of Manifest Destiny.

The South wished to see the acquisition of Mexico serve its own destiny too, by extending the reaches of the slave and plantation systems there. Thus its own economic and political power within the Union would be increased.

The power of the South had been steadily growing. The cotton crop trebled in value from 1850 to 1860, from $78 to $236 million a year. The South still hoped to limit the imbalance between herself and the North in terms of population, industrial wealth, capital, and farming; but without the support of additional territories provided with the interests of plantation economy and slave labor, the balance became increasingly unfavorable.

The rapid development of the country continued to probe the sensitive issue of the relative power of its two sections. Texas and California were added to the Union; huge, newly acquired territories in the Far West were organized. The Wilmot Proviso was introduced by Congressman David Wilmot to prohibit slavery in the new territories as they were admitted into the Union. The North feared the same eventuality that it had been warning of since 1820, at the time of the Missouri compromise. An embittered northern congressman, Bayard Taylor of New York, had put these fears into eloquent words then:

> On implied power to acquire territory by treaty, you raise an implied right to erect it onto States, and imply a compromise by which slavery is to be established and slaves represented in Congress. Is this just? Is this fair? Where will it end? . . . Your lust of acquisition is not yet satiated. You must have the Floridas. Your ambition rises. You covet Cuba, and obtain it; you stretch your arms to the other islands in the Gulf of Mexico, and they become yours. Are the millions of slaves inhabiting those countries to be incorporated into the Union and represented in Congress? Are the freemen of the old States to become the slaves of the representatives of foreign slaves?

The thrust of northern sentiment which produced the Wilmot Proviso was stalled in the Senate. Nevertheless, the poor long-range prospects for the expansion of her system filled the South with a brand of pessimism which made her citizens listen more intently to the rising clamor of extremists advocating secession. South Carolina led the trend, actually hesitating as to whether to secede alone or wait for other states to join her. A southern union was envisioned, encompassing Cuba and Mexico. Who knew, even Brazil might be added to a gigantic conglomeration of plantation states relying on slave labor.

These serene dreams of a slave empire stretching southwards were often interrupted by the intrusion of a brutal reality—as, when in 1856, some slaves of Texas took their fate into their own hands and resolved to march across the border out of the United States to Mexico and freedom.

What actually happened in this case is not easy to determine from the available reports in such papers as the Galveston *News*. At the time the southern newspapers played down any news of slave unrest if they printed it at all. There was a need to avoid sensationalism of any kind, lest the abolitionist interests in the North should take advantage of it for propaganda purposes.

What is known of the plot is this: During a meeting of the citizens of Colorado County, Texas, to investigate an alleged slave conspiracy, it was revealed that the local slaves had organized into something like military formations, elected captains and officers, agreed on secret signals and passwords, and had set the date of an insurrection for September 6, 1856. Late in the night, the warriors were to take the white population by surprise, kill all the men and elderly women, and spare the young females for their wives. They would then plunder all households, collect all arms, and force their way through Texas to Mexico.

The citizens' meeting deliberated on these "facts" produced by a committee for their consideration. Moderation in dealing with the slaves was decided upon—perhaps because the price of slaves was high and their loss would be too large for the citizens who owned them—but some exemplary punishments were to be meted out. Thus, although it was asserted at this meeting that over 200 Negroes had committed crimes punishable with death, only three ringleaders were condemned at the trial on September 5. Three more slaves were hanged and two whipped to death a week later.

Rumors of conspiracies such as this one continued to spread, and the irritation of the citizenry of Texas increased. The public saw the connivance of white abolitionists behind the conspiracies, and dealt ruthlessly with suspected abolitionists, or anyone in favor of emancipation. Toward the end of the 1850s excitement in Texas had reached a level of public hysteria again. A series of suspicious fires blazed devastatingly at Dallas, Denton, Waxahachie, Kaufman, and other places. According to Rupert N. Richardson, a historian of the state, the public expected some great awakening of the rebellious spirit:

> It was charged that the fires were the work of certain Abolitionists who proposed to demoralize the people by fire and assassination, making ready for a revolt of the slaves that soon was to follow.

There were the usual distorted stories of plots circulated: uprisings, mass poisonings, arsonists, without much evidence of their existence in fact. Yet, in 1860, three more Negroes were hanged in Dallas "in the presence of a large crowd," and three white men in Fort Worth, "because they were tampering with slaves."

In the older states of the Union, courts had shown reticence in sentencing white citizens who had allegedly taken part in slave plots, usually requiring only that the offender leave the state. In the western localities, no community feeling had developed as to the sanctity of the white citizen which might give the benefit of the doubt to the accused, or weigh the evidence in his favor more carefully.

Texas and Louisiana appeared to be the principal trouble spots all during the years preceding the Civil War.

Tennessee, from 1856 on, experienced a number of suspected slave "conspiracies," said to be instigated by abolitionist agitators. "A terrible example should be made," the Clarksville (Tenn.) *Jeffersonian* insisted in its issue of December 3, 1856, "in every neighborhood where the crime can be established and if necessary, let every tree of the county bend with negro meat."

A conspiracy in Tennessee was in fact discovered in November of 1857: sixty slave laborers at the Cumberland Iron Works had been involved; four were condemned to hang, and the mob hanged five others.

The Montgomery (Alabama) *Advertiser* of December 18 of the same year was equally bloodthirsty:

> Simply tarring and feathering and ejecting an Abolitionist is but a child's remedy. Better to hang two or three Abolitionists than to be in continual danger of having our throats cut.

The Missouri *Democrat* lamented in its issue of December 4, 1857 that such states as Texas and Arkansas, so far immune from "abolition contagion" had now become the scene of slave disturbances. This boded ill for those states that had suffered under their impact often in the past. "What may we expect," the paper asked, "who are infested with them, all round us? It becomes us to be as wise as serpents and as harmless as doves, lest we alarm the Freedom Shriekers of the North."

A pessimistic account of the situation in Kansas, written in 1856 by a certain E. W. Clark, found its way into the State Papers of Virginia on December 25, 1856:

> The Southern emigrants are leaving by hundreds. I think from the moving of the waters that the South will abandon that

land to the North, and strike for something south to enlarge their favored institution.

But the writer predicted nothing good to come for the South:

> I think they will soon find that they have all that they can attend to at home. The slaves are in the state of insurrection all over the country. Every paper brings us accounts of their plots for a general uprising. They cannot accomplish that object at present. This ball is moving and they have heard the sound, and they are ready to keep it a moving as their rising content seems to indicate they will surely accomplish their object before long.

At approximately the same time, there was reported in the New York papers a rebellion in New Orleans, with twenty slaves hanged as a result; details had been supplanted by violent denunciations of the "murderers in the guise of philanthropy," meaning the abolitionists and their secret supporters, whom the southerners deemed responsible for all upheavals. The real enemy was now these northern white men, but they were remote from punishment and hard to lay hands on. Another group could be persecuted instead: the free Negroes, who were isolated by perversely refined legal restrictions and by the suspicion of the general public. They were the perennial whipping boys when all other scapegoats failed. In Tennessee, the legislature narrowly defeated a bill that stipulated the sale into slavery of any free Negro who had not left the state by May of 1861. Similar alternatives were proposed in other states; but it was another development that in fact threatened to undermine the livelihood of the free Negro and compel him to leave his state, or starve, or enter slavery again.

As the free Negro became increasingly irritating to the whites, the slaves slowly pushed him out of his customary manner of livelihood. Masters, especially in the border states, found it more remunerative to lend their slaves to craftsmen or to contractors for roadbuilding, and receive wages for their labor, than to have them work at home. A small part of the wage was allotted to the slave as incentive money. The custom of employing slaves in such a way was quite old, but it had come into more common practice since the industrialization of the South had opened new mines and sent railway spurs into the mountains. Slaves enjoyed more freedom at such jobs than in the fields; they had the additional advantage of learning a skill. Though they still could be sold at a moment's notice, such assignments gave them a measure of self-respect.

Faced with cheap competition, the status of the free Negro rapidly deteriorated. South Carolina and Georgia created legal provisions by which it was assumed that every Negro was a slave unless he proved the contrary: the freedom of a Negro was made to hinge on the existence of his papers of manumission; should he lose them—or a malevolent hand tear them to shreds—he was incapable of proving his free status.

A measure taken in Arkansas illustrates how unpopular the free Negro became before the Civil War: in 1859, the state decreed that all free persons of color should sell their belongings and leave the state by New Year's Day of the next year. Those who failed to comply would be hired out for a year. Louisiana followed suit, but having 18,000 free Negroes and still needing their skills, its ordinances remained only on paper.

The fervor of the northern abolitionists may have had little effect on the slaves, but the restlessness of their masters sooner or later produced the same state of mind in the

Negroes. At this time the white people were in great excitement and weariness of spirit; the Mexican War had stirred in the slaves the hope of change or escape into the region of the Gulf of Mexico. The great western migrations, though distant, also sent a current of agitation through the slave quarters.

There are several colorful descriptions of life on the plantations and the physical and mental state of the Negro in the last years before the Civil War. John B. Cade of Southern University of Scotlandsville, Louisiana, and his students, interviewed eighty-two former slaves and their children. As published in the *Journal of Negro History* in 1935, these personal memories confirm the reports of travelers from the North and abroad; yet they have an insight into both the vitality and anguish of the slave's life.

One former slave from Louisiana described eating habits on his plantation:

> We children ate at the big house. Our food was put in one big trough together; syrup, milk and other odd food were mixed in this trough and we children stood around eating like little pigs.

On the plantations, some old woman, too old for field work, usually fed the children.

> The food was poured into a dugout made from the body of a tree. They ate with their hands or fingers and put their little heads down into the trough to sip up the milk or pot licker. The more enterprising children went to the creek and got mussel shell for spoons.

"Some slaves got plenty to eat; some did not. Some masters wouldn't give dey slaves enough to eat," said one of the interviewed. Most agreed. A favorite slave received permission from the master to hunt; he was supposed to offer to the master's family the game he bagged. Some of it he received back as a reward and so could improve his diet with a little variety.

Little boys wore heavy linen dresses and "Wahoo" hats made from the bark of trees. Men's clothes were made of burlap. In general the material made at home into garments was heavy-grade cotton.

No matter how large a family had grown, it occupied but a single room in the cabin.

A slave marriage came about in this way: A man slave would tell his master of his intended bride and await consent. Sometimes a master exchanged slaves and let the man take his wife with him to his own master's place. Some men claimed several wives. It made little difference whether or not a man and his so-called wife lived in the same hut. The man was not responsible for the support of his wife and children anyway; they all belonged to the owner.

Some masters encouraged celebrations at weddings and contributed extra food to the event or made it memorable by a sort of rite, especially if the master had picked the girl for the slave or had given him the woman of his choice.

In some cases, both man and wife had to indulge in some silly ritual, such as jumping over a broom together, before being considered married. The master was also sometimes called upon to read one or two verses from the Bible.

Religious worship was relegated to underground meetings. If slaves wanted to sing or pray, they stole off to the woods to do so. If a master heard the singing, he might fetch his whip and whip the slaves all the way home. But this would not stop the meetings; when one hiding place was discovered, they could easily find another one.

An old woman, a former slave, described one form of secret worship:

> If dey had prayer meeting dey would turn a wash pot down to ketch the sound to keep the marsters from hearing um. Didn't have no church; sometimes a white man would go around through the quarters preaching to the slaves, telling dem to obey dey marsters and missus and dey would be good to dem.

Another woman remarked that preachers didn't have a chance to speak at prayer meetings; everyone else was too anxious to inject his own opinions into the proceedings.

In another variation on religious camouflage the slaves would wet old quilts, and rags, hang them up, and huddle behind them to pray, preach, or sing. The sound of their voices would be muffled by the sodden cloth.

There were still the gala Sunday occasions, when the fear of the whip, the monotony of work, and the constant suspicions of the whites were forgotten:

> They had socials or balls occasionally. The dances that were done in those days were quadrille and other square dances. An accordion often furnished the music. On rare occasions there were fiddles, fifes, and sometimes a drum.

The past, of course, often becomes a brighter color in reminiscence: To one old lady, the very idea of slavery itself did not seem to be too bad in retrospect. Born in Athens, Louisiana, she said she had seen more slavery since emancipation than before. But for most of the Negroes interviewed by Cade, time could not make up for the sense of injury, nor could good treatment, sufficient food, or merry Sundays: "We were sold just as our masters would see fit,

228

and many of us were driven and kicked about like dogs," one old man recalled.

The worst indignity was the lash.

Travelers had told of terrible beatings by brutal overseers, but one short anecdote should stand alone to show to what extremes fear of the whip could carry its victim:

> Betty was brought from Alabama and sold in Louisiana. She was very high tempered. She weighed about 180 pounds. She was the mother of one child named Simon. She once got into dispute with Molly McAmore, tall with coal black hair, about the age of thirty. Betty struck Molly with her hoe, cutting the flesh from her face. Her punishment was so severe she would stand it no longer. She threw her little son, Simon, in the well. They whipped her terribly about the disappearance of the child. She would not tell where the child was. An old slave felt sorry for her and begged her to tell where the child was because he had heard the overseer say that night would be his last time to whip her because he was going to kill her. So she told him where her little son was. He rushed to the well and pulled him out. Tried by the court she was condemned to die. On the day she was hanged they asked her what she had to say. She only said, "I want to eat breakfast in hell tomorrow morning with Molly McAmore."

Many travelers witnessed in horror how hordes of slaves were driven to the Deep South from Maryland or Virginia, and remembered the scenes years later. One man recalled:

> Dey would carry them in droves just like dey do cattle and horse today. A man would be riding in front and one behind. Natchez, Mississippi, was one of the big slave markets. Dey would take chillum from dey mothers. Dey would examine men, women and chillum just like dey would cattle and horses before buying um. Sometimes dey would give $1500; $1800 for one slave.

Then there was the pathetic case of Mrs. Harriet Robinson, a Texas slave. Mrs. Robinson was sold four times. Being considered an excellent mother for breeding, she always brought high prices, was well cared for, and never whipped; she was constantly brokenhearted because of her degrading use and the fact that her children were always taken from her.

Slavery, the issue, increasingly became the crux of the controversy over a balance of power between North and South. Harriet Beecher Stowe's *Uncle Tom's Cabin* brought home to the people of the North the humiliations that the Negro had to bear as a slave in the South. Perhaps no book in history made such a powerful impact upon as large a public as did this novel.

In 1858, the Negro seemed for a moment to have gained a leader in rebellion even more powerful and subversive to the interests of the South than Mrs. Stowe's book.

The man was, of course, John Brown, to whom *Uncle Tom's Cabin* and all of the abolitionist propaganda were but empty words when action was needed to bring the time to a decision.

Brown had been born in Torrington, Connecticut, in 1800. His grandfathers on both sides had fought in the Revolutionary War. Brown inherited a stern Puritan temperament and some of the insanity which ran in both lines of his family.

Setting up as a tanner in Ohio, he married at twenty, moved to Richmond, Pennsylvania, in 1826, and had seven children by his first wife, five of them surviving their mother, who died in 1832. Brown married an eighteen-year-old girl from Meadville, Pennsylvania, the next year, and this girl stoically endured the idolatry with which the seven sons and six daughters born from this marriage surrounded their father.

Brown worshipped heroes, and every day he was home, gave family readings from the Psalms of David, from a history of Oliver Cromwell, or from Nat Turner's *Confessions*.

Brown dedicated his life to the liberation of the slaves. He did not believe, as many abolitionists did, that the slaveholder could be convinced by any moral or rational arguments to free slaves. In his view, slavery in the United States was already a war of one part of the population against another and, in war, force alone was effective. Only force could check the abuses of the slaveowners.

He moved as a warrior in four states, trying at the same time, and not always by irreproachable means, to support the large family he was raising in the spirit of great moral principles. In fact, his sons became the nucleus of his army of liberation.

In Kansas in 1856 Brown staged the first memorable raid based on the creed of terror. Kansas was then already a battlefield of pro- and antislavery guerrilla factions. With his four sons and two other men, he set on some poor whites from Tennessee, sitting peacefully in their cabin on the Pottawatomie Creek. His men killed five people and he lost one of his sons in the raid. Brown said the boy died for a sacred cause, though many people considered the death sheer murder on the part of the father.

Brown lost two other children, who died in his arms. He had no fear of death, and his disciples, uncritical of his methods, were totally devoted to him and to his cause. Highly educated northerners believed him to share in the pure moral qualities of Socrates, that he was possessed of a genius which was too much for him. "Nature," wrote Bronson Alcott, the transcendentalist, "was obviously intent in the making of him ... tall, eyes of deep gray, dauntless yet kindly; nose trenchant and Romanesque, set lips, his voice suppressed

231

yet metallic, decided mouth, power throughout. His flying beard gives the soldiery and the port of an apostle."

Ralph Waldo Emerson found him "a man to make himself felt wherever in the world courage and integrity are esteemed—the rarest of heroes, and yet a pure idealist." Lewis W. Washington, great-grandnephew of the first President and Brown's hostage at Harpers Ferry, said of him that he was

> the coolest and firmest man he ever saw in defying danger and death. With one son dead by his side, and another shot through, he felt the pulse of his dying son with one hand, and held his rifle with the other . . . his was the most determined face I ever beheld. His lips were like the lips of fate, and yet they met together as lightly as rose petals.

In 1858 Brown began planning a massive attack on slavery in Virginia. Working from the home in Rochester, New York, of Frederick Douglass, the one-time fugitive slave who became a great orator and Negro leader, Brown worked out a sort of Constitution for the territories to be liberated, which he intended to present to a convention of his followers for approval. Douglass later wrote that Brown's plan had much to recommend it, but, perhaps prudently, he refused to join in its execution.

Brown's "constitutional convention" was held in Chatham, Canada, not far from Detroit. Though there were at that time about 45,000 fugitive slaves living in freedom in Canada, only thirty-four Negroes participated in the meeting, with twelve whites, mostly of Brown's party.

Keeping the details of his plan secret, Brown solicited and received sums of money from important and respectable individuals for its execution. He bought some rifles and a large number of pikes. He decided on Harpers Ferry, a little town at the meeting point of the Shenandoah and Potomac rivers, as his jumping-off place.

In July, 1858, one of Brown's men leased the Kennedy farm, about five miles outside of Harpers Ferry, where Brown went with some of his followers and two female members of his own family to dispel suspicion. As the rebels gathered there, arms also arrived under the guise of farm tools.

On Sunday, October 16, at 8:00 A.M., Brown swept down on Harpers Ferry, cut the telegraph lines, seized the arsenal and the railroad station, and put sentries on the Potomac bridge. Some of his men rounded up slaveowners, took forty of them as hostages, and declared to the slaves that they were now free. For the occasion, the commander borrowed from Colonel Washington, one of the hostages, the historic sword which Frederick the Great had given to the Colonel's great-great uncle.

The continuation of Brown's plan called for a march to the Virginia mountains, bearing with them the food and arms confiscated from slaveholders' property and the armory. From their mountain hideout the guerrilla groups could swoop down on plantations, liberate their slaves, and move toward the heart of the South. Such panic and confusion would be created by their growing hordes that the slaveholders could do nothing but accept the fact that slavery ceased to exist.

John Brown held Harpers Ferry safely. The road to the mountains was free. His sons blindly accepted all their father's decisions, but his captains urged him to leave the town before reports reached authorities nearby who could alert the militia or the federal army. Yet Brown stalled. He let a train which had been held in the Harpers Ferry station for hours proceed to Maryland and, of course, there the word was spread of the sensational happenings at the little town.

Instead of fleeing, Brown remained in the engine house of the railroad station, where he entered into polite discussion with his hostages and fortified the structure against an attack which soon materialized and brought disaster to his plan.

On Monday afternoon, October 17, the militia from neighboring Charleston arrived. A few hours later a great force of militia from Baltimore reached Harpers Ferry followed by ninety U.S. marines who brought two field cannon with them. Altogether, 1,500 armed men converged on the town. At 7:00 P.M. the marines smashed the doors of the engine room, arrested the wounded John Brown and those of his band who had survived the preceding skirmishes.

Only one member of Brown's party escaped, Osborne P. Anderson, a Negro. All the rest were either shot and drowned on that day or later tried and hanged.

When all was over and he stood for trial in Charleston, on grounds of conspiracy, murder, and treason, Brown told the jury that he had had twenty-two men under his command, but that he had expected large reinforcements from other slave states, and also from the free states. He had thought it necessary only to seize the public arsenal and place them in the hands of Negroes and nonslaveholders, then he would be able to recruit his forces indefinitely.

When the court inquired why he had deviated from his avowed intent to flee to the mountains after his first success, Brown admitted that he had made a grave mistake, but that he had yielded to the wishes of his hostages, who had implored him not to drag them to the mountains. For this mistake he declared himself ready to take the consequences. And, since the cause they were to die for was a sacred one,

Brown had no regrets that his men were to die with him in atonement for his error in judgment.

John Brown did not comment on what might have been the real reason for his fatal blunder. He had been deeply disappointed that the slaves in and around Harpers Ferry had not quit their masters and flocked to the party that was bringing them freedom. He had wanted to wait until these slaves could escape to him under the protection of darkness. When none had come Sunday night, he wished to give them another chance on Monday. Without the cooperation of the slaves, his whole plan was foolish. It was built on the assumption that wherever the armed band went offering freedom to the slaves and the opportunity to fight for their fellows, Negroes would heed the call. Yet they had failed to come.

If the slaves around Harpers Ferry refused to join their liberators, how could Brown believe that his raids would be more successful further south?

Brown's legions had not materialized:

> And this is the only consolation I have to offer you in this disgrace [Governor Henry A. Wise addressed the citizens in Richmond] that the faithful slaves refused to take up arms against their masters; and those who were taken by force from their happy homes deserted their liberators as soon as they could dare to make the attempt. Not a slave around was found faithless.

Senator J. M. Mason, making his own investigation of the effect of the raid on the Negro population, complied in this judgment, concluding that "on the part of the negroes, it is certain that the only emotion evinced by them was alarm and terror and their only refuge was sought at their masters' homes."

The slaves' lack of response to Brown's raid was not an exceptional phenomenon. Not even the largest slave revolts succeeded in spreading to areas where the leader or his close associates were not known personally. Slaves would follow only men they trusted and who were able to exercise the sort of hypnotism that made them oblivious to fear. Denmark Vesey had prepared his revolt with patient strategy, selecting slaves who enjoyed the confidence of fellow Negroes on the plantation, and had proven their force of persuasion at Sunday meetings and barbecues. And Nat Turner's lieutenants had made no attempt to recruit leaders far from the Travis plantation. As a consequence, the slaves a short distance away had hidden from the rebels and refused to join.

Indeed, why should the slaves of Harpers Ferry have trusted a white man, a complete stranger? The local militia and the federal troops were powerful and close by; in comparison, the little band of whites and Negroes led by the man with the beard made no sense.

As was inevitably the case, however, the white population reacted with doubled vigilance in the wake of the raid. *The New York Times* reported from Richmond:

> The heavy property holders begin to see that the subject of slavery is destined to produce interminable strife in that State in the future, and materially decrease the value of property. Families are accordingly preparing to leave the State; panic pervades all classes of citizens; there is no freedom of speech; suspicion and distrust are abroad. The country, according to this representation, is in fact one degree removed from anarchy.

John Brown exhibited a dignified unconcern for his personal fate during the six weeks of his trial; he affirmed the ideals his life was dedicated to, even on the scaffold. "He was an apostle and a hero," said the French poet, Victor

Hugo, speaking for the great body of the liberal public in the North and in western Europe who protested his execution.

But the southern whites were aroused and stung by the glorification of this man. For them he was an archenemy, an adventurer and criminal trying to arm black slaves to massacre the whites. The rapid myth growing around John Brown outside the South gave credence to the extremists within who insisted that the Union threatened not only their property and the southern mode of life, but their own skins as well. Only secession was left as a reasonable path.

The emotional turmoil following John Brown's raid helped to sharpen further the political division of North and South and prepared for the ultimate break. Abolitionists in the North and secessionists in the South asserted their conviction that no coexistence was possible between the two regions.

The legal advantages won by the extension of the slavery concept to the West worked to the disadvantage of the slave system in practice. By 1860, the slaveholding citizens of the Kansas and Nebraska territories had in great part either left the region or sold their slaves away. This development, however, while appeasing the passive citizens in the North did not appease the moral passions of the abolitionists; and the latter had added a serious economic interest to their idealism.

By 1860, 400,000 slaves were living in southern towns, working not only in the iron mines and on the railroads, but in textile mills and other new light industries. Northern industrialists were jealous of the cheap slave labor available in the South, fearful of being underbid in prices, and hopeful that with emancipation a market of three million new customers might be created. Not all economic interests in the North favored abolition, however; many of the merchants and bankers who were involved in the overseas trade of cotton opposed it.

237

The substance of North-South animosity continued to focus on slavery as the most spectacular difference between the two ways of life. Yet the large majority of the population of the South had no economic interest in it. Six million whites inhabited the slaveholding states; only about 350,000 of them owned slaves, and most of these less than 10. Not more than 1,400 white men owned over 100 slaves each, and only 400 could be considered plantation aristocrats. However, the latter succeeded in having their own social and political vision accepted by the entire southern white population as its own. In all events, the southerner could now not give up that vision, for his identity had been established in it. "We are two peoples," Nathaniel Hawthorne said of the two ways of life.

The Republican Party was formed in 1854 with the intent of excluding slavery from the West. The southerners considered the new party as an organized attack on their way of life. Though ambiguously formulated, Lincoln's "House divided" speech made during the campaign of 1858 for the Senate had but a single meaning for the South:

> Either the opponents of slavery will arrest further spread of it, and place it where the public mind shall rest in the belief that it is in the course of ultimate extinction; or its advocates will push it forward, till it shall become alike lawful in all the States; old as well as new, North as well as South.

To the South, this was a declaration of war on its way of life, despite Lincoln's assurance that he would not expedite the final extinction of slavery in the states where it existed, but merely prevent its expansion.

The South reacted to Lincoln's election promptly. The legislature of South Carolina resolved to call a convention with the purpose of taking a stand on the event. Meeting on December 20, 1860, the convention unanimously passed a fateful resolution: it declared that the Union between the State of South Carolina and all other states was dissolved. On that day, the state flag floated from the houses of Charleston; cannons boomed, the church bells pealed, and the citizens, radiant with relief, hailed the secession. Few believed, however, that the action would lead to war either in South Carolina or in the ten other states that eventually seceded.

In a message to Congress on December 3 of that year, President Buchanan had explained that the southerner's state of mind could be attributed to the fear of slave insurrections caused by the activities of abolitionists: "Many a matron throughout the South retires at night in dread of what may befall herself and her children before the morning." In his Inaugural Address on March 4, Lincoln tried to reassure the failing ranks of southerners, stating that he had "no purpose, directly or indirectly, to interfere with the institution of slavery in the States where it exists."

Nevertheless, southern guns opened fire on Fort Sumter on April 12, and the Great Conflict began.

XI

THE NEGRO AWAITS HIS FATE

JEFFERSON DAVIS, before being elected president of the Confederacy, but after secession, feared a fifth column of slaves. He told his wife that "an immense standing army would be necessary if the slaves were to be kept in bondage."

The slaves' attitude was even more disconcerting, if one takes the testimony of Scipio, an old slave belonging to James R. Gilmore of South Carolina: "Dey'll fight wid only one hand. When dey fight de Norf wid the right hand, dey'll have to hold the nigga wid de leff."

However threatening such prophecies may have been, the white fears of Negro treachery during the war seem to have been misplaced; the planter went to war, and more often than not, entrusted his family to the domestic slaves.

Henry W. Grady, postwar editor of the *Atlanta Constitution,* wrote:

> A thousand torches would have disbanded the Southern army, but there was not one. For the blacks knew that they were being watched very closely . . . A beleaguered country, the Confederacy bristled with every gun and mortar she could build or run through the Union blockading squadron. A garrison, Dixie was armed to the teeth.

There were a few disturbances. In Georgia, a conspiracy was discovered in August, 1864. A people's court sentenced three Negroes to hang. A month later, in Amite County, Mississippi, it was reported that a crowd of Negroes, armed and singing, was marching towards the Mississippi River, but was intercepted by the militia. At Christmas time, slaves rioted near Troy, Alabama.

But the whites, highly pleased over the faithfulness of their slaves during the war, were soon disappointed as Union troops began to occupy their lands. The slaves believed they were better off than their masters, who faced death and the miseries of warfare. They could wait quietly until arms had decided their fate for them.

The fate that awaited the Negro depended on the victor. The South, with her population of eight million, could have won in the conflict only if her initial advantages had forced an early decision. The South believed that England would become her ally if only because her cotton kept England's textile mills humming. One-tenth of Britain's capital was invested in that industry and its produce formed a half of all her exports. In addition, there were the strong sympathies of the English ruling classes with the rural southerners over the ill-mannered, ruthless egalitarian Yankees. The British government wanted the South to win the Civil War, because it would mean the splitting of the United States for good. No immediate interest impelled the British to intervene in favor of the South. Contrary to southern calculations, England did not depend on American cotton. Great Britain had a stock of cotton to last for two years. During the Civil War, Indian cotton, having no competition, thrived and made up for the shortage.

Moreover, antislavery sentiment grew strong in Britain. Intervention in favor of the South would have been extremely unpopular in a struggle viewed by Europeans as an attempt to abolish slavery in the entire land. This sentiment abroad, incidentally, was repeatedly outraged by Lincoln's insistence that his government did not intend to abolish slavery where it existed. Lincoln's paramount consideration was "to save the Union and . . . not either to save or destroy slavery . . . what I do about slavery, and the colored race, I do because I believe it would help to save the Union."

The Emancipation Proclamation, when issued on January 1, 1863, freed slaves only in states and regions that were found on that date to be in rebellion. It did not free the slaves in the border states that had not seceded or in regions of the South that were then occupied by the Union Army. Consequently, the Proclamation had no practical effect, as the Europeans were quick to point out in disappointed and indignant reactions. Lord John Russell, the British Foreign Secretary, was correct in his assertion that he missed "a declaration of principle adverse to slavery in this proclamation."

Lincoln, in fact, envisaged a gradual process of emancipation that would end some time around 1900, organized by the states, with indemnity to the slaveholders. He did not believe that white people and former black slaves could live in the same community. His close family ties to the South may have been responsible for his efforts to save southern sensibilities. Possibly, he was anxious to keep the border states secure within the Union and tempt others that had joined the South back into the fold.

Whatever his motives, Lincoln's prejudice against immediate creation of a population of free colored people had its source in his experiences in the Midwest, where there had been savage hostility among white people toward free

Negroes. This experience accounts, perhaps, for his statement in August of 1862 to a deputation of free Negroes, quoted by J. G. Randall in his book *Divided Union*. Lincoln there expressed his doubts to the former slaves on the possibilities of coexistence between the two races in the one society; doubts that, a hundred years later, would still be a hindrance to their integration in the same society:

> You and we are different races. Your race suffers very greatly ... by living among us, while ours suffers from your presence. On this broad continent, not a single man of your race is made the equal of a single man of ours. It is better for us both, therefore, to be separated.

Lincoln reiterated that personally he was favorable to complete equality of the two races, and when his acts deviated from his convictions they were motivated not only by his main endeavor, to restore the Union, but also by his careful appraisal of how much equality the country would accept. He observed that it was the lowest classes that put up the strongest resistance toward work with free Negroes, fearing Negro competition and a degraded status in society. Labor leaders and labor publications supported emancipation and explained to the white workers that slavery caused disrespect of manual work and the perpetuation of low wages. Though it was not too difficult to infuse sympathy in workers for slaves, it was almost impossible to break down their opposition to free Negroes.

If Lincoln doubted that the two races could coexist in peace, it is logical that he reflected upon resettling the free Negroes elsewhere. Although the abolitionists protested, as always, against the concept of foreign colonization of Negroes, Richard N. Current, in *The Lincoln that Nobody Knows*, asserts that "federal aid, gradual emancipation, and voluntary colonization ... were indispensable features of the Lincoln plan"; further, that Lincoln held that "freed Negroes must be shipped out of the country and colonized abroad, but they must be persuaded to go willingly." Lincoln had in mind "a climate congenial to the Negroes," such as the land on the American Isthmus claimed by the Chiriqui Improvement Company, which Lincoln suggested be purchased. The President later became interested in the Île à Vache (Haiti) as an appropriate place to resettle the Negroes. But the Chiriqui colony proved too costly, and the project in Haiti met with fierce hostility on the part of Negroes native to the island. Furthermore, the 400 Negroes shipped to the Île à Vache were decimated by smallpox and entangled in a maze of administrative corruption.

Lincoln also had a tentative plan of setting up freed Negro colonies in Texas and Florida, but in the end only Haiti and Liberia would accept American Negroes as citizens. Congress, though it would not vote money for a vast colonization project, did vote appropriations for voluntary colonization of free Negroes of Washington, D.C., and all Negroes whom the army had freed.

The Emancipation Proclamation may, in fact, have only sanctioned the *status quo* in the states where the Union armies had arrived, but for the slaves it meant something more: the advent of freedom, pure and simple, the message that swept away in its grandeur any qualifications offered to it. Since the federal troops were believed to be bearers of the message, for the slaves they were the army of liberation. When news of the approach of Union troops reached the slaves in southern rural districts, they left their plantations, their masters' households, collected their children and all the possessions they could carry, and, like a flood of refugees, streamed toward the army camps and freedom:

Negroes of all ages and every variety of physical condition, from the infant in his mother's arms to the decrepit old man, joined the columns,—from plantations and cross-roads, singly, and in large groups, on foot, on horseback, and in every description of vehicle. The vehicles were discarded as obstructing the progress of our very long column. The decrepit, the aged, and the feeble, were told of the long journey before them, and advised to remain behind [Brigadier General H. S. Williams reported].

The advance of Sherman's army was known far and wide many miles in advance. It was natural that these poor creatures, seeking a place of safety, should flee to the army and endeavor to keep in sight of it. Every day, as we marched on we could see, on each side of our line of march, crowds of these people coming to us through roads and across the fields, bringing with them all their earthly goods, and many goods which were not theirs. Horses, mules, cows, dogs, old family carriages, carts, and whatever they thought might be of use ... were ... brought to us. They were allowed to follow in rear of our column, and at times they were almost equal in numbers to the army they were following. [So General H. W. Slocum described the Negro migration to freedom.]

The hordes of exultant Negroes led to much confusion and many misplaced children among the slaves on the road. There were pathetic scenes of the young and the old, lost, wandering without a thought as to what the object of their journey was. There were many scenes of reunion. It seemed to one observer as if the mass migrations were a constant human drama, where "the dead was alive and the lost was found," as the dead souls of former slaves suddenly became alive, and many found their families who had been sold to other masters.

Slaves also deserted plantations in the border states at

the coming of the Union armies, running counter to the U.S. government's policy of sparing the nonrebel slaveholders. Despite official insistence on the war's single purpose to salvage the Union, the general run of the population, both Negro and white, believed that it was in fact being waged to wipe out slavery. Thus, the slaves of the loyal slave states vanished from their plantations in large numbers. Quick-thinking owners in the border states sold many into the Deep South, but more slaves left for the North. Many enlisted in the army. From Kentucky and Maryland well over 100,000 slaves fled; 32,000 enlisted. Missouri lost 90,000 of her 112,000 slaves between 1860 and 1864. In the Confederacy as a whole, a total of more than a half-million slaves fled their owners.

The army used the refugees for every conceivable odd job around the camps, and in return fed them and their families. Since the Negroes were in continual fear of being reenslaved, they were always eager to be near northern troops.

In the early years of the war, the Negroes were impatient to enlist, feeling that they owed their service to their country at war for their freedom, and wishing to enhance their self-respect. Humiliating disappointment was in store for them. Though the abolitionists urged President Lincoln to admit Negroes into the army as the first step in their integration into the nation, Lincoln was reluctant, for the same reasons that prevented him from emancipating slaves before victory. Armed Negro units would enrage the southerners and drive them to fight to the bitter end rather than accept compromise; Negro recruits would also anger the border states that were loyal, and would keep those within the Confederacy from changing sides when defeat approached for the South. As always, Lincoln was holding a finger to the pulse of the nation to find out how radical his approach to the slavery question should be: what he found was far from encouraging for those who would have him take the first steps toward raising the Negro to citizenship.

In 1861 the military in Washington, D.C. had refused to allow Negroes to enlist. Pennsylvania also rejected the offer of a group of free Negroes to go South and, as guerrillas, incite the slaves to rise against their masters to flee.

The necessities of warfare and logic of developments resolved the problem of whether or not Negroes should be admitted into the armed forces. In August of 1862, Lincoln admonished that, if the country had resigned herself to bear the disadvantages of the emancipation, she should not refuse its benefits, but let the Negroes and whites share together the dangers and weariness of war.

In the South, Louisiana utilized free Negro soldiers from the very beginning of the conflict. Its Native Guards, active since the time of the war against the Natchez Indians, consisted almost entirely of mulattoes who had served with the French and Spanish troops. The Guards reported for service as the war began; when the Federal Navy appeared and the Confederate troops were evacuated, the Guards refused to quit New Orleans and offered their services to the Union Army. General Benjamin F. Butler in May, 1862, accepted this colored militia on behalf of the United States; the General justified this measure, to which he had not been empowered, by asserting that the Negroes of the Native Guards were free, had been used as soldiers by the enemy, and now had every reason to become loyal to the United States.

In September, a regiment of free Negroes was assembled in Louisiana and put under the command of Union Brigadier General Godfrey Weitzel. General Weitzel, in a report to Washington, confirmed what many there and in the army command had feared in connection with using colored men as soldiers: that "symptoms of servile insurrections were evident following the arrival of colored soldiers."

Tennessee had already passed a law in 1861 to permit the use of Negroes between the ages of fifteen and fifty in military service. And in Kansas, General James H. Lane enrolled Negroes into his troops and formed companies of colored men.

The "First Regiment of South Carolina Volunteers" was organized by General David Hunter, successor of Sherman in South Carolina, an abolitionist, who praised his group enthusiastically in his reports. But several congressmen in Washington condemned his action and demanded an investigation into the matter. Upon receipt of the inquiry, General Hunter wrote a defiant answer, stating that the men in his regiment were no fugitive slaves but "loyal persons whose former masters are fugitive rebels." When the congressmen read the general's statement, they referred it to the President, who promptly ordered the regiment disbanded.

Colonel Thomas Wentworth Higginson, the prolific political writer and abolitionist, was also the commander of a Negro regiment. In his *Memoirs,* Higginson gave what was probably the most acceptable answer to the much disputed question of how good Negro soldiers had been as fighters: "As to the simple fact of courage and reliability," he wrote, "I think no officer in our camp ever thought of there being any difference between black and white."

Nevertheless, the Negroes in the Union armies had to endure discrimination throughout the Civil War. Even their white officers met contempt in the officers' corps. A Negro soldier did not receive as much pay as a white soldier did. His monthly paycheck was $7, plus $3 for clothes, while a white soldier received $13 plus an additional $3.50. A Negro commissioned officer (there were about 100, mostly in the Louisiana forces) received the same pay as a white private.

Some Negro troops staged impressive protests against the discrimination leveled against them. Colored soldiers from Massachusetts refused to accept their inferior pay grade, and served a whole year without reimbursement rather than accept a humiliating distinction. This was a sustained example of insistence on equal rights with equal duties. Black and white men faced the same danger and miseries of soldiers in a general war.

From time to time the abuse of the Negro in the corps became violent and senseless, and the soldiers registered their discontent en masse. Two colored soldiers of the Fourth Regiment, Corps d'Afrique at Fort Jackson, Louisiana, were whipped with a cart whip by Lieutenant Colonel Benedict on December 9, 1863. Half of the regiment rushed to the defense of the two recruits, firing into the air on the parade grounds and shouting insults directed at the officer. These mutineers were court-martialed and seven of them were found guilty of mutiny. Two were condemned to die, but execution of the sentence was suspended. Five defendants received a punishment of hard labor instead. Negro witnesses were not admitted at the trial, but justice seems to have been done: Lieutenant Colonel Benedict was also court-martialed as a result, found guilty of inflicting cruel and unusual punishment, and dismissed from service.

The State Convention of Colored People, held in New Orleans in January, 1865, chose as its topic discrimination against colored men in the army. A committee was appointed to inquire of the authorities "why we are commanded and cannot command." The answer lay in the Constitutional flaw, which after over half a century of discussion, was mended with the passing of the Thirteenth Amendment in

December, 1865, abolishing slavery for good in all the United States.

In all, 186,017 Negro soldiers had served in the Union Army; of these, half had originated in the seceded states.

These soldiers fought in Negro regiments in 449 engagements. Thirty-nine of them were major battles. Seventeen Negro soldiers and four Negro sailors were awarded Congressional Medals of Honor.

While many Negro groups offered their services to the Union Army with enthusiasm, others issued resolutions expressing indignation and protest, warning the Negroes not to join the white men's fight unless on the same terms as they enjoyed. "Until then we are in no condition to fight under the flag which gives us no protection," one of the many resolutions insisted, urging the Negroes to stay neutral.

In the South, the southerners had heeded the call to the army without a murmur, but had protested the conscription of their slaves.

The soldiers of the Confederacy took along black servants of their households to act as butlers and perform all menial work. Those who had no slaves often hired one as a body servant. Many slaves were requisitioned for the construction of fortifications. President Davis allowed a draft of 40,000 slaves in 1864 to serve as "pioneer and engineer laborers." This was done, however, at the risk of incurring slaveowners' resentment. Governmental disposition of their personal property was detested.

The attitude of the Confederacy toward Negroes in northern fighting units was one of abhorrence. The Confederate army issued orders to handle white officers of Negro units as outlaws, and to send Negro soldiers who had been fugitives from southern masters to their own state to be punished. When the Government of the United States countered with a threat of retaliation, these orders were disregarded by southern commanders. Southerners were so enraged by the sight of Negro soldiers in arms that they were apt to massacre them straightway when captured.

As the war progressed and the shortage of manpower became more acute in the South, the admission of Negroes to the Confederate armies was proposed, discussed, and rejected, ever more frequently, but six Confederate states subsequently passed laws providing for the impressment of free Negroes into labor batallions.

General Patrick R. Cleburn, commander of a division, suggested in January of 1864 "that we retain in service for the war, and that we immediately commence training a large reserve of the most courageous of our slaves; and further, that we guarantee, within a reasonable time, freedom to convey on slaves who shall remain true to the Confederacy in this war." Otherwise, he reasoned, it would be impossible to muster and maintain an army sufficiently powerful to overcome the federal forces. Cleburn's proposal was bitterly opposed by most officers, who considered it incendiary. President Davis had it suppressed promptly.

The shortage of men available to fight for the cause of the Old South continued to bring the question into the open. Everyone was aware of the validity of President Davis' arguments against considering Negroes as soldiers in the Confederate armies: "When we establish the fact that the negroes are a military people we destroy our theory that they are unfit to be free, and when we arm them then we abandon slavery." But something had to be done. In February, 1865, Virginia desperately adopted a law permitting Negroes to serve in the army. The Confederate Congress was divided on the issue. At last, shortly before Appomattox, when the entire issue abruptly became academic, the southern Congress passed a law sanctioning the call of as many as 300,000 slaves to serve in the Confederate armies—but gave no promise that slaves who served faithfully thus might eventually receive freedom.

In this manner the Confederacy stubbornly went down, with its principle of a master race upheld.

XII

IN RETROSPECT

THE enslaved Negro on the North American continent rarely revolted against his master. The reasons, as we have seen, were many. The native African, torn from his homeland and mixed indiscriminately with Negroes of other tribes and languages, was hardly able to comprehend his new status, much less to make common cause against the enslavers.

Later, when Negroes in America had come to form a subculture of their own, the barriers to revolt remained almost insuperable. Slaveowning whites were vigilant in guarding against such an occurrence, to the point of imagining numerous conspiracies that did not exist. Any gathering of slaves was looked upon suspiciously.

Every prospective Negro rebel leader constantly faced the danger of betrayal by one of his confidants. The difficulty was that slaves would only follow a leader whom they knew personally; yet each person admitted into the conspiracy increased the danger of betrayal. Denmark Vesey sought to solve this problem by directing lieutenants and yet keeping the master plan to himself. But Vesey's caution did not prevent his conspiracy from being foiled by the betrayal of a single man.

Leaders of slave revolts showed high native intelligence as well as qualities of imagination and command, but lacked understanding of the wider world. They were uneducated— often, like Gabriel, illiterate. They derived strength from the belief that they had been chosen by God and were able to convey this quality to their followers, but only Denmark Vesey knew how to move confidently in both free and slave, white and colored worlds. The South reasoned correctly in fearing that the educated, free Negro presented a great danger to the existing order.

Negroes who rebelled against their condition also found great difficulty in seeking refuge. In contrast with the slaves on San Domingo, the slaves on the continent did not outnumber white men. Thus the continental slaves sought sanctuary rather than a general massacre of their oppressors. In this respect, the colonial years offered rebellious slaves the best opportunities for escape. In fact, as we have seen, fugitive slaves formed common cause with the Indians in Florida in both the 18th and 19th centuries. In addition, the rivalry of European nations during colonial times offered some chance for slaves to gain their freedom through military service.

These opportunities ended with the creation of the United States and the spread of the plantation system throughout the South. The conspiracies of Gabriel Vesey and Nat Turner indicate an increase of such plots as a result of the fact that individual slaves found it practically impossible to escape from their masters.

The final phase saw the contribution of conscience-stricken whites, in the creation of the Underground Railway and John Brown's conspiracy. Forces larger even than the institution of slavery itself were acting to break the chains of the slave. After more than two hundred years, the awful curse was lifted. The new freedmen were condemned usually to poverty and often to peonage, but never again would they be chattels. It is the basic human yearning for freedom that provides meaning to this account of Negro resistance to slavery in America.

NOTES ON SOURCES

The books listed here have been selected because of specific information they convey relative to the subject matter.

Slavery and slave trade in general and in countries other than the United States:

Ail, Abd Elwahed, *Contribution à une Théorie Sociologique de l'Esclavage*, Paris, 1931.

Barinetti, Carlo, *A Voyage to Mexico*, New York, 1841.

Blake, William O., *A History of Slavery and Slave Trade*, Columbus, 1848.

Block, M., *Comment et Pourquoi Finit l'Esclavage Antique*, Paris, 1947.

Channing, William E., *Slavery*, Boston, 1835.

Cobb, T., *A Historical Sketch of Slavery*, Phila., 1858.

Continental Congress, *Journals of no. 13* Phila., 1800–1801.

Copley, E., *A History of Slavery and Its Abolition*, London, 1844.

Coupland, R., *East Africa and its Invaders*, Oxford, 1938.

Dawson, T. C., *South American Republics*, vol. 1, New York, 1903.

Farrington, B., *Greek Science*, vol. 2, London, 1949.

Federal Convention of 1787, *Debates*, New York, 1920.

Fletcher, Sir George, *Slavery through the Ages*, London, 1938.

NOTES ON SOURCES

Foulks, T., *18 Months in Jamaica,* London, 1833.

Gales and Seaton, *Register of Debates in Congress,* vol. 1, Washington, 1834.

Hard, John C., *Laws of Freedom and Bondage,* 2 vols., Boston, 1857.

Hart, A. B., *Slavery and Abolition,* New York, 1906.

Herskovits, M. J., *The Myth of the Negro Past,* New York, 1941.

House of Commons, *Analysis of Reports of the Commission,* London, 1853.

Howard, Warren S., *American Slavers and the Federal Law,* Univ. of California, 1963.

Humboldt, A. von, *The Island of Cuba,* New York, 1856.

Jobson, Richard, *The Golden Trade,* London, 1623.

Laroque, Patrice, *De l'Esclavage chez les Nations Chrétiennes,* Paris, 1848.

Lee, C., *Papers,* vol. 1, New York, 1872.

Letourneau, C. J. M., *Evolution de l'Esclavage,* Paris, 1897.

Martin, Gaston, *Histoire de l'Esclavage dans les Colonies Fr.,* Paris, 1948.

Mathieson, W. L. *British Slavery and its Abolition,* London, 1844.

Mousnier, Jehan, *Journal de la Traite des Noirs,* Paris, 1957.

Ramos, A., *The Negro in Brazil,* Washington, 1939.

Scelle, Georges, *Histoire Politique de la Traite,* 2 vols., Paris, 1902.

Schoelcher, Victor, *Esclavage and Colonizacion,* Paris, 1948.

Southey, Robert, *Chronological History of the British W. Indies,* 2 vols, London, 1826.

Wyndham, H. A., *The Atlantic and Slavery,* London, 1935.

Early Spanish and Portuguese Slavery:

Adams, H. B., *Columbus and his Discovery,* Baltimore, 1892.

Azurara, Gomes Bannes de, *Chronicle of Conquest,* London, 1896.

Brion, Marcel *Bartolomé de Las Casas,* New York, 1929.

Hahn, T. "Early Explorers," *Cape Quarterly Review,* 1881.

Harrisse, H., *Notes on Columbus,* Cambridge, 1866.

Helps, Arthur, *Spanish Conquest in America,* 3 vols., London, 1885.

Helps, Arthur, *The Life of Las Casas,* Phila., 1868.

Herreray T. A. de, *Description des Indes Occidentales,* Amsterdam, 1622.

Lowery, Woodbury, *The Spanish Settlements . . . of the U.S.,* New York, 1905.

Pinkerton, John, *A General Collection of Voyages and Travels,* London, 1812.

Thacher, J. B., *Christopher Columbus,* New York, 1903.

Revolts on the Sea:

Churchill, A., *Collection of Voyages and Travels,* vols. 1 & 3, London, 1746.

Donnan, Elizabeth, *Documents Illustrative of the History of Slave-Trade in America,* 4 vols., Phila., 1930–1935.

Green, Lorenzo J., *Mutiny on the Slave Ships in Phylon,* 1944.

Jensen, Merrill, in Douglas, David C., *English Historical Documents,* vol. 9, New York, 1955.

O'Callaghan, E. B., *Transatlantic Voyages of Slavers,* Albany, 1867.

San Domingo Revolts:

American Historical Association, *Annual Report,* vol. 2, 1903.

Beard, J. K., *The Life of Toussaint,* London, 1853.

Hardy, C. O., *The Negro Question in the French Revolution,* Menasha, 1919.

Korngold, R., *Citizen Toussaint,* Boston, 1944.

Montague, L. L., *Haiti and the U.S.,* Durham, 1940.

Steward, T. G., *The Haitian Revolution,* New York, 1914.

Stoddard, T. L., *The French Revolution in San Domingo,* New York, 1914.

Trendley, Mary, "The U.S. and San Domingo," *Journal of Race Development,* vol. 7.

NOTES ON SOURCES

Gabriel's Revolt:

Calendar of Virginia State Papers, vols. 6 & 9.
Callender, J. T., *Jefferson 1798–1802,* Brooklyn, 1897.
Higginson, T. W., *Travellers and Outlaws,* Boston, 1889.
Howison, R. H., *A History of Virginia,* 2 vols., Richmond, 1848.

Vesey's Insurrection:

The Corporation of Charleston, *An Account of the late intended Insurrection,* Charleston, 1822.
Grimke, H., "The Martyrs . . . ," *American Negro Academy Occosional Papers,* no. 7, Washington, 1900.
Higginson, T. W. *Op. Cit.*
Lofton, J. M., Jr., "Negro Insurrectionist," *Antioch Review,* 1958.

Nat Turner's Revolt:

Bibb, Henry, *The Insurrection and Massacre in Southampton Cy.,* New York, 1831.
Cromwell, J. W., "The Aftermath of Turner," *Journal of Negro History,* 1920.
Drewry, W., *The Southampton Insurrection,* Washington, 1900.
Gray, T. R., *The Confession of Nat Turner,* Richmond, 1832.
Warner, S., *An Authentic Narrative of the Attempted Revolt in Southampton,* New York, 1831.

On Slave Revolts and Conspiracies in America:

Aptheker, Herbert, *American Negro Slave Revolts,* New York, 1943, published an account of over two hundred cases reported in contemporary papers, official records, and private correspondence. A great number of them existed, however, only in the frightened imagination of white people or were never even alleged to have been more than unfulfilled conspiracies.
Carroll, J. C., *Slave Insurrections in the U.S. 1800–1860,* Boston, 1938.

NOTES ON SOURCES

Coffin, J., *An Account of some of the Principal Insurrections in America*, New York, 1960.

Wish, Harvey, *American Slave Insurrections before 1861*, Washington, 1927, treated the subject, Carroll more emotionally, the others more discriminately.

Slavery in the United States:

Adair, J., *History of the American Indian*, Johnson City, 1930.

Adams, C. F., ed., *The Works of J. Adams*, vol. 2, Boston, 1850.

Adams, J. T., *America's Tragedy*, New York, 1945.

American Anti-Slavery Society, *Annual Report*, New York, 1854–1859.

Bancroft, Frederic, *Slave Trading in the South*, New York, 1959.

Barnes, J. H., *The Anti-Slavery Impetus*, London, 1933.

Basler, Roy P., *Collected Works of Abraham Lincoln*, vol. 3, New Brunswick, 1953.

Bassett, J. S., *Slavery in the State of North Carolina*, Baltimore, 1899.

Bell, I. W., *Southern Negroes, 1861–65*, New Haven, 1938.

Bower, A. R. & Bower, A. H., "Day to Day Resistance to Slavery," *Journal of Negro Hist.*, vol. 27.

Brawley, B. G., *A Social History of the American Negro*, New York, 1917.

Breyfogle, W., *Make Free*, New York, 1958.

Buckingham, J. S., *The Slave States in America*, 2 vols., London, 1842.

Catteral, Helen T., *Judicial Cases Concerning the Negro and American Slavery*, vol. 2, Washington, 1926–1937.

Chambers, W., *American Slavery and Colour*, London, 1857.

Cromwell, J. W., *The Negro in American History*, Washington, 1914.

Dawson, D., *The Mexican Adventure*, London, 1935.

Douglass, Frederick, *The Life and Times of Frederick Douglass*, Boston, 1892.

DuBois, W. E. B., *Black Reconstruction*, New York, 1939.

NOTES ON SOURCES

DuBois, W. E. B., *The Negro*, New York, 1915.

Elkins, S. M., *Slavery*, Chicago, 1959.

Filler, Louis, *The Crusade against Slavery*, New York, 1960.

Foster, L., *Negro-Indian Relationships*, Phila., 1935.

Frazier, Franklin E., *The Negro in the U.S.*, New York, 1949.

Gordell, W., *The American Slave Code*, New York, 1853.

Gross, Bella, *Clarion Call*, New York, 1947.

Hanna, K. A., "The Role of the South in the French Intervention in Mexico," *Journal of Southern History*, 1954.

Hay, T. R., "The South and the Armory of Slaves," Mississippi Valley Historical Review, 1929.

Hildreth, R., *Despotism in America*, Boston, 1901.

Hodgson, A., *A Journey Through North America*, New York, 1827.

Hunter, F. L., "Slave Society on the Southern Plantation," *Journal of Negro History*, 1902.

Locke, M. S., *Anti-Slavery in America*, Boston, 1901.

Lloyd, Arthur Young, *The Slavery Controversy*, Chapel Hill, 1939.

Lyell, Sir C., *A Second Visit to the U.S.A.*, vol. 2, New York, 1849.

McDougall, M. G., *Fugitive Slaves*, Boston, 1891.

McPherson, James M., *The Negro's Civil War*, New York, 1965.

Macy, J., *The Anti-Slavery Crusade*, New Haven, 1920.

Mellon, M., *Early American Views on Negro Slavery*, Boston, 1934.

Montagne, L. L., *Haiti and the U.S.*, Durham, 1940.

Nordholt, J. W. Schulte, *The People that Walks in Darkness*, New York, 1960.

Olmsted, F. L., *A Journey in the Seaboard States*, New York, 1856.

Olmsted, F. L., *A Journey in the Back Country*, New York, 1860.

Phillips, U., *American Negro Slavery*, New York, 1918.

Porter, K. W., *Relations between Negroes and Indians in the U.S.*, Washington, 1933.

Priest, W., *Travels in the U.S. 1793–97*, London, 1802.

Quarls, B., *The Negro in the Civil War*, Boston, 1953.

Reuter, E. B., *The American Race Problem*, New York, 1927.

Siebert, W. A., *The Underground Railroad*, New York, 1898.

Sinclair, W. A., *The Aftermath of Slavery*, Boston, 1905.

Spears, J. S., *The American Slave Trade*, London, 1907.

Stampp, K. M., *The Peculiar Institution*, New York, 1956.

Stanton, W., *The Leopard's Spots*, Chicago, 1959.

Staudenraus, P. J., *The African Colonization Movement*, Columbus, 1961.

Sydnov, C. S., *The Development of Southern Sectionalism*, Baton Rouge, 1948.

Tannenbaum, F., *Slave and Citizen*, New York, 1947.

Tillinghast, J. A., *The Negro in Africa and America*, New York, 1900.

Valdo, S. P., *Memoirs of Andrew Jackson*, Hartford, 1819.

Villard, O. G., *John Brown*, Boston, 1910.

Weatherford, W. D., *The Negro from Africa to America*, New York, 1924.

Webb, R. D., *The Life and Letters of Captain John Brown*, London, 1841.

William and Mary College Quarterly, "Notes from Colonial Papers," 1902.

Williams, G. W., *A History of the Negro Race in America*, New York, 1883.

Williams, S. C., *History of the American Indians*, Johnson City, 1930.

Wilson, H., *Rise and Fall of the Slave Power in America*, New York, 1924.

Witkins, G., *The History of the Negro Race in America*, New York, 1883.

Source Material from These Works and Collections of Documents:

Angle, P. M., *Created Equal*, Chicago, 1959.

Beard, C. A., *An Economic Interpretation of the Constitution of the U.S.*, New York, 1959.

Commager, H. S., *Documents of American History*, New York, 1963.

Dubos, R. *The Torch of Life*, New York, 1962.

Jefferson, T., *Writings*, vol. 6., L. Ford ed., New York, 1899.

Miller, J. C., *The Federalist Era*, New York, 1960.

Nevins, A., *The Emergence of Modern America*, New York, 1927.

Nevins, A., *Ordeal of the Union*, vol. 1, New York, 1947.

Radcliffe College, *Monographs*, nos. 3 & 11, Boston, 1891, 1901.

U.S. Government, *Official Records of the Rebellion*, Ser. I. II. 1953–1954.

Woodward, C. V., *Reunion and Reaction*, Boston, 1951.

Regional History:

Archives of New Jersey, *Second Series*, vol. 3.

Ashe, S. A'court, *The History of North Carolina*, vol. 1, Greensboro, 1908.

Ballagh, J. S., *A History of Slavery in Virginia*, Baltimore, 1902.

Bassett, J. C., *Slavery in North Carolina*, Baltimore, 1899.

Brackett, J. R., *The Negro in Maryland*, Baltimore, 1899.

Brock, R. A., *Virginia 1606–1689*, Boston, 1884.

Calendar of Virginia State Papers, vols. 5, 6, 9, 10.

Colonial Records of Georgia, vols. 4 & 5.

Cooley, H. S., *A Study of Slavery in New Jersey*, Baltimore, 1896.

Crane, V. W., "A Lost Utopia," *Suwanee Review*, vol. 27.

Everett, D. E., Ben Butler and the Louisiana Native Guard, *Journal of Southern History*, vol. 20.

Flanders, R. B., *Plantation Slavery in Georgia*, Chapel Hill, 1932.

Flinter, G. D., *An Account of the Present State of Puerto Rico*, London, 1834.

Foster, Laurence, *Indian and Negro Relationship in the Southwest*, Phila., 1935.

Gayarré, C. E. A., *History of Louisiana*, 4 vols., New Orleans, 1903.

Hewatt, A., *An Historical Account of the Rise and Progress of South Carolina and Georgia*, 2 vols., London, 1779.

Jackson, L. P., "Virginia Soldiers and Seamen," *Journal of Negro History*, vol. 27.

NOTES ON SOURCES

Johnson, G. G., *Ante-Bellum North Carolina*, Durham, 1937.

Jones, C. C., *The History of Georgia*, Boston, 1883.

McCrady, E., *South Carolina under the Royal Government*, New York, 1901.

McPherson, J. H. T., *History of Liberia*, Baltimore, 1897.

Martin, F. X., *The History of Louisiana*, New Orleans, 1882.

Massachusetts Historical Society, *Proceedings*, no. 44, Boston, 1910–1911.

Moore, G. H., *Notes on the History of Slavery in Massachusetts*, New York, 1866.

Patterson, C. P., *The Negro in Tennessee*, Austin, 1922.

Pennsylvania Archives, ed. S. Hazard, First Ser. vol. 4.

Pierce, E., *The Freedom of Port Royal in South Carolina*, New York, 1863.

Porter, K. W., "Negroes and the E. Florida Annexation," *Journal of Negro History*, vol. 30.

Public Records of South Carolina, vol. 8.

Richardson, R. N., *Texas the Lone Star State*, New York, 1943.

Rose, Willie Lee, *Rehearsal for Reconstruction*, New York, 1964.

Russell, John, H. *The Free Negro in Virginia*, Baltimore, 1903.

Skinner, C. L., *Pioneers of the Old Southwest*, New Haven, 1920.

Stevens, W. B., *A History of Georgia*, 2 vols. New York, 1847.

White, G., Rev., *Historical Collection of Georgia*, Atlanta, 1854.

Information pertaining to specific phases, areas, and aspects of slavery was supplied to a large extent by scholarly journals, sometimes identified in the text. The following magazines complete the list of sources:

American Anthropologist, vol. 63, no. 3.
Florida Historical Quarterly, nos. 8, 9, 10.
Louisiana Historical Quarterly, vol. 20.
Magazine of American History, vols. 12, 25.
Magazine of History, vol. 13.
The Negro History Bulletins, no. 6.

NOTES ON SOURCES

North Carolina Historical Review, vol. 38.
South Atlantic Quarterly, vol. 25.
Southwestern Historical Quarterly, vol. 26.

From contemporary newspapers, *The Liberator,* Boston; *Niles' Weekly Register,* Boston; *Raleigh Register; Richmond Enquirer; Richmond Whig; Houston State Gazette* are quoted or referred to.

INDEX

INDEX

INDEX

INDEX

McAmore, Molly, 229
McDowell, James, 137
Magazine of American History, 32–33
Maine admitted to the Union, 115
Maitland, Colonel, 60
Manumission, 40, 112, 225
Martin (Negro slave), 90, 91
Martin, Alexander, 52
Martin, Luther, 56
Martinique, 62, 187
Mary (schooner), 95
Maryland, 31, 246
  anti-slavery attitudes, 43
  early agriculture in, 5–6
  escape routes from, 211
  freed Negroes in, 114
  Negro arsons in, 135
  plan to return Negroes to Africa, 196
  restrictions on importation of slaves, 36
  slave breeding in, 101, 217
  slavery recognized by, 4
Maryland Colonization Society, 196
Mason, George, 57
Mason, J. M., 235
Massachusetts, 213–214
  petition from slaves, 46–47
  slavery laws, 36–37
Mathieson, W. L., 185
Meade, Richard W., 207
Medals of Honor, 250
Memoirs (Higginson), 248
Memoirs (Jackson), 107
Methodists, 92
Mexican War, 226
Mexico, 219, 220
Michigan, 215
Mirabeau, Honoré, 63
Miscegenation, 4, 34, 178
Mississippi, uprisings in, 204, 241
Missouri, 246
  slavery approved for, 115–116
Missouri Compromise, 212–213
Molasses, 73
Monroe, James, 76, 87–88, 93–96, 98, 187, 192

Montiano, Governor, 18
Moore, Mr., 182
Moravians, 23, 24
Morris, Gouverneur, 54–55
Mosby, Major, 88–89, 93
Mulattoes, 62–84
  white marriages, 34
Murrel, Captain, 7

Nancy (Negro slave), 158, 159
Napoleon I, 81–83, 100
Natchez (sloop), 170
Natchez Indians, 32
Nebraska, 212, 237
Necker, Jacques, 63
Negroes
  African chieftains, 119
  coexistence with Indians, 107–110
  death penalties for, 34–37
  first slaves in North America, 1–2
  freed, 98–134
    education of, 148
    expulsion of, 148
    guardians for, 136
    help to slaves, 215–216
    mortality rate, 114
    number of (1820), 112
    plan to return to Africa, 114–116, 193
    in Puerto Rico, 138
    right to vote of, 200
    sold into slavery, 136
    unpopularity of, 225
  military service of, 247–252
  in the Revolutionary War, 47–53
  in San Domingo, 60–97
  white marriages, 34
  See also Slavery; Slaves
Nelson (Negro slave), 175
New England Abolition Society, 190
New Jersey, Negro arsonists in, 86
New York, Negro arsonists in, 86
New York Times, The, 236
Newport Mercury, 9–10
News (Galveston newspaper), 221
News Letter, The, 10
Nicholls, Edward, 109

271

INDEX